ADVANCE PRAISE FOR

INSURGENT SOCIAL STUDI
SCHOLAR-EDUCATORS DISRUPTIN(

---

"Why and how social studies education has continued to fail to serve as a curriculum of humanity and justice for all children is laid bare by *Insurgent Social Studies: Scholar-Educators Disrupting Erasure and Marginality.* Neither natural nor inevitable, social studies that serves the status quo of white settler supremacy is always promoted by those who benefit from it. In this unapologetically insurgent book, the most important scholar-educators of our time name the beneficiaries of this system and guide us to take back the curriculum that has harmed our children and communities for far too long. Join the struggle. The time for insurgency is NOW!"

Sohyun An
Professor of Social Studies Education
Kennesaw State University

"The call for a more radical social studies has been clear since even before the field's existence. *Insurgent social studies* is building from the radical tradition of scholars and teachers from historically and systemically excluded backgrounds who have used the classroom to challenge how humanity is defined. For the editors and authors of this book, they seek not for approval or permission from the social studies establishment, which for far too long has straddled the fence with those who want power and exhibit hegemony. The book forces us to rethink and reconsider what is social studies education. Insurgent outlines an ideological and pedagogical revolution with teachers, students, professors, and parents. The time is not to surrender or curtail from political pressure but to continue to do what is right for our children and citizens alike. *Insurgent social studies* will be a timeless classic that will influence social studies education for many years."

LaGarrett J. King
Associate Professor, Social Studies Education
Director, Center for K-12 Black History and Racial Literacy Education
University at Buffalo

"*Insurgent Social Studies: Scholar-Educators Disrupting Erasure and Marginality* is a powerful and timely volume on Critical Social Studies Education. The authors of this book provide a diverse assortment of chapters, all seeking to theorize, conceptualize and challenge majoritarian stories told about history education and social studies as a whole. This book is a must-read for all educators inside and outside the academy committed insurgent pedagogy."

Anthony Brown
Professor, Department of Curriculum and Instruction,
and the Center for African and African American Studies
University of Texas, Austin

# INSURGENT SOCIAL STUDIES

# INSURGENT SOCIAL STUDIES

## Scholar-Educators Disrupting Erasure and Marginality

BY NATASHA HAKIMALI MERCHANT,

SARAH B. SHEAR, AND WAYNE AU

*Gorham, Maine*

Published by Myers Education Press, LLC
P.O. Box 424
Gorham, ME 04038



**Myers Education Press** is an academic publisher specializing in books, e-books and digital content in the field of education. All of our books are subjected to a rigorous peer review process and produced in compliance with the standards of the Council on Library and Information Resources.

Library of Congress Cataloging-in-Publication Data available from Library of Congress.

13-digit ISBN 978-1-9755-0455-7 (paperback)
13-digit ISBN 978-1-9755-0456-4 (library networkable e-edition)
13-digit ISBN 978-1-9755-0457-1 (consumer e-edition)

Printed in the United States of America.

All first editions printed on acid-free paper that meets the American National Standards Institute Z39-48 standard.



*Cover design by Shelby Gates Designs.*

# *Dedication*

This book is for the generations of students who have, and continue to be, harmed in social studies spaces. We dedicate this text to you and will continue to work to change social studies for future generations of learners.

## *Contents*

INTRODUCTION

# We Won't Wait Any Longer: An Introduction and Invitation to Insurgency for Social Studies

*Natasha Hakimali Merchant, Sarah B. Shear, and Wayne Au*

SOCIAL STUDIES EDUCATION IN THE United States is a problem. When we look closely at the last hundred years of curriculum and teaching, it is clear who history, geography, economics, and civics (to name the big four subject areas) was written by and for—white, able-bodied, Christian, English-speaking, pro-capitalist, cis men and, in proximity, the women who look and behave in a manner befitting their heteropatriarchal society (e.g., Busey & Walker, 2017; Calderón, 2014; Epstein, 2009; King & Chandler, 2016; Ladson-Billings, 2003; Rains, 2006; Tyson & Park, 2008; Vickery, 2015; Vickery & Duncan, 2020).

This singular actor speaks a singular story. The social studies problem is a violent act of white settler supremacy that is repeated generation after generation in classrooms across the United States from kindergarten through graduate school and in media spaces too many to list. Although there have been movements of resistance, and to varying degrees successes, to address these crimes, social studies education is still largely a curriculum designed to erase or otherwise marginalize voices, bodies, and experiences not accepted by or created for the benefit of white supremacist society.

We, the editors and contributors of this volume, recognize that as a new(er) generation of insurgents in social studies we build from a robust legacy of resistance practiced by many educators on a daily basis. With deep respect we acknowledge the work of scholars, especially scholars of color, who have fought for years to engage social studies education in meaningful change, but their efforts were met by a field largely resistant and unwelcoming. Many scholars of color left the halls of the College and University Faculty Assembly of the National Council for the Social Studies, taking their wisdom to other lanes of education; some stayed and continued the fight, working to build the capacity for social studies education and research to be a space where change was possible, where scholars of color and allied critical partners felt welcome (e.g., Ooka Pang et al., 1998). Yet, we lament that the pace of change has been horrifically slow in our publications, professional organizations, and curriculum. More than writing to convince those who continue to usurp ideas and space, we write to root ourselves within a practice of insurgent social studies and forge a stronger, collective bond as a community that is unyielding to the forces who would maintain white settler supremacy in any part of the world in which we live. We won't wait any longer for social studies to wake up and do the work necessary to make our subject areas ones where students learn the truth, hear from a multiplicity of voices and experiences, see themselves reflected in the pages of their texts, feel inspired to dream big dreams that will create a better world for us all. We won't wait any longer. The time for insurgency is now, and we invite you to join us in growing our understanding of its applications.

## Insurgent Social Studies

The idea for this collection stemmed from Au's (2021) conception of a *pedagogy of insurgency*. In his article, Au first outlines the current social and political context of the United States, highlighting the rise of authoritarian populism as expressed through a particularly virulent strand of capitalist, white supremacist, nationalist, patriarchal, conservative Christian, heteronormative, and violent ideology. The rising threat and power of this ideology has manifested as increasing violent hate crimes and hate speech over the last several years and encompasses the election of Donald J. Trump as the 45th president of the United States. In terms of policy, the rise of authoritarian populism has also resulted in attacks on the rights of immigrants of all races, Muslims, the LGBQTIA community, the poor, non-white peoples, and many others. Not surprisingly, as this ideology seeps and is reproduced through various institutions, it has also made its way into schools. Au highlights research and other evidence clearly demonstrating the increase in authoritarian populist politics through hate speech happening in schools, perpetrated by both students and teachers alike.

Using the example of teacher, school staff, and community organizing for Black Lives Matter at School in Seattle, Washington, Au (2021) outlines a framing of a *pedagogy of insurgency* that he argues is needed to combat educational and social injustice in this historical moment. In his conception, Au suggests that a *pedagogy of insurgency* requires the following:

- *Bravery and risk*, as rebellious educators take the step of fighting back against social and educational injustice in public and visible ways;
- *Allies, accomplices, and solidarity*, as educators and community members come together across different identities in order to build a broader-based and effective movement for educational justice. This, in turn, also helps mitigate risk;
- Understanding *organizing, protest, and demonstrations* as a valuable and worthwhile form of pedagogy and curriculum in itself;
- Using *critical analyses of power* as a central approach for teaching and learning about social and educational injustice;
- Developing a *curriculum of insurgency* for educators, students, and the community to engage in critical analyses of power in schools and society;
- *Embracing* schools as sites of both oppression and liberation and in the process also *reimagining* the role that schools can play in broader social change; and
- *Connecting to broader social movements*, as educators, students, and communities see and understand that their own struggles for justice and liberation are part of broader, historic traditions in the fight for change.

Taken as a whole, a *pedagogy of insurgency* seeks to understand and at least partially explain the ways that teachers have the power—through pedagogy, curriculum, and community activism—to actively resist injustice while also working toward a more radically just world.

Given the rise of authoritarian populism in the larger social-political context, its ongoing influence in schools, and the state of the field of social studies outlined earlier, we envisioned the importance of collecting and uplifting voices that can articulate what *Insurgent Social Studies* looks like in both theory and practice. We did this with the express intent of highlighting newer social studies scholars whose work and perspectives have been marginalized in the field with the hope that this act would potentially move the field. Perhaps more important, we collected these voices because we wanted to defend our children and their communities against the ever-encroaching tide of injustice and inequality that we all face.

## Overview of Chapters

The contributors to this volume live with the tension of affiliating with the current problematic landscape of the social studies while also striving to join forces with those who dare to theorize, write, teach, and build toward a radical future in which truth telling, building solidarity, and cultivating a liberatory impulse are among the measurable outcomes of social studies. Although separating this collection into distinct topical foci is difficult, our editorial team strongly felt that certain chapters be particularly acknowledged due to the landscape of injustice undergirding the entire trajectory of what is commonly referred to as United States history. For this reason, the first two chapters in this volume center Indigenous and Black liberation.

We begin this volume with a chapter written by the Turtle Island Social Studies Collective. In this chapter, the authors draw from two liberatory projects stemming from traditions of Indigenous scholarship. First, the authors call on Quechua scholar Sandy Grande's "Red Pedagogy" as a framework for decolonial pedagogy. They then turn to the Red Nation's platform named the Red Deal, which insists on Indigenous sovereignty and liberation at its core. The authors of this chapter resist commonplace additive notions of Indigenous representation and instead unapologetically center Indigenous knowledge and priorities, noting that liberation through Red Insurgency is true liberation for all.

In the second chapter of this volume, Tiffany Mitchell Patterson challenges social studies educators to move beyond a curriculum that encourages performative activism. Noting the whitewashed ways in which Black movement work is often approached in social studies, Patterson discusses how discounting the power, strategy, and multidimensionality of movement-building work is yet another way to curtail and minimize the full flourishing of Black life. To this end, Patterson draws from the Black Lives Matter movement as a master study of building solidarity as an essential component of liberation. Despite the widespread anti-Blackness found across the social studies, in schools generally and in broader public life, Patterson's experience as an educator suggests that demonstrating courage and bravery in tackling anti-Blackness and teaching for Black liberation is generally well received and, moreover, is absolutely necessary for educators everywhere.

In their chapter, Rodríguez and Kim utilize Asian American critical race theory to expose the racialization of Asian Americans across U.S. history and the salient tropes that continue to constrain conceptions of Asian Americans. The racialization of Asian Americans told through well-chosen examples in this chapter demonstrates that the current rise in hatred against Asian Americans, far from surprising, is a consistent pattern that is easily stoked for political and economic gain. Rodríguez and Kim delve into the complexity of Asian American identity including the myriad ways Asian Americans have responded to white supremacy. To challenge essentialist narratives about who Asian Americans are and how they've been constructed by white supremacy, Rodríguez and Kim provide eye-opening examples that typify all that is missing from coverage of Asian Americans in social studies curricula.

The theme of combating essentialism continues in our next chapter, *"Existence Is Resistance": Palestine and Palestinians in Social Studies Education.* In this chapter, Hanadi Shatara highlights how the field of social studies education has either ignored or represented Palestine through reductionist tropes and points us in the direction of how to better teach about Palestine and Palestinians. Beginning with a study of *Theory and Research in Social Education*, Shatara exposes the dearth of work on Palestine and its people, save the highly problematic instances of mention which synonymize Palestine with conflict and controversy. As the title of her work suggests, an insurgent politics must include a full acknowledgement of Palestine and Palestinians. Shatara closes her chapter by supplementing the absence of robust coverage on Palestine and Palestinians by offering an abundance of resources for educators.

Pedagogies of insurgency can be applied to politics as well as poetics. In our next chapter, La Familia Aponte-Safe Tirado Díaz Beltrán Ender Busey and Christ invite you, the reader, to humbly observe their conversation while setting aside your own expectations and agenda. Much of what is discussed in this chapter will resonate for insurgent scholars who are socially and politically located at the margins. Instead of thinking of the margins as a stuck space, this chapter highlights what some of the authors talk about as "crevices" and "cracks" within which sustaining conversations and knowledge production are spun. Within this particular crevice, the authors meditate on the manifestations of insurgency in their lives as scholars, teachers, and public intellectuals. Grappling with the academy's obsession with categorization as a prerequisite for visibility and the struggles of articulations of truth in ways legible to those who perpetuate epistemological violence are among the many topics discussed in this chapter.

Following the reflective chapter by La Familia comes another introspective chapter by Natasha Hakimali Merchant who presents a conceptual mapping around the inquiry that has occupied her career: *how best to teach about Islam in secondary social studies*. Through the charting of her explorations comes a conceptual mapping of four worthy paths to teaching about Islam. Although the journey through these paths is nonlinear, in-depth engagement with each shapes a set of critical interruptions to typical curricula on Islam. These interruptions include deconstructing commonsense notions of "religion," utilizing textbooks as data of dominance, and intentionally building in (seemingly) contradictory examples and manifestations of Muslim belief and practice.

Challenging disciplinary norms continues in the next chapter by Tadashi Dozono, who flips the idea of historical inquiry as it is typically conceived and practiced in social studies. Informed by his students' agentive experiences in response to erasure within curriculum, Dozono lays out a pedagogy of queer worlding. Incorporating elements of freedom dreaming and the construction of genealogies of histories and future, Dozono expands on the concept of queer worlding by drawing from queer artists of color who use art as a mode of reconstructing speculative genealogies, giving new shape to, or queering, historical inquiry. Ultimately, Dozono calls educators to consider how the idea of queer worlding can be part of the social studies classroom, particularly through artistic interventions.

The next chapter examines civics, a curricular area typically thought of as exclusively belonging in the field of social studies. In their chapter, Antero Garcia, Nicole Mirra, and Mark Gomez argue that civic learning should not be confined to social studies and that doing so limits expansive understandings of civic learning and civic life. The authors also assert that typical notions of civics as learning about the three branches of government and participation in the electoral system favor notions of incremental progress thus socializing students to accept the status quo in the hopes that change will come through steadfast loyalty to institutions. Instead, the authors contend that interdisciplinary take-up of speculative civic education offers opportunities for students and teachers to go beyond the false nostalgic notions of what America is.

Thus far, our chapters have imagined a largely U.S.-based audience of educators and students. The next chapter in our volume demonstrates the hegemonic power of the United States in shaping curriculum outside of its own constructed borders. Jennice McCafferty-Wright broadens our awareness of imperial social studies by introducing the ways in which the U.S. government utilizes social studies education (through diplomacy programs sprouted from counterterrorism efforts) in order to further U.S. political and economic interests. She calls these educational efforts "cultural bombs," as they are an ideological state apparatus of imperialism, aiming to control ideology and movement, particularly for non-elite Muslim youth. Ultimately, McCafferty-Wright draws attention to the ways in which social studies is a weapon of war and urges social studies educators to object to the ways in which social studies education is weaponized across the world as part of U.S. foreign policy.

We conclude our volume on insurgent social studies with a chapter on whiteness. We include this as the last chapter to signify that whiteness (particularly as an invisible default) should be deprioritized if not eradicated in an insurgent agenda. We have decided to include this chapter with the knowledge that most social studies teachers are white and in order to adopt an insurgent orientation, must gain basic competency on whiteness. Written by Andrea Hawkman, this chapter begins with a discussion of four ways that whiteness functions in pursuit of white supremacy. Next, the author calls into question the ways that whiteness functions in social studies teaching and learning. To conclude, the author suggests that in order for insurgency to be possible, whiteness must be acknowledged, decentered, and replaced with an ideology focused on intersectional justice.

## References

Au, W. (2021). A pedagogy of insurgency: Teaching and organizing for radical racial justice in our schools. *Educational Studies*. Advanced online publication. https://doi.org/10.1080/00131946.2021.1878181

Busey, C., & Walker, I. (2017). A dream and a bus: Black critical patriotism in elementary social studies standards. *Theory & Research in Social Education, 45*(4), 1–33. https://doi.org/10.1080/00933104.2017.1320251

Calderón, D. (2014). Uncovering settler grammars in curriculum. *Educational Studies: Journal of the American Educational Studies Association, 50*(4), 313–338. https://doi.org/10.1080/00131946.2014.926904

Epstein, T. (2009). *Interpreting national history: Race, identity, and pedagogy in classrooms and communities*. Routledge.

King, L. J., & Chandler, P. T. (2016). From non-racism to anti-racism in social studies teacher education: Social studies and racial pedagogical content knowledge. In A. R. Crowe & A. Cuenca (Eds.), *Rethinking social studies teacher education in the twenty-first century* (pp. 3–22). Springer.

Ladson-Billings, G. (2003). Lies my teacher still tells: Developing a critical race perspective toward the social studies. In G. Ladson-Billings (Ed.), *Critical race theory perspectives on social studies: The profession, policies, and curriculum* (pp. 1–14). Information Age Publishing.

Ooka Pang, V., Rivera, J. J., & Gillette, M. (1998). Can CUFA be a leader in the national debate on racism? *Theory & Research in Social Education, 26*(3), 430–436. https://doi.org/10.1080/00933104.1998.10505858

Rains, F. V. (2006). The color of social studies: A post-social studies reality check. In E. W. Ross (Ed.), *The social studies curriculum: Purposes, problems, and possibilities* (pp. 137–155). State University of New York Press.

Tyson, C., & Park, S. (2008). Civic education, social justice and critical race theory. In J. Arthur, I. Davies, & C. Hahn (Eds.), *The SAGE handbook of education for citizenship and democracy* (pp. 29–56). SAGE.

Vickery, A. E. (2015). It was never meant for us: Towards a Black feminist construct of citizenship in social studies. *Journal of Social Studies Research, 39*(3), 163–172. https://doi.org/10.1016/j.jssr.2014.12.002

Vickery, A. E., & Duncan, K. E. (2020). Lifting the veil: On decentering whiteness in social studies curriculum, teaching, and research. In A. M. Hawkman & S. B. Shear (Eds.), *Marking the "invisible": Articulating whiteness in social studies education* (pp. xiii–xxiii). Information Age Publishing.

ONE

# Insurgence Must Be Red: Connecting Indigenous Studies and Social Studies Education for Anticolonial Praxis

*The Turtle Island Social Studies Collective*[1]

FOR THIS COLLECTED VOLUME, WE were invited to write about insurgence, and we are grateful to be in community and conversation with this critical collective of scholars whose work pushes our own thinking in generative ways. For our contribution to this volume, this moment, and this movement, we will take the opportunity to frame social studies within and beyond insurgence and in terms of what Indigenous studies scholars call resurgence, that is, the reinvestment in Indigenous knowledges and lifeways to inform "transformative and revolutionary" movement out of colonialism (Simpson, 2011, p. 24).

Settler narratives have long framed Indigeneity as a problem in the United States, both in popular rhetoric and in federal policy (i.e., the "Indian Problem"). Rather than a problem, our thinking comes from a legacy of scholarship that poses Indigeneity as the *solution* to the social, economic, and ecological crises we are facing. To be clear, we are not advocating for mining Indigenous communities for the knowledges and practices that may save the planet and all it sustains—this is an extractive practice itself steeped in colonial entitlement. Rather, if we are to pursue an insurgent social studies, we believe we must foreground foundational concepts and commitments in Indigenous studies, which live both in- and outside the academy: rematriating Indigenous homelands, respecting Indigenous sovereignty, restoring systems of Indigenous governance, recognizing and valuing Indigenous leadership, centering diverse Indigenous perspectives and knowledge systems, investing in Indigenous languages, and nourishing place-based, intergenerational forms of learning (Cook-Lynn, 1997; Lomawaima, 2007; McCoy et al., 2020; Rowe & Tuck, 2017). Native nations and communities actively engage in these concepts and commitments in their struggles to protect their lands and lifeways, as made visible through hashtags such as #LandBack, #WaterIsLife,

#HonorTheTreaties, #MMIWG2S, and #NativeVote that speak to the ongoing Indigenous insurgent and resurgent movements occurring across Turtle Island and beyond.[2]

We recognize, however, that we may not yet be in a place to think about resurgence in the social studies. We remain wary of how people continue to relate to Indigenous communities in ways that are extractive and exploitative and that not only mine Indigenous lands but also mine Indigenous people for their insights without also taking on responsibility for their struggles and commitments. We are wary, but we remain hopeful. We view ourselves, as the Red Nation (TRN, 2020) shares in their own principles of unity, as "the 'permanent persuaders' who believe revolutionary change is not only possible but inevitable" (p. 2). We hold a stubborn hope that a future beyond settler-colonial and heteropatriarchal systems is possible, that such a future is in fact already underway. We hope that one day—once Indigenous lands are returned, Indigenous leaders recognized, Indigenous knowledge systems valued—we can think about life on Turtle Island differently, that we can think about the types of relationships and autonomy that we would need to sustain more respectful and reciprocal relations with land and with each other.

We want to be clear that rather than advancing a new vision for insurgent social studies, we are drawing our readers' attention to well-established theories from Indigenous scholars, in part, to highlight that the erasure of Indigenous scholarship is part of the problem. Although some of this chapter draws on recent scholarship, much of what we are offering has already been generously offered by those before us. Quechua scholar Sandy Grande's (2000, 2008, 2015) theory of Red Pedagogy has been available to social studies scholars for two decades, yet it has been largely ignored or dismissed by scholars in the field. As a discipline, social studies has not seen itself in relationship and conversation with Indigenous studies. Drawing on Lenape/Potawatomi scholar Susan Dion's (2008; marchiggins, 2012) concept of "perfect stranger," a theory to describe how non-Native preservice teachers place Native people and "their" concerns outside of themselves (n.p.), we argue that as a discipline, social studies has positioned itself as a "perfect stranger" to Indigenous peoples and the discipline of Indigenous studies. To be insurgent, the field of social studies must not only interrogate this positioning but also reckon with the challenges Indigenous studies pose, including questions of colonization, land, and sovereignty among others.

Social studies, across K–12 education, teacher education, and curriculum (e.g., state content standards, textbooks), has long been a weapon of colonialism and assimilation, spreading the ideology of white supremacy and manifest destiny time and time again. Research continuously reveals the insidious nature of social studies to erase, reframe, or recast the histories and experiences of Black, Indigenous, and People of Color in the United States (e.g., Brown & Brown, 2010, Hawkman, 2017; Rains, 2006; Sabzalian, 2019; Sabzalian & Shear, 2018; Shear et al., 2015), and it is high time that the discipline takes responsibility for its role in miseducating generations of students about how the United States acquired its nationhood and who this country has always served. Still, we move with stubborn hope. Grassroots efforts in places like Montana, Washington state, and Oregon have brought changes in those states' social studies standards and the implementation of Indigenous studies curriculum for all students. Additional movements to bring Native-specific curriculum are gaining footholds in other U.S. states and several others are beginning the hard work to address and correct inaccurate and harmful content across their K–12 social studies standards. Educators, too, have taken powerful steps to lead needed pedagogical changes by sharing their work publicly in order for their fellow classroom teachers and teacher educators to infuse Indigenous studies into their social studies teaching.

## Interrogating Colonial Logics

The aforementioned projects have offered important interventions into how social studies education is imagined, theorized, and enacted, yet we must remain vigilant that these interventions—often founded in premises of inclusion and multiculturalism—not inadvertently reinforce the assumed permanence of the nation-state. Ongoing projects must seek to create more just practices that openly and honestly attend to Indigenous dispossession and the denial of Indigenous sovereignty.

To set the context for how an insurgent social studies must interrogate colonial logics that tacitly (or at times explicitly) frame social studies, we draw attention to three concepts: *settled expectations* (Mackey, 2016), *settler futurity* (Tuck & Gaztambide-Fernández, 2013; Tuck & Yang, 2012), and *Indigenous futurity* (Saranillio, 2014; Tuck & Gaztambide-Fernández, 2013; Tuck & Yang, 2012). Together, these concepts reveal the ways that political and pedagogical projects often remain deeply tethered to and invested in the nation-state and continue to disavow Indigenous sovereignty, despite their critical and liberal intent.

*Settled expectations*

In the 2005 Supreme Court case *City of Sherrill v. Oneida Indian Nation of New York*, the Oneida Nation sought to declare land they had purchased within their traditional territory as "Indian Country" (a declaration that would remove the lands from the tax rolls of Sherrill County; Mackey, 2016). The City of Sherrill opposed Oneida's claim, an opinion shared by the Supreme Court, which ruled in favor of the City of Sherrill.

Of interest here is the logic used by the Supreme Court to deny the Oneida Nation's claim. As Mackey (2016) observes, the court argued on the (rarely used) basis of "laches," the idea

> that the Oneida had waited too long to make their claim and that it was, therefore, ineligible. Further, using language that reveals a powerful sense of settler entitlement, the court was unwilling to disrupt what it called the "settled expectations" and "justifiable expectations" of the current non-Indian occupants of the land. (p. 151)

The court framed Indigenous sovereignty as an outdated project, a point emphasized repeatedly throughout the opinion by characterizing sovereignty as "ancient" and asserting that the Oneida were trying to "rekindl[e] embers of sovereignty that long ago grew cold" (*City of Sherrill v. Oneida Indian Nation of New York*, 2005, para. 24). This is a misreading of tribal sovereignty. Indigenous sovereignty is *inherent* (Lomawaima, 2000, 2013; Wilkins & Stark, 2010); it was not granted or gifted to Indigenous nations but "comes from within a people or culture" (Kickingbird et al., 1999, p. 2). Tribal sovereignty is *also* recognized and affirmed by the treaties between the United States and Native nations, treaties recognized by Article VI of the U.S. Constitution as the "supreme law of the land." As such, tribal sovereignty involves the *ongoing* "ability to govern and to protect and enhance the health, safety, and welfare of tribal citizens within tribal territory" and beyond (National Congress for American Indians, 2020, p. 23).

Coupled with the discursive and legal erosion of Indigenous sovereignty through this opinion is the legal assertion of settler entitlement to Indigenous homelands. Because settlers have come to call a place home, in this case the City of Sherrill, an "expectation" to remain on those lands has developed over time, a "justifiable expectation" according to the court. As Mackey (2016) writes, "the legal, political, and cultural defence of the 'settled expectations' of current inhabitants (descendants of those who deliberately *un*settled Indigenous nations over centuries) . . . almost always supersede the just desires of Indigenous nations for recognition of their historic rights to their land" (p. 8).

The framework of "settled expectations" is an apt description for the assumptions of settler entitlement and permanence that underlie social studies education. It is imperative to examine how social studies theories, practices, and curricula similarly frame Indigenous sovereignty as an "ancient" or outdated project and take for granted the "settled expectations" of non-Indigenous peoples. Social studies researchers and practitioners must ask ourselves: *How does social studies disavow Indigenous sovereignty? And how does social studies continue to justify occupation?* Mainstream theories of democratic citizenship education, for example, are "silent to occupation" (Calderón, 2014, p. 321) and often "erase Indigenous nationhood and sovereignty and presume that inclusion into the nation-state is a shared aspiration" (Sabzalian, 2019, p. 314). To make these erasures and settled expectations more visible, we turn to the concept of settler futurity.

### *Settler futurity*

Closely coupled with the idea of *settled expectations* is the concept of *settler futurity* (Tuck & Yang, 2012). Settler futurity is not only about the expectations of settlers to claim Indigenous homelands but about the normalization of the nation-state as well. Settler futurity presumes, for example, that the United States is a given and that social studies and theories must accommodate that reality. As Tuck and Gaztambide-Fernández (2013) write, "anything that seeks to recuperate and not interrupt settler colonialism, to reform the settlement and incorporate Indigenous peoples into the multicultural settler colonial nation state is fettered to settler futurity" (p. 80). Here, we see an analysis that is broadened, away from the settled expectations of individuals and institutions to the societal presumption that the settler state will always exist.

Settlement and the nation-state may feel like a given, a taken-for-granted part of the legal, political, and cultural backdrop of the United States. But, as Kahnawà:ke Mohawk scholar Audra Simpson (2011) argues, "settlement was wrought through violent and bloody dispossession and now maintains itself through the threat of military force and the force of the law" (p. 208). Maintaining the United States *as* a nation-state requires a great deal of work (Moreton-Robinson, 2015), as the "precarious and illogical claims to settler sovereignty must be constantly reinvented and defended" (Mackey, 2016, p. 36).

An insurgent social studies must recognize the ways in which Indigenous peoples' persistence "fundamentally interrupts what is received, what is ordered, and what is supposed to be settled" (Simpson, 2011, p. 209). The nation-state is merely the present, not a given. Indigenous sovereignty is inherent and enduring. To be insurgent, social studies must interrupt settler futurity and work toward Indigenous futurities.

### *Indigenous futurity*

When settler futurities are presumed, Indigenous desires for decolonization are framed not only as outdated but also as too impractical, too fantastical (Tuck & Yang, 2018). *"Where would everyone go?"* people often wonder or say aloud when confronted with Indigenous calls for decolonization. *"What will be the consequences of decolonization for the settler?"* (Tuck & Yang, 2012, p. 35). Of course, Indigenous peoples have advocated repeatedly that Indigenous decolonization does not require the same violence, the same exclusions, the same removals it took to acquire Indigenous homelands: "Indigenous futurity does not require the erasure of now-settlers in the ways that settler futurity requires of Indigenous peoples" (Tuck & Gaztambide-Fernández, 2013, p. 80).

Social studies educators should look to examples of Indigenous futurity in practice. In 2005, for example, the Onondaga Nation asserted its rights to land in New York state. In their complaint for a declaratory judgment, the Nation wrote, "We want justice. . . . But we will not displace any of our neighbors—the Ononadaga know too well the pain of being forced to leave our homes and do not wish that on anyone" (Onondaga Nation, as cited in Mackey, 2016, p. 145). The Onondaga were fighting primarily for their right to caretake Onondaga Lake. From an Indigenous standpoint, this fight was about sovereignty and land stewardship, which, at its core, is a "request to be responsible" for Indigenous lands, waters, and more-than-human relations (Monture-Angus, 1999, p. 36). The court denied the Onondaga Nation's claim, in part because of the colonial logics of "settled expectations" discussed earlier. The court could not *hear* the Nation's claim because it could only understand title in a Western framework that relies on domination and exclusion. Important to note, however, is that the Onondaga Nation was fighting for the life of their Nation and lands and explicitly sought a way to "*share* territory" without "compromis[ing] their autonomy" (Mackey, 2016, p. 150).

Indigenous futurity is about *life*, about a future in which the lives, lifeways, and lands of Indigenous peoples persist and thrive. When the state is taken for granted and transformation is contained and confined within the settler state's imaginary, transformative (or decolonial) action is treated as impossible (Saranillio, 2014). To be insurgent, social studies must upset settled expectations and assumed settler futurities. An insurgent social studies must explicitly work toward Indigenous futurities and liberation.

## Insurgence Must Be Red

Learning comes from laboring with Indigenous analyses, and social studies practitioners and researchers must commit to doing this work. To truly partner in building toward Indigenous futures, educators must confront and lean into the myriad ways the U.S. education system broadly and social studies specifically have operated as weapons for assimilation and the attempted genocide of Indigeneity. Indigenous peoples have already offered beautiful theories and visions of liberation. In this section, we turn to two: Quechua scholar Sandy Grande's theory of Red Pedagogy and the Red Deal proposed by TRN. We argue that both projects, which view themselves as extensions of legacies of Indigenous activism that came before them, offer social studies a way to imagine itself on different terms, on Indigenous terms. Unless social studies conceives of itself as a project dedicated to the liberation of Indigenous life and lands, it can never be insurgent. Furthermore, Indigenous liberation is an inclusive goal, one that accounts for multiple and interrelated experiences of oppression and modes of resistance. As TRN (2020) writes, "the Red Deal is 'Red' because it prioritizes Indigenous liberation, on the one hand, and a revolutionary left position, on the other. It is simultaneously particular and universal, because Indigenous liberation is for everybody" (p. 11).

### *Red Pedagogy*

Insurgent social studies explicitly seeks to distinguish itself from conservative, and even critical, conceptions of social studies. Grande's scholarship, which has creatively navigated the tensions and resonances between critical and Indigenous theories, offers an important intervention into discussions of insurgent social studies, in particular, by reminding social studies scholars and practitioners to question the deep-seated colonial assumptions and institutions that remain taken for granted from within critical, radical, even revolutionary projects.

Some might assume that an insurgent social studies is a radical practice. Grande (2013) argues that for a movement to be truly "radical" or "revolutionary," it must "propose something distinct from or counter to the settler state," a challenge given that many movements toward social justice in the United States "ultimately [retain] a liberal (which is to say Eurocentric) center" and are primarily focused on "a politics of inclusion that seeks to absorb Indigenous peoples" (Grande, 2013, p. 370). For social studies to be insurgent, it must engender relations and practices that aren't tethered to empire, that aren't reliant on capitalism and colonialism, that are rooted not on Indigenous erasure or absorption but instead on the promotion of Indigenous land and life.

As a framework, Red Pedagogy calls for

> (1) the subjection of the processes of whitestream schooling to critical pedagogical analyses; (2) the decoupling and dethinking of education from its Western, colonialist contexts; and (3) the institution of Indigenous efforts to reground students and educators in traditional knowledge and teachings. (Grande, 2015, p. 74).

More specifically, Grande (2008) has offered seven precepts for thinking about Red Pedagogy as a decolonizing pedagogy and praxis:

1. Red pedagogy is primarily a pedagogical project.
2. Red pedagogy is fundamentally rooted in indigenous knowledge and praxis.
3. Red pedagogy is informed by critical theories of education.
4. Red pedagogy promotes an education for decolonization.

5. Red pedagogy is a project that interrogates both democracy and Indigenous sovereignty.
6. Red pedagogy actively cultivates praxis of collective agency.
7. Red pedagogy is grounded in hope. (p. 250)

Grande (2008) frames pedagogy as "inherently political, cultural, spiritual, and intellectual" (p. 250) and advocates for interrogating the legacies and ongoing impacts of colonization while thinking alongside other traditions of revolutionary thought and practice. In thinking about our classroom practice, Red Pedagogy offers us pathways out of colonization, looking toward "equity, emancipation, sovereignty, and balance" (p. 250), not as loose or abstract concepts but as tangible commitments in our daily lives and work. Such commitments are grounded in intersectional approaches to solidarity and seek to realize a vision of a world liberated from "imperialist, colonialist, and capitalist exploitation" (p. 250). As it points us toward the better future that we can help create through our classrooms, Red Pedagogy demands that we trust "the beliefs and understandings of our ancestors, the power of traditional knowledge, and the possibilities of new understandings" as we build new educational structures that better serve all students (Grande, 2008, p. 250).

Red Pedagogy urges us to remember that we are theorizing and teaching on Indigenous homelands and thus engage in scholarship and pedagogies that aren't rooted in the ongoing dispossession of Indigenous peoples, and that actively work to dismantle global capitalist and colonial relations. Red Pedagogy recognizes land as our ancestor, our relation, our source of life. Red Pedagogy understands the universe to be spiritual, an understanding that shapes our processes of inquiry and pursuit of sovereignty. Informed by Red Pedagogy, an insurgent social studies would explicitly work to cultivate land-based solidarities around a "decolonial imaginary" that envision and work toward "a way of life free from exploitation and replete with spirit" (Grande, 2015, p. 243).

### *TRN and the Red Deal*

TRN (n.d.) is a "coalition of Native and non-Native activists, educators, students, and community organizers advocating Native liberation" ("Who We Are"). Recognizing "the invisibility and marginalization of Native struggles within mainstream social justice organizing," the coalition formed to advance Native liberation as a necessary intervention to "the targeted destruction and violence towards Native life and land" (TRN, 2020, p. 3).

TRN developed a program called the Red Deal based on U.S. Representative Alexandria Ocasio-Cortez's "Green New Deal," a congressional resolution that simultaneously seeks to address economic, environmental, and racial inequalities and that was itself inspired by Ocasio-Cortez's participation in the NoDAPL fight at Standing Rock in 2016. The Red Deal moves beyond the Green New Deal to imagine a world beyond the present, a world in which relationality, justice, and care take priority over profit and competition. This builds on Indigenous histories and values, amplifying demands that are decades (and, in some cases, hundreds of years) old. In this sense, the Red Deal is "not the 'Red *New* Deal' because it's the same '*Old* Deal'—the fulfillment of treaty rights, land restoration, sovereignty, self-determination, decolonization, and liberation" (TRN, 2020, p. 11, emphasis added).

In developing a vision of an insurgent social studies, we turn to the Red Deal for its unapologetic centering of Indigenous liberation while also forwarding a vision of justice grounded in solidarity with other struggles. The Red Deal attends to both the liberation of Indigenous land and lives and to the liberation of other oppressed peoples, as the authors envision "a coming Indigenous future, a future in which many worlds fit" (TRN, 2020, pp. 1–2). Its vision is intersectional, feminist, anticolonial, anti-imperial, and anticapitalist, as seen in its 10 priorities:

1. The re-instatement of treaty rights;
2. The full rights and equal protection for Native people;
3. The end to disciplinary violence against Native peoples and all oppressed peoples;
4. The end to discrimination against the Native silent majority: youth and the poor;
5. The end to the discrimination, persecution, killing, torture, and rape of Native women;
6. The end to the discrimination, persecution, killing, torture, and rape of Native lesbian, gay, bisexual, transgender, queer, and two-spirit people (LGBTQ2+);
7. The end to the dehumanization of Native peoples;

8. Access to appropriate education, health care, social services, employment, and housing;
9. The repatriation of Native lands and lives and the protection of nonhuman relatives; and
10. The end to capitalism-colonialism. (TRN, 2020, pp. 4–8)

Taken as a whole, the authors offer "a platform so that our planet may live" (TRN, 2020, p. 10). Recognizing the disproportionate violence enacted on Native women, Native LGBTQ2S+ people, Native youth, and Native people who are presently unsheltered, the Red Deal provides tangible steps toward imagining and realizing a different future—one in which the current extreme funding allocated to the military and police is redistributed to social services, including health care and education. We encourage readers to dive more deeply into the Red Deal and engage with the justifications, urgent areas of focus, and action items related to each area of struggle. As they do, we hope they take specific note of the ways Indigenous liberation benefits others.

Taking seriously calls for justice and ways of being, knowing, and doing that do not further capitalist and colonialist relations may feel impossible for some social studies theorists and practitioners. However, for Indigenous peoples, decolonization has always been a stubbornly hopeful and practical vision. Indigenous peoples have been gracious and generous in sharing these visions and practical strategies to enact decolonial futures. However, these analyses are often sidelined, deemed important only to Indigenous peoples (if at all). To be insurgent, we argue that Indigenous analyses must be *central* to how we theorize and enact social studies.

It is here that many of you may be wondering: *How* do we center Indigenous analyses? What does this *look like* in practice? What do I *do* with these frameworks of Red Pedagogy and liberation? Rather than offer another list—a "how-to" or "honey-do list" (Tuck, 2006, p. 156)—we invite social studies scholars and practitioners to "pause" (Patel, 2016) with what we have offered. Pausing "can be a productive interruption" (Patel, 2016, p. 1) into the way things have always been. Pausing can also be generative and help us "reach beyond" what social studies is, to what social studies could be. In reflecting on listening to an Anishinaabe woman's experiences of colonization and genocide and the implications of that narrative to her own understanding of slavery, Tiffany King (2019) writes,

> When I felt around and realized the new and unfamiliar about the slavery with which I had become so comfortable, it changed me—and I do not mean changed in a neat, orderly, or containable way. It unmoored and disassembled me in ways that I and others did not expect . . . When I say unmoored, I meant that I could not continue life as I knew it. (p. ix)

To be insurgent, social studies must become *unmoored*. Social studies scholars and practitioners *cannot continue life as they knew it*. We recognize that this will feel unsatisfying to read, particularly for those who are already convinced that this work is important and who crave steps to enact and implement the theories and practices of Indigenous liberation we have shared. However, we pose that a "pedagogy of pausing . . . which involves intentionally engaging suspension of one's own premises and projects, but always with a sense of futurity" (Tuck, 2016, p. xii) *is* the path and practice we need to take in order to imagine and enact insurgent social studies. There is no prescription, no template, for this work.

A locally responsive and "place-based Indigenous politics" (Aikau et al., 2015, p. 86) requires that educators take up insurgent social studies within their own contexts and with respect to the specific decolonial struggles Indigenous peoples are facing in their "own backyard" (Aikau et al., 2015, p. 85). We therefore invite educators to pause, to labor with, to learn, and to think with Red Pedagogy and the Red Deal. Here, we offer three scenarios. As you read them, consider a response grounded in your specific place, context, and a praxis that thinks alongside both frameworks. For each, ponder: What practices are no longer viable for you? What practices do you need to unlearn or learn? What relational work do you need to invest in to be able to do this work ethically, and where can you go to learn how to do the work needed to build these practices?

1. As a teacher, your social studies standards ask your students to name major state geographical features like rivers and mountain ranges. You have heard about efforts from land-based educators like Megan Bang (Ojibwe and Italian descent), Emma Elliott-Groves (Cowichan), and Meixi (Hokkien/Hokchiu) to restore Indigenous land-based educational practices. You are wondering how to reach beyond the standards to help your students understand the significance of the place where they are learning. Thinking with Red Pedagogy and the Red Deal, what strategies

might you employ in the classroom to help students interrogate ideas of ownership, dispossession, and capitalist division of people from place? How can you help your students see themselves in relation to place? How will you facilitate your students grounding themselves in relationality and reciprocity with our lands and more-than-human relations?

2. As an administrator, you recognize the importance of building relationships with representatives of local Native nations. You understand that your work, in part, is to meet requirements stated in the Every Student Succeeds Act. You also understand that the political landscape of tribal nations, urban Native organizations, districts, and state agencies for consultation is complex. Thinking with the teachings of Red Pedagogy and the Red Deal, how will you both educate yourself and find learning opportunities that push your understanding of the complex experiences of Indian education in your state? How will you seek consultation with tribal leaders in your area? How will you work to build relationships that are mutually beneficial rather than extractive? How will you ensure that all of your school's or district's leadership teams hold space for the time, hard work, and listening necessary to foster meaningful and mutually beneficial relationships, especially when it is inconvenient or time-consuming? How will you share decision-making power with nearby tribal nations?
3. As a teacher educator and researcher, you have learned that Indigenous knowledge systems are valid bodies of knowledge, with equivalent rigor and credibility as Western knowledge systems. You recognize the hegemonic role Western knowledge has played in defining what counts as knowledge, in general, and social studies, in particular. You believe that all students can learn from Indigenous knowledge systems, and you want to ensure your teaching and research don't reinforce Eurocentrism and epistemic supremacy. How will you challenge Eurocentric knowledge systems in your discipline, curriculum, pedagogy, and research? How will you anticipate and work against the frequent commodification of Indigenous knowledges? How can you move beyond using Indigenous knowledges to "diversify" Eurocentric curricula? How will you ensure your teaching is grounded in relationality and mutual obligation? How will you create space for Indigenous knowledges to be valued and understood on their own terms?

While inviting you to think with these theories, we also want to acknowledge that Red Pedagogy and the theories of action and liberation outlined by the Red Deal are *already* happening in educational spaces; they are just not always named as social studies. Instead, they live on the margins of social studies, many times after school, and are often found within the fields of Indigenous studies or Indigenous education or ethnic studies. Insurgent social studies will require moving these existing practices from the margins to the center. It will also require defying the rigid disciplinary boundaries that typically frame social studies—history, geography, economics, civics—and engage in interdisciplinary approaches that may involve literature, land-based, environmental, or science education. Indigenous educators have shown us that Red Pedagogy and the Red Deal's commitments are "doable" in practice: repatriating fire technologies with Native youth at an Urban Indian Center in Chicago (Bang et al., 2013); "water walks" led by Indigenous Elders that draw attention to water issues and enlist community members in its protection (http://www.motherearthwaterwalk.com/); community walks, again with Elders, in which youth learn from and develop right relations with Land (Bang et al., 2014); and STEAM (science, technology, engineering, the arts, mathematics) activities (http://indigenouseducationtools.org/) that invite students to explore relations with their "water, food, plant and bird relatives," learn across generations, learn through story, think civically about their responsibility to water, and connect their local understanding of water to social movements to protect water. These pedagogies point us toward a resurgent praxis that foregrounds Indigenous relations, knowledge, and lifeways.

We recognize that some educators may not yet feel prepared to enact the concepts and commitments that we have outlined. We believe the lack of preparedness on the part of most educators to take up this work has direct implications for teacher education programs who should be actively recruiting, preparing, and retaining educators *already* versed in the knowledges and skills we are foregrounding and who are willing to lean into these commitments. Teacher education programs must also center Indigenous studies within their programs so that each and every educator who graduates has a grounding in Indigenous studies theories and understands that learning is a process they must continue long after they leave the university. And while we recognize that some educators don't yet feel prepared to take up this work, we worry that the process of waiting, of not engaging in the work until the right book(s) have been read or enough professional development workshops attended, can absolve educators of the responsibility of taking this work up now. The positioning of Indigenous studies as always on the horizon is another form of erasure, another form of displacement. It removes Indigenous knowledges by framing them always as something we will get to when we've done *enough* work. We must implicate ourselves in the learning with, in the learning now, in the vulnerability of learning while doing. This is the work of insurgency—embracing the complex messiness of learning alongside our students rather than waiting until we know enough because waiting is yet another tool of oppression. The time to lean into the work is now. It requires willingness, commitment, reflection, relationships, humility, and accountability.

## Dreaming of Resurgence: Beyond an Insurgent Social Studies Praxis

> The theory and practice of Indigenous anticolonialism, including Indigenous anticapitalism, is best understood as a struggle primarily inspired by and oriented around *the question of land*—a struggle not only *for* land in the material sense, but also deeply informed by what the *land as system of reciprocal relations and obligations* can teach us about living our lives in relation to one another and the natural world in nondominating and nonexploitative terms.
>
> —*Coulthard (2014, p. 13)*

By looking to Red Pedagogy and the Red Deal, we can see that an insurgent social studies grounded in Indigenous theories is inclusive, intersectional, land-based, and attentive to the needs of both our human and more-than-human relatives. The tag line, "All Relatives Forever," that sits beneath TRN on its site is not a metaphor but an inclusive vision and principled commitment.

To begin, an insurgent social studies requires that educators attend to relations of power within the classroom, including their own positionality and complicity in colonialism. Non-Native teachers need to critically interrogate their own "colonization stories" (Tuck & Yang, 2012, p. 6). Even those whose histories result from violence or forced migration must reflect on what it means to live responsibly in diaspora (Haig-Brown, 2009). Looking deeply at their own relationship to the United States and reflecting on their family histories, educators should ask themselves: Upon whose homelands am I living and working? How does my family's historical and ongoing relationships to property maintain the dispossession of Indigenous nations? What are my responsibilities and actions as a result of this work? An insurgent social studies cannot proceed without first wrestling with these questions, histories, and inheritances.

Cowichan scholar Emma Elliott-Groves asks her students to imagine themselves from an Indigenous perspective: Would Indigenous peoples see them as a neighbor, ally, or uninvited guest? We hope teachers would aspire to becoming what Mashpee Wampanoag Elder gkisedtanamoogk calls "neighbors with legitimacy" (Mazo et al., 2018). To enter into this type of right relationship with Indigenous peoples, settler educators must consider the racist and colonial structures that continue to shape where and how they live and work. This is about more than apologies and acknowledgments: Teachers have an individual role to play in how they model grappling with these issues for their students, and their actions in the classroom have ramifications for how we proceed as a society in the generations to come.

Potawatomi ecologist Robin Wall Kimmerer offers a useful framing for this responsibility, drawing on the relationships between endemic and invasive species. Kimmerer (2013) writes,

> Our immigrant plant teachers offer a lot of different models for how not to make themselves welcome on a new continent. Garlic mustard poisons the soil so that native species will die. Tamarisk uses up all the water. Foreign invaders like loosestrife, kudzu and cheat grass have the colonizing habit of taking over others' homes and growing without regard to limits. But plantain is not like that. Its strategy was to be useful, to fit into small places, to co-exist with others around the dooryard, to heal wounds. Plantain is so prevalent, so well-integrated that we think of it as native. It has earned the name bestowed by botanists for plants that have become our own. Plantain is not Indigenous, but naturalized. This is the same term we use for the foreign-born when they become citizens in our country. (p. 214)

Such a deeply relational view reflects Indigenous understandings of our obligations to one another, both to our human relations and to our more-than-human relatives. We recognize that this approach often feels at odds with forms of activism that prioritize individual agency rather than networks of mutual obligation, forms of activism that are likely more familiar to the reader of this volume.[3] And yet, this neoliberal approach to advocacy, one that emphasizes the rights of individuals, largely fails to engage with the foundational elements of community organizing through relationship building. Such relationship building can serve as an entry point for understanding how treatied relationships have been nurtured in the past and can be maintained in the current moment.

This requires intention, as even an insurgent social studies can still normalize the presence of the nation-state and its power hierarchies, even as it seeks to invert or realign them. Rather than colonial frameworks, which imagine redistributing existing power more equitably, an insurgent social studies built through Indigenous frameworks imagines undoing hierarchies of power entirely in favor of more just systems of relationality.

There are ways in which even an insurgent social studies does not go far enough in stretching us toward Indigenous futures. At the start of this chapter, we argued that we may not yet be ready for a social studies praxis based in resurgence. And yet, we are left wondering: What might a social studies praxis focused on Indigenous futures and resurgences look like? How might such a practice of social studies lead us to land-based practices of social studies that tightly link history, geography, and civics within our obligations to our human and more-than-human relations? That takes seriously understandings of sovereignty beyond the boundaries of colonial legal thought?[4]

In the aftermath of 2020, a world beset by a pandemic brought on by deforestation, by wildfires made worse by ignoring Indigenous ecological practices that promote healthy burns to reduce more destructive inflagrations, and by a global rise in autocratic leaders whose singular focus on profit occludes compassionate care for one another, it is clearer than ever that colonization kills all of us. It just kills some of us faster.[5] Indigenous teachings around land practices and governance are important for our collective survival in this moment.

Insurgence responds to colonialism. Resurgence moves beyond settler presence to Indigenous futures. Recognizing this, how might we ground social studies in Indigenous resurgence? Looking to Michi Saagiig Nishnaabeg scholar Leanne Betasamosake Simpson (2011), what if we worked alongside our students toward practices of Indigenous resurgence that "propel and maintain social, cultural and political transformative movement through the worst forms of political genocide" (p. 24). Grounded in Indigenous languages, epistemologies, and networks of relationality, a resurgent social studies would "diagnose, interrogate, and eviscerate the insidious nature of conquest, empire, and imperial thought in every aspect of our lives" and seek to learn from and invest in the health of "traditional cultures, knowledge systems, and lifeways in the dynamic, fluid, compassionate, respectful context within which they were originally generated" (Simpson, 2011, pp. 17–18).

This shift requires a commitment to humility, to becoming a "neighbor with legitimacy." A resurgent Indigenous social studies centers Indigenous approaches to relationality, responsibility, and collective renewal. Recognizing the importance of restoring Indigenous models for education and governance, it recognizes that land-based, relationship-oriented approaches to social studies are good for *all* students and, by extension, the future of our collective society.

## Notes

1. We rise and resist together, fighting against settler colonialism in education. Following Quechua scholar Sandy Grande's (2018) call to "commit to collectivity," we write as a scholarly collective under the nom de guerre "Turtle Island Social Studies Collective." Our hope is to further collective "insurgence and resurgence (and not individual recognition)" (Grande, 2018, p. 61).

2. We use the term *Turtle Island* for the continent of North America to draw attention to the importance of ongoing relationships between Indigenous peoples and lands and to the importance of land in Indigenous theories and practices of decolonization.

3. The category of the activist is primarily concerned with the individual, appearances, and exclusivity because there is no specificity attached to it. Taylor (2016) succinctly summarizes that despite "notable exceptions, many strands of contemporary activism risk emphasizing the self over the collective" (n.p.).

4 In this, we can follow Lumbee scholar Malinda Maynor Lowery, who has commented, "Sovereignty is culturally-embedded, it's place-specific, and it does not lend itself towards neoliberal, rights-based conceptions of citizenship. What it lends itself to is permission and reciprocity" (#ScholarStrike2020, 2020, 30:03). This has clear ramifications for how we teach citizenship—citing Māori scholar Nēpia Mahuika, Lowery continues: "No one has citizenship in a nation unless Indigenous people have offered that, have invited you, have acknowledged your presence legally within their own systems of knowledge and cultural constructs" (#ScholarStrike2020, 2020, 30:03).

5. This idea builds from Kelly Wickham Hurst's (2020) tweet that "Racism kills all of us. Some faster than others."

## References

Aikau, H. K., Arvin, M., Goeman, M., & Morgensen, S. (2015). Indigenous feminisms roundtable. *Frontiers: A Journal of Women Studies, 36*(3), 84–106.

Bang, M., Marin, A., Faber, L., & Suzukovich, E. S. (2013). Repatriating Indigenous technologies in an urban Indian community. *Urban Education, 48*(5), 705–733.

Brown, K. D., & Brown, A. L. (2010). Silenced memories: An examination of the sociocultural knowledge on race and racial violence in official school curriculum. *Equity & Excellence in Education, 43*, 139–154. https://doi.org/10.1080/10665681003719590

Calderón, D. (2014). Uncovering settler grammars in curriculum. *Educational Studies: Journal of the American Educational Studies Association, 50*(4), 313–338. https://doi.org/10.1080/00131946.2014.926904

City of Sherrill v. Oneida Indian Nation of New York, 544 U.S. 197. (2005). Supreme Court of the United States. https://supreme.justia.com/cases/federal/us/544/197/#F8

Cook-Lynn, E. (1997). Who stole Native American studies? *Wicazo Sa Review, 12*, 9–28. https://doi.org/10.2307/1409161

Coulthard, G. S. (2014). *Red skin, white masks: Rejecting the colonial politics of recognition.* University of Minnesota Press.

Dion, S. D. (2008). *Braiding histories: Learning from Aboriginal peoples' experiences and perspectives.* UBC Press.

Grande, S. (2000). American Indian identity and intellectualism: The quest for a new red pedagogy. *International Journal of Qualitative Studies in Education, 13*(4), 343–359. https://doi.org/10.1080/095183900413296

Grande, S. (2008). Red pedagogy: The un-methodology. In N. K. Denzin, Y. S. Lincoln, & L. T. Smith (Eds.), *Handbook of critical and Indigenous methodologies* (pp. 233–254). SAGE.

Grande, S. (2013). Accumulation of the primitive: The limits of liberalism and the politics of Occupy Wall Street. *Settler Colonial Studies, 3*(3–4), 369–380. https://doi.org/10.1080/2201473X.2013.810704

Grande, S. (2015). *Red pedagogy: Native American social and political thought* (10th anniversary ed.). Rowman & Littlefield.

Grande, S. (2018). Refusing the university. In E. Tuck & K. W. Yang (Eds.), *Toward what justice? Describing diverse dreams of justice in education* (pp. 47–66). Routledge.

Haif-Brown, C. (2009). Decolonizing diaspora: Whose traditional land are we on? *Culture and Pedagogical Inquiry, 1*(2), 4–21.

Hawkman, A. M. (2017). Race and racism in the social studies: Foundations of critical race theory. In P. Chandler & T. Hawley (Eds.), *Race lessons: Using inquiry to teach about race in social studies* (pp. 19–31). Information Age.

Hurst, K. W. (2020, August 27). *Racism kills all of us. Some faster than others* [Tweet]. Twitter. https://twitter.com/mochamomma/status/1298974772601200641

Kickingbird, J., Kickingbird, L., Chibitty, C. J., & Berkey, C. (1999). Indian sovereignty. In J. Wunder (Ed.), *Native American sovereignty* (pp. 1–13). Garland.

Kimmerer, R. W. (2013). *Braiding sweetgrass: Indigenous wisdom, scientific knowledge, and the teachings of plants*. Milkweed Editions.

King, T. L. (2019). *The black shoals: Offshore formations of Black and Native studies*. Duke University Press.

Lomawaima, K. T. (2000). Tribal sovereigns: Reframing research in American Indian education. *Harvard Educational Review, 70*(1), 1–21. https://doi.org/10.17763/haer.70.1.b133t096714n73r

Lomawaima, K. T. (2007, May 3–5). *Remarks for Friday morning plenary session*. Indigenous & Native studies meeting, University of Oklahoma, Norman, Oklahoma, USA. https://www.naisa.org/wp-content/uploads/2018/01/Lomawaima_Plenary_Remarks_OU_0.pdf

Lomawaima, K. T. (2013). The mutuality of citizenship and sovereignty: The Society of American Indians and the battle to inherit America. *American Indian Quarterly, 37*(3), 333–351.

Mackey, E. (2016). *Unsettled expectations: Uncertainty, land and settler decolonization*. Fernwood.

marchiggins. (2012, July). *Dr. Susan D. Dion: Introducing and disrupting the "perfect stranger"* [Video]. Vimeo. http://vimeo.com/59543958

Mazo, A. (Director), Pender-Cudlip, B., & Duthu, N. B. (Producers). (2018). *Dawnland* [Film]. Upstander Films.

McCoy, M., Elliott-Groves, E., Sabzalian, L., & Bang, M. (2020). *Educating for right relations and land return* [Invited Testimony]. Center for Humans and Nature. Libertyville, IL. https://www.humansandnature.org/restoring-indigenous-systems-of-relationality

Monture-Angus, P. (1999). *Journeying forward: Dreaming First Nations' independence*. Fernwood.

Moreton-Robinson, A. (2015). *The white possessive: Property, power, and indigenous sovereignty*. University of Minnesota Press.

National Congress of American Indians. (2020). *Tribal Nations and the United States: An introduction*. https://www.ncai.org/about-tribes

Patel, L. (2016). *Decolonizing educational research: From ownership to answerability*. Routledge.

Rains, F. V. (2006). The color of social studies: A post-social studies reality check. In E. W. Ross (Ed.), *The social studies curriculum: Purposes, problems, and possibilities* (pp. 137–156). State University of New York Press.

The Red Nation. (2020). *The Red Deal: Indigenous action to save our Earth. Part 1: End the occupation*. https://therednation.org/

The Red Nation. (n.d.). *About*. http://therednation.org/about

Rowe, A., & Tuck, E. (2017). Settler colonialism and cultural studies: Ongoing settlement, cultural production, and resistance. *Cultural Studies ↔ Critical Methodologies, 17*(1), 3–13. https://doi.org/10.1177/1532708616653693

Sabzalian, L. (2019). *Indigenous children's survivance in public schools* (Indigenous and Decolonizing Studies in Education). Routledge.

Sabzalian, L., & Shear, S. (2018). Confronting colonial blindness in civics education: Recognizing colonization, self-determination, and sovereignty as core knowledge for elementary social studies teacher education. In S. Shear, C. M. Tschida, E. Bellows, L. B. Buchanan, & E. E. Saylor (Eds.), *(Re)Imagining elementary social studies: A controversial issues reader* (pp. 153–176). Information Age Press.

Saranillio, D. I. (2014). The Kēpaniwai (damming of the water) Heritage Gardens: Alternative futures beyond the settler state. In A. Goldstein (Ed.), *Formations of United States colonialism* (pp. 233–263). Duke University Press.

#ScholarStrike2020. (2020, September 9). *Mark Simposon-Vos interview with Malinda Maynor Lowery 9/9/2020* [Video]. YouTube. https://www.youtube.com/watch?time_continue=1846&v=Ky_jlJjd2GA

Shear, S. B., Knowles, R. T., Soden, G. J., & Castro, A. J. (2015). Manifesting destiny: Re/presentations of Indigenous peoples in K–12 U.S. history standards. *Theory & Research in Social Education, 43*, 68–101. https://doi.org/10.1080/00933104.2014.999849

Simpson, L. (2011). *Dancing on our turtle's back: Stories of Nishnaabeg re-creation, resurgence and a new emergence.* Arbeiter Ring.

Taylor, A. (2016, Quarter 1). Against activism. *The Baffler, 30*. https://www.thebaffler.com

Tuck, E., & Gaztambide-Fernández, R. A. (2013). Curriculum, replacement, and settler futurity. *Journal of Curriculum Theorizing, 29*(1), 72–89.

Tuck, E., & Yang, K. W. (2012). Decolonization is not a metaphor. *Decolonization: Indigeneity, Education and Society, 1*, 1–40.

Tuck, E., & Yang, K. W. (2018). (Eds.). *Toward what justice?: Describing diverse dreams of justice in education.* Routledge.

Wilkins, D., & Stark, H. K. (2010). *American Indian politics and the American political system* (3rd ed.). Rowman & Littlefield.

TWO

# *Solidarity* Is a Verb: What the Black Lives Matter Movement Can Teach Social Studies About the Intersectional Fight Against Anti-Black Racism

*Tiffany Mitchell Patterson*

> We've got to face the fact that some people say you fight fire best with fire, but we say you put fire out best with water. We say you don't fight racism with racism. We're gonna fight racism with solidarity.
>
> —*Fred Hampton (1969)*

> You're either in the movement or you're not, and in order to achieve justice everyone needs to feel as if they have something at stake when it comes to Black liberation.
>
> —*Thandiwe Abdullah (2020)*

SOLIDARITY (N.D.) IS DEFINED AS "unity (as a group or class) that produces or is based on a community of interests, objectives and standards." Although solidarity is fundamental to social movements, as a concept it can be ambiguous or vague if used without specifying what it means in a particular context. Fred Hampton and Thandiwe Abdullah, youth activists in the Black Panther Party and Black Lives Matter (BLM) Youth Vanguard, respectively, both emphasize the capacity of solidarity to be utilized for racial justice, specifically anti-Black racism. Amid a pandemic that disproportionately impacts Black (Laurencin & Walker, 2020), Indigenous, Latinx/e/o/a, and People of Color, state-sanctioned Black violence and death still persist—a reminder that anti-Black racism is as violent, relentless, widespread, and fluid as it is endemic systemically and enacted by individuals (Gillborn, 2018). Solidarity, both Black and cross-racial, with the political goal of racial justice is not new; there are many examples of grassroots organizations and multiracial coalitions within Black liberation movements (Clayton, 2018; De

Lissovoy & Brown, 2013; Middlebrook, 2019), so we must teach it, as these social histories are often minimized and erased in textbooks and curriculum.

The unprecedented multiracial uprisings of 2020 sparked global dialogue on police brutality, systemic racism, and anti-Blackness. An increasing number of BLM statements began to appear on websites and in corporate ad campaigns, schools, and institutions of higher education. Few statements delineated clear action steps. Many invoked *solidarity* and *BLM* as performative buzzwords while their track records remained in opposition to deeply complex and sustained action-oriented institutional practices anti-Black racism demands (Jan et al., 2020). Liberation and antiracism require that solidarity be a continual praxis (Mayorga & Picower, 2018)—a *verb*. This message is especially important for social studies educators. The social studies teaching force continues to be disproportionately white (84%) and male (58%; Hansen et. al., 2018), consistent with decades of overall teacher demographic data (Busey & Waters, 2016). Not that white teachers can't teach the perils of anti-Blackness and white supremacy deeply and concretely; some may feel very comfortable navigating this terrain. However, recent research reminds us that many teachers have the same racial biases as the broader society (Starck et al., 2020), which leaves many ill equipped to teach racial justice.

The long civil rights movement or Black Freedom Struggle is an example of antiracist solidarity within a continuous social movement that has existed for generations. There is much we can learn from the ongoing fight against anti-Black racism that is often missing or not presented holistically within the social studies curriculum. This movement's history is especially important as we are living in the era of BLM. A major disservice in how social movements are presented in curricular materials and taught is that often, the transformative nature of the people as a collective group is dismissed; people, not just individuals, push society forward (Bigelow, 2011). The disregard of organizing and explicit teaching of solidarity within social movements is a missed opportunity that can leave students with a limited understanding of the power of collective action for radical change (Westheimer, 2014). This gap highlights the continued need for this discourse within the field of social studies. Students should have opportunities to learn about social movements and civil disobedience as critical components of civic education similar to more traditional forms of political education such as voting (Wheeler-Bell, 2014). Moreover, antiracist-focused social movements provide an avenue for students to critically examine systemic racism, power, and the ways collectives challenge racial injustice.

As social studies educators tasked with preparing students to be democratic citizens and teaching current events, the BLM movement is an example of antiracist civic engagement that directly confronts anti-Black racism. Still in 2020, a Texas school district reprimanded an educator for displaying BLM and LGBT+ posters in its virtual Bitmoji classroom (Gowdy, 2020), and another Texas educator was fired for repeatedly wearing a BLM mask in solidarity with students and the movement (Elassar, 2020). Simply mentioning or displaying BLM can lead to punitive repercussions, coupled with pressures from parents or community members, and educators may experience some trepidation about teaching this movement—but that can't serve as an excuse to not engage in this critical work. Being in solidarity against white supremacy and anti-Blackness both personally and professionally is difficult, complex, and necessary. This chapter seeks to *continue a conversation* about anti-Black racism in social studies curriculum, the importance of the BLM movement in the fight for intersectional racial justice, and why teaching solidarity will support student understanding of how change truly happens.

## Anti-Black Racism in Social Studies

Racism is endemic, pervasive, and a permanent function of American society (Bell, 1992) with anti-Black racism being "one of the many pernicious aspects of racisms" (Dei, 2017, p. 31). *Anti-Blackness* and *anti-Black racism*, terms often used interchangeably, are both systemic and ideological, as they speak to the specific racial prejudice, discrimination, and socially constructed stereotypical beliefs about Black people. A vestige of chattel slavery, in which Black people were considered property, anti-Blackness dehumanizes Black life and promotes the systematic marginalization of Black people. It undergirds white supremacy and consequently advances hatred, racist ideologies and institutional practices, racialized violence, and Black suffering (Dumas, 2016; Dumas & ross, 2016). To put it plainly, anti-Black racism has been here, is here, and ain't going nowhere unless we truly reckon with it.

Anti-Black racism remains ever present in institutions such as education and is deeply embedded in K–12 schools, colleges, and universities (Warren & Coles, 2020). The unadulterated truth is that anti-Black racism takes many forms in education, including tracking, curriculum violence, the school-to-prison pipeline, zero-tolerance policies, and under-resourced schools. Black children relentlessly encounter anti-Blackness, as Love (2016) says, from the moment they enter school, which can be spirit murdering for Black children by not providing them with safety, inclusion, love, and protection from racism. The false equivalence is often drawn between a perceived "achievement gap" and Black intellectual inferiority. In many places, Black students do not even have a lot of chances to be taught by Black teachers or teachers of color. Teachers in K–12 settings (82%), preservice teachers (75%), and education leaders (80%) are overwhelmingly white as the student population of public schools are increasingly diverse (U.S. Department of Education, 2016). Black students are often over-disciplined while simultaneously underrepresented in Advanced Placement courses. The culture of discipline in schools is an example of how anti-Black racism organizes policies and punitive outcomes for Black children in both formal and informal ways (Wun, 2016). These are just a few examples of how Black children—and all children—are steeped in spaces that consciously or subconsciously reinforce anti-Blackness. Naming matters. Kirkland (2021) reminds us that everything that occurs in schools in relation to Black life is neither neutral nor universal and that it must be named also. Educators can't continue to ignore anti-Black racism, as Howard (2020) clearly explains our critical charge:

> There is a pressing need for educators to develop a propensity, some knowledge, and the courage to discuss, name, and describe the levels of exclusion, oppression, hostility, and racism in the United States that have afflicted Black people for centuries. (para. 10)

The purpose of social studies as defined by the National Council for the Social Studies (n.d.) is to "help young people develop the ability to make informed and reasoned decisions for the public good as citizens of a culturally diverse, democratic society in an interdependent world" (para. 2). Much can be interpreted about this purpose, but what we do know is that the goals outlined can't be achieved without grappling with anti-Black racism and how it *lives* in the profession. Nowhere is this more prevalent than in the curriculum, which is violent and anti-Black. The social studies curriculum is steeped in anti-Blackness, and textbooks are fraught with problematic representations, minimization, and even complete erasure of Black life and experiences

(Khan et. al, 2020; King, 2014). For example, the National Women's History Museum (2017) reported 62% of women named in state social studies standards were white women and 25% were Black women. This means that Black women are largely missing from social studies standards. Furthermore, when they appear in the curriculum it's typically a famous few. Three Black women, Rosa Parks, Harriet Tubman, and Sojourner Truth, are cited multiple times (White, 2019), with Rosa Parks being the most-cited woman in state social studies standards (National Women's History Museum, 2017). While this might appear as progress, students are only exposed to a few Black women and often their intersectional experiences are vastly missing and/or incomplete in the social studies (Vickery & Salinas, 2019). Parks's activism is often reduced to a reductionist idea that she was tired and sat down on the bus, a history totally disconnected from her lifelong commitment to political and community activism that is unfortunately largely diminished in the national memory and curriculum (Theoharis, 2013). Brown and Brown (2021) note the way in which the history and lived experiences of Black people are incorporated; or mostly the lack thereof renders their stories dispensable and even worse: subhuman. There are so many Black experiences and historical narratives that have yet to be told, which highlights the need for counter-storytelling in social studies. We can take cues from how many Black social studies educators have navigated systems of white supremacy (Busey & Vickery, 2018; Duncan, 2020; Nyachae, 2016) and make instructional decisions in the classroom that center Blackness and teach outside of whitewashed dominant narratives. When the full spectrum of Black life and experiences, including joy, resistance, and love, are not fully reflected in the social studies curriculum, white supremacy, inaccurate revisionist historical narratives, and anti-Blackness are maintained.

## BLM Movement and the Intersectional Fight Against Anti-Black Racism

In the following quote, Unita Blackwell, activist politician, member of the Student Nonviolent Coordinating Committee (SNCC), delegate of the Mississippi Freedom Democratic party in 1964, and the first African American and woman mayor of Mayersville, Mississippi, reminds us of what movements can teach us:

> Change depends on people knowing the truth. Change depends on people speaking that truth out loud. That's what movements do. Movements educate people to the truth. They pass along information and ideas that many others do not know, and they cause them to ask questions, to challenge their own long-held beliefs. Movements are the way ordinary people get more freedom and justice. Movements are how we keep a check on power and those who abuse it. (Blackwell & Morris, 2006)

Movements can teach about oppression and resistance as they are both closely bound. As Collins (2000) states, "the shape of one influences that of the other" (p. 274), and we should teach that. Much can be gleaned about the current BLM movement as it focuses on a lot of the same anti-Black racism previous Black liberation movements addressed, including police brutality, the criminalization of Black people, and how expendable their lives are (Clayton, 2018). The reality is our students are living and coming of age in the era of #BlackLivesMatter, in what has recently been termed as "the Trayvon Generation'" (Alexander, 2020). It is important to engage students beyond the rhetoric and dive into what the movement can teach us about the intersectional fight against anti-Black racism.

The BLM movement, which emerged as a hashtag in 2013, is a continuation of the long Black Freedom Struggle to eradicate white supremacy and end systemic oppression (Clayton, 2018; Ransby, 2018) that has grown and sparked a global intersectional movement (Asmelash, 2020; BLM, n.d.; Lebron, 2017) against anti-Black racism. The decentralized BLM movement and nominee for the 2021 Nobel Peace Prize is often mischaracterized and misunderstood, yet their goals are stated clearly, as follows:

> #BlackLivesMatter was founded in 2013 in response to the acquittal of Trayvon Martin's murderer. Black Lives Matter Global Network Foundation, Inc. is a global organization in the US, UK, and Canada, whose mission is to eradicate white supremacy and build local power to intervene in violence inflicted on Black communities by the state and vigilantes. By combating and countering acts of violence, creating space for Black imagination and innovation, and centering Black joy, we are winning immediate improvements in our lives. (BLM, n.d., para. 1)

The hashtag, started by three women, two of whom identify as queer, has intentionally declared from the outset that the movement affirms all Black lives, meaning "the lives of Black queer and trans folks, disabled folks, undocumented folks, folks with records, women, and all Black lives along the gender spectrum" (BLM, n.d., para. 3). Audre Lorde (1982) said it best: "There is no such thing as a single-issue struggle because we don't live single-issue lives" (Blackpast, 2012, para. 13). The BLM movement is deeply shaped by Black feminist thought and rooted in intersectionality, a term coined by Crenshaw (1989), in which individuals face multiple and intersecting forms of structural racism. The following statement on its website signals its commitment to making space for *all* Black lives in the movement:

> As organizers who work with everyday people, BLM members see and understand significant gaps in movement spaces and leadership. Black liberation movements in this country have created room, space, and leadership mostly for Black heterosexual, cisgender men—leaving women, queer and transgender people, and others either out of the movement or in the background to move the work forward with little or no recognition. As a network, we have always recognized the need to center the leadership of women and queer and trans people. To maximize our movement muscle, and to be intentional about not replicating harmful practices that excluded so many in past movements for liberation, we made a commitment to placing those at the margins closer to the center. (BLM, n.d., para. 4)

BLM is also a member of the Movement for Black Lives, a coalition of more than 50 Black organizations working toward a common vision and policy agenda for Black liberation that amplifies the work of the African American Policy Forum and the Center for Intersectionality and Social Policy Studies #SayHerName campaign, to name a few.

With the statements and commitments of the BLM movement as a starting point, we can learn from the movement about naming and including the intersectional lives of Black folks in the pursuit of racial justice. The intersectional approach of fighting anti-Black racism through the BLM movement can serve as an example of what we should strive for in our social studies classrooms.

## Teaching *Solidarity* as a Verb

During the summer of 2020, BLM protests over police brutality and racism erupted in all 50 states, in U.S. territories, and in countries around the world. This visual display of unity against anti-Black racism provides us with an example and opportunity to teach the complexities of solidarity. Robin D.G. Kelley emphasizes that "solidarity is not a market exchange" (Kelley et al., 2018, p. 592), meaning it is not transactional or charity; it is the belief that everyone deserves human dignity regardless of if it directly connects to your lived experience. *Solidarity* is a verb; it's an action that requires critical analysis of systems of oppression, empathy, listening, visioning, sacrifice, learning, or, more important, unlearning.

Teaching social movements offers a window into teaching the opportunities and challenges with sustaining solidarity for anti-Black racism. Solidarity offers a chance to be in community with like-minded individuals who share the same goal of justice to a particular cause. Solidarity can be shown in myriad ways: It can be protesting, boycotting, raising awareness, providing mutual aid and financial support, organizing, and essentially utilizing one's time, talents, and treasures to a cause and in this case fighting anti-Blackness. Solidarity is not without its challenges and can be hard to sustain. De Lissovoy and Brown (2013) offer this critical perspective: "authentic solidarity requires both a deeper commitment to transformation and a deeper understanding of whiteness, in global and historical terms" (p. 557). Often, space is not made for this work in teacher preparation programs or in service professional development. Sometimes, there is a difference of opinion on the best path forward. People have different, overlapping identities and values that sometimes compete with each other and require negotiation (Hooker, 2009). Oppression is unrelenting and takes no days off; thus, activists may experience burnout. We know this from the lived experiences of activists, primary and secondary sources from previous movements such as abolition, Reconstruction, the nadir of race relations in the early 20th century, the civil rights movement, and the current BLM movement. There is so much power in teaching students to grapple with these complexities of what it means to be in solidarity with Black liberation and racial justice and it is not always a smooth experience or kumbaya moment.

Taking informed action for ourselves and our students is critical to the inquiry design model promoted by the National Council for the Social Studies.

A shining example of this is the BLM at School movement and the ongoing fight to tackle anti-Black racism in schools. The BLM at School movement started in Seattle when thousands of educators and hundreds of students, families, and community members wore "Black Lives Matter: We Stand Together" T-shirts in 2016 (Au & Hagopian, 2018). Their activism became national news and organizing began in Philadelphia the same year. A small working group titled the Caucus of Working Educators' Racial Justice Committee expanded the day into a week, with the movement continuing to grow and expand at all educational levels, from Pre-K to higher education participating in the movement in cities all around the country (BLM at School, n.d.). A common misconception of the BLM movement is that its goals are singular in nature. The goal of BLM at School is to expand student understanding of 13 guiding principles that emphasize justice, affirm all Black lives, and honor the legacies of Black communities and families. The principles guide the fight against anti-Black racism in schools with four demands (Hagopian, 2020): (1) end "zero tolerance" discipline (which disproportionately impacts Black youth and youth of color) and implement restorative justice, (2) hire more Black teachers, (3) mandate Black history and ethnic studies in K–12 curricula, and 4) fund counselors, not cops. Around the country, educators and students have been working to change the curriculum, advocate for Black history courses, and campaign for police-free schools—this is taking informed action. Getting connected to local or national BLM at School efforts is a concrete action step to combating anti-Black racism within our sphere of influence—education.

## Conclusion

I have taught in urban and rural settings, in middle school and higher education, and when asked about BLM, students have an array of perspectives from lived experiences to incomplete media sound bites. I have found that creating space to unpack the BLM movement, teaching social movements for Black liberation, and naming anti-Black racism to be well received. Social studies teachers and teacher educators must make pedagogical choices, implement instructional practices, and cultivate an environment that mirror that commitment and that affirm that all Black lives matter (King et al., 2016). Reflect on the ways Black people *are* dehumanized and the work that needs to be done to humanize Black lives in the social studies curriculum, in our practice, and in the broader profession. We must directly confront anti-Black racism as a field, now more than ever.

Some educators may be apathetic about the need to fight anti-Black racism. Some may feel constraints on what can be taught for myriad reasons, including standardized testing, curriculum pacing, administrative, parental, and community pressures. Some may feel like they are not prepared. Whatever the reason may be, the first step starts with us. It is critical that as educators, we examine our positionalities, preconceived notions, biases, politics, and instructional practices when teaching about the BLM movement (Austin et al., 2016; Hollstein, 2016). Consider what you need to learn and, more importantly, unlearn. Reflective practitioners recognize unlearning as an iterative process with learning (McLeod et al., 2020). You must be radically honest with yourself about the ways anti-Blackness manifests in your teaching practice. Know that there is support available for this work. There are a lot of online resources to support teaching and learning about movement history, Black lives, and intersectionality, including BLM at School, Rethinking Schools, Learning for Justice, Zinn Education Project, the Abolition Teaching Network, the Education for Liberation Network, and Teaching for Change, among many others. Two highly recommended books to support educators in this work are *Teaching for Black Lives* (Watson et al., 2018) and *Black Lives Matter at School: An Uprising for Educational Justice* (Jones & Hagopian, 2020); both offer background information on the movement, lesson plans, and testimonials.

Scholars of color have continued to lead scholarship in the field of social studies by analyzing race and racism (Navarro & Howard, 2017), and we must heed their words. As a field we must constantly challenge ourselves to think about what it means to be in solidarity for all Black lives and disrupt anti-Black racism. Ideally, we along with our students may be inspired to take informed action and in solidarity seek collective solutions to combat anti-Black racism in and outside of the classroom. Howard (2020) reminds us that individual acts must transform into collective action, and students and educators can be a part of that. As the next generation of activists emerge in the movement, let the words of Black student activist Marshé Doss (BLM in Schools, 2020) guide us as we continue this much-needed conversation in our field:

> But how do you make Black lives matter in schools when the whole system wasn't even built for us? I will tell you how. You tear it down and build it into something that *is* made for us. And so that's what we are doing. Step by step, policy by policy, person by person, we're tearing it down and rebuilding it into a system that is meant to make sure that Black Lives Matter in schools. (p. 241)

## References

Alexander, E. (2020, June 15). The Trayvon generation. *The New Yorker*. https://www.newyorker.com/magazine/2020/06/22/the-trayvon-generation

Asmelash, L. (2020, July 26). *How Black Lives Matter went from a hashtag to a global rallying cry.* CNN. https://www.cnn.com/2020/07/26/us/black-lives-matter-explainer-trnd/index.html

Au, W., & Hagopian, J. (2018). How one elementary school sparked a citywide movement to make Black students' lives matter. In D. Watson, J. Hagopian, & W. Au (Eds.), *Teaching for Black lives* (pp. 22–31). Rethinking Schools.

Austin, P., Cardwell, E., Kennedy, C., & Spencer, R. (2016, Fall). Introduction: Teaching Black Lives Matter. *Radical Teacher, 106*, 13–17. https://doi.org/10.5195/rt.2016.340

Bell, D. (1992). *Faces at the bottom of the well: The permanence of racism*. Basic Books.

Bigelow, B. (2011). "If there is no struggle": Teaching a people's history of the abolition. *Our Schools / Our Selves, 20*(3), 205–219. https://www.zinnedproject.org/materials/if-there-is- no-struggle-abolition-movement-history/

Black Lives Matter. (n.d.). *About Black Lives Matter*. https://blacklivesmatter.com/about/

BLM at School. (n.d.). *Black Lives Matter at School.* https://www.blacklivesmatteratschool.com/

Blackpast. (2012, August 12). (1982) *Audre Lorde, "Learning from the 60s."* Blackpast. https://www.blackpast.org/african-american-history/1982-audre-lorde-learning-60s/

Blackwell, U., & Morris, J. A. P. (2006). *Barefootin': Life lessons from the road to freedom*. Crown.

Brown, K. D., & Brown, A. L. (2021). Anti-Blackness and the school curriculum. In C. A. Grant, A. N. Woodson, & M. J. Dumas (Eds.), *The future is Black: Afropessimism, fugivity and radical hope in education*. Routledge.

Busey, C. L., & Vickery, A. E. (2018). Black like me: Race pedagogy and Black elementary social studies teacher educators. In S. Shear, C. Tschinda, E. Bellow, L. Buchanan Brown, & E. Saylor (Eds.), *(Re)imagining elementary social studies: A controversial studies reader* (pp. 25–48). Information Age.

Busey, C. L., & Waters, S. (2016). Who are we? The demographic and professional identity of social studies teacher educators. *Journal of Social Studies Research, 40*(1), 71–83. https://doi.org/10.1016/j.jssr.2015.07.001

Clayton, D. M. (2018). Black Lives Matter and the civil rights movement: A comparative analysis of two social movements in the United States. *Journal of Black Studies, 49*(5), 448–480. https://doi.org/10.1177/0021934718764099

Collins, P. (2000). *Black feminist thought: Knowledge, consciousness, and the politics of empowerment.* Routledge.

Crenshaw, K. (1989). Demarginalizing the intersection of race and sex: A Black feminist critique of antidiscrimination doctrine, feminist theory and antiracist politics. *University of Chicago Legal Forum, 1*(8), 139–167. http://chicagounbound.uchicago.edu/uclf/vol1989/iss1/8

Dei, G. J. S. (2017). Towards a (re)theorization of Blackness, anti-Blackness, and Black solidarities. In G. J. S. Dei (Ed.), *Reframing Blackness and Black solidarities through anti-colonial and decolonial prisms* (pp. 31–63). Springer International. https://doi.org/10.1007/978-3-319-53079-6_2

De Lissovoy, N., & Brown, A. L. (2013). Antiracist solidarity in critical education: Contemporary problems and possibilities. *The Urban Review, 45*(5), 539–560. https://doi.org/10.1007/s11256-013-0235-8

Dumas, M. J. (2016). Against the dark: Antiblackness in education policy and discourse. *Theory Into Practice, 55*(1), 11–19. https://doi.org/10.1080/00405841.2016.1116852

Dumas, M. J., & ross, k. m. (2016). "Be real Black for me": Imagining BlackCrit in education. *Urban Education, 51*(4), 415–442. https://doi.org/10.1177/0042085916628611

Duncan, K. E. (2020, July 23). "That's my job": Black teachers' perspectives on helping Black students navigate white supremacy. *Race Ethnicity and Education*. Advanced online publication. https://doi.org/10.1080/13613324.2020.1798377

Elassar, A. (2020, September 26). *A Texas teacher was fired for wearing a Black Lives Matter face mask.* CNN. https://www.cnn.com/2020/09/26/us/texas-teacher-fired-black-lives-matter-mask-trnd/index.html

Gillborn, D. (2018). Heads I win, tails you lose: Anti-Black racism as fluid, relentless, individual and systemic. *Peabody Journal of Education, 93*(1), 66–77. https://doi.org/10.1080/0161956X.2017.1403178

Gowdy, S. (2020, August 27). Texas teacher reinstated after BLM, LGBTQ virtual posters controversy. *Houston Chronicle*. https://www.houstonchronicle.com/news/houston-texas/education/article/Texas-teacher-placed-on-leave-for-Black-Lives-15519139.php

Hagopian, J. (2020). Making Black lives matter at school. In D. Jones & J. Hagopian (Eds.), *Black Lives Matter at School: An uprising for educational justice* (pp. 1–24). Haymarket Books.

Hansen, M., Levesque, E., Valant, J., & Quintero, D. (2018). *The 2018 Brown Center report on American education: How well are American students learning?* The Brookings Institution. https://www.brookings.edu/multi-chapter-report/the-2018-brown-center-report-on-american-education/

Hollstein, M. (2016). Black Lives Matter in the social studies. *Ohio Social Studies Review, 53*(1), 28–37. https://ossr.scholasticahq.com/article/964.pdf

Hooker, J. (2009). *Race and the politics of solidarity*. Oxford University Press.

Howard, T. C. (2020, June 4). How to root out anti-Black racism from your school. *Education Week.* https://www.edweek.org/leadership/opinion-how-to-root-out-anti-black-racism-from-your-school/2020/06

Jan, T., McGregor, J., Merle, R., & Tiku, N. (2020, June 13). As big corporations say "Black lives matter," their track records raise skepticism. *Washington Post*. https://www.washingtonpost.com/business/2020/06/13/after-years-marginalizing-black-employees-customers-corporate-america-says-black-lives-matter/

Jones, D., & Hagopian, J. (2020). *Black Lives Matter at School: An uprising for educational justice.* Haymarket Books.

Kelley, R. D. G., Amariglio, J., & Wilson, L. (2018). "Solidarity is not a market exchange": A *RM* interview with Robin D. G. Kelley, part 1. *Rethinking Marxism, 30*(4), 568–598. https://doi.org/10.1080/08935696.2018.1552420

Khan, N. M., Simmons, C., & Busey, C. L. (2020). A critical race theory analysis of representations of Black history in mainstream secondary textbooks across the Americas. In L. J. King (Ed.), *Perspectives of Black histories in schools* (pp. 127–149). Information Age.

King, L. J. (2014). When lions write history: Black history textbooks, African-American educators, & the alternative Black curriculum in social studies education, 1890–1940. *Multicultural Education, 22*(1), 2–11. https://files.eric.ed.gov/fulltext/EJ1065311.pdf

King, L. J., Warren, C. A., Bender, M., & Finley, S. (2016). #BlackLivesMatter as critical patriotism. In W. Journell (Ed.), *Teaching social studies in an era of divisiveness: The challenges of discussing social issues in a non-partisan way* (pp. 93–110). Rowman & Littlefield.

Kirkland, D. E. (2021). A pedagogy for Black people: Why naming race matters. *Equity & Excellence in Education, 54*(1), 60–67. https://doi.org/10.1080/10665684.2020.1867018

Laurencin, C. T., & Walker, J. M. (2020). A pandemic on a pandemic: Racism and COVID-19 in Blacks. *Cell Systems, 11*(1), 9–10. https://doi.org/10.1016/j.cels.2020.07.002

Lebron, C. J. (2017). *The making of Black Lives Matter: A brief history of an idea.* Oxford University Press.

Love, B. L. (2016). Anti-Black state violence, classroom edition: The spirit murdering of Black children. *Journal of Curriculum and Pedagogy, 13*(1), 22–25. https://doi.org/10.1080/15505170.2016.1138258

Mayorga, E., & Picower, B. (2018). Active solidarity: Centering the demands and vision of the Black Lives Matter movement in teacher education. *Urban Education, 53*(2), 212–230. https://doi.org/10.1177/0042085917747117

McLeod, K., Thakchoe, S., Hunter, M. A., Vincent, K., Baltra-Ulloa, A. J., & MacDonald, A. (2020). Principles for a pedagogy of unlearning. *Reflective Practice, 21*(2), 183–197. https://doi.org/10.1080/14623943.2020.1730782

Middlebrook, J. A. (2019). Organizing a rainbow coalition of revolutionary solidarity. *Journal of African American Studies, 23*(4), 405–434. https://doi.org/10.1007/s12111-019-09454-6

National Council for the Social Studies. (n.d.). *About the National Council for the Social Studies.* https://www.socialstudies.org/about

National Women's History Museum. (2017). *Where are the women? A report on the status of women in the United States curricula.* https://www.womenshistory.org/social-studies-standards

Navarro, O., & Howard, T. C. (2017). A critical race theory analysis of social studies research, theory and practice. In M. M. Manfra & C. M. Bolick (Eds.), *The Wiley handbook of social studies research* (pp. 209–226). John Wiley & Sons.

Nyachae, T. M. (2016). Complicated contradictions amid Black feminism and millennial Black women teachers creating curriculum for Black girls. *Gender and Education, 28*(6), 786–806. https://doi.org/10.1080/09540253.2016.1221896

Ransby, B. (2018). *Making all Black lives matter: Reimagining freedom in the twenty-first century*. University of California Press.

Solidarity. (n.d.). In *Merriam-Webster's*. Retrieved September 12, 2020, from https://www.merriam-webster.com/

Starck, J. G., Riddle, T., Sinclair, S., & Warikoo, N. (2020, April 14). Teachers are people too: Examining the racial bias of teachers compared to other American adults. *Educational Researcher*. Advanced online publication. https://doi.org/10.3102/0013189X20912758

Theoharis, J. (2013). *The rebellious life of Mrs. Rosa Parks*. Beacon Press.

U.S. Department of Education. (2016, July). *The state of racial diversity in the educator workforce*. https://www2.ed.gov/rschstat/eval/highered/racial-diversity/state-racial-diversity-workforce.pdf

Vickery, A. E., & Salinas, C. (2019). "I question America . . . is this America": Learning to view the civil rights movement through an intersectional lens. *Curriculum Inquiry, 49*(3), 260–283. https://doi.org/10.1080/03626784.2019.1614878

Warren, C. A., & Coles, J. A. (2020). Trading spaces: Antiblackness and reflections on Black education futures. *Equity & Excellence in Education, 53*(3), 382–398. https://doi.org/10.1080/10665684.2020.1764882

Watson, D., Hagopian, J., & Au, W. (2018). *Teaching for Black lives*. Rethinking Schools.

Westheimer, J. (2014). Teaching students to think about patriotism. In E. W. Ross (Ed.), *Social studies curriculum: Purposes, problems, and possibilities* (pp. 127–138). State University of New York Press.

Wheeler-Bell, Q. (2014). Educating the spirit of activism: A "critical" civic education. *Educational Policy, 28*(3), 463–486. http://doi.org/10.1177/0895904812465113

White, A. (2019, March). What schools teach about women's history leaves a lot to be desired. *Smithsonian Magazine*. https://www.smithsonianmag.com/history/what-schools-teach-womens-history-180971447/

Wun, C. (2016). Unaccounted foundations: Black girls, anti-Black racism, and punishment in schools. *Critical Sociology, 42*(4–5), 737–750. https://doi.org/10.1177/0896920514560444

THREE

# The Audacity of Equality: Disrupting the Distortion of Asian America in Social Studies

*Noreen Naseem Rodríguez and Esther June Kim*

> "These things happen, and these things will continue to happen. That's the price we pay for being here." My dad's from that generation where he feels like if you come to this country, you pay the American dream tax. You endure racism, and if it doesn't cost you your life, pay it. There you go, Uncle Sam. But for me . . . I actually have the audacity of equality. I'm like, "I'm in honors gov, I have it right here: Life, liberty, pursuit of happiness. All men created equal." It says it right here, I'm equal. *I'm equal.* I don't deserve this.
>
> —*Hasan Minhaj (2017)*

THE EPIGRAPH FROM HASAN MINHAJ'S comedy special *Homecoming King* (Minhaj & Storer, 2017) has stuck with Noreen (first author) since she first heard the live performance in Washington, D.C. Seated next to a childhood friend in a sea of Brown faces, they cried tears of laughter and sorrow listening to Minhaj's masterful and hysterical account of growing up as a Brown-skinned South Asian Muslim in the overwhelmingly white Christian city of Davis, California. Although she and her childhood friend grew up in Texas, the cultural and intergenerational clashes Minhaj described with his peers and family reflected their experiences as second-generation immigrants and first-generation U.S. citizens.

We rarely enjoyed such public moments, when the feelings and frustrations of our youth were not only expressed by others on a major platform but were also affirmed and confirmed by the majority in our midst. In fact, we are accustomed to *not* having our identities and family histories reflected in our places of work and, in particular, school. Such is the experience of many Asian Americans across the United States, even when they live in areas with dense concentrations of Asian Americans. Asian Americans make up just over 2% of the public school teaching force (National Center for Educational Statistics, 2019) and are rarely present in K–12 educational standards or curriculum (An, 2016; Rodríguez, 2018).

As a child, Noreen was acutely aware that the cultures, languages, and histories of the peoples from whom she descended were glaringly absent in school. The Desi[1] Muslim community and Filipino communities her family socialized with on weekends and during the summer and school holidays offered her a very different sense of who "we" were and what was important to us. In these spaces, multilingualism and multiculturalism abounded. Yet in school, we were unmentioned and made invisible—not a part of the national story, not woven into multicultural narratives.

Not until 9/11 was Islam a common topic outside a cursory unit on world religions; afterward, it became a target on our backs and the source of ridicule and vitriol. Such vitriol is what prefaced the Minhaj quote that opened this chapter: In the days, weeks, and months after the attacks on the World Trade Center and Pentagon, Muslims (and those perceived to be Muslim) across the United States were the targets of anti-Muslim racism, harassment, and physical violence. Minhaj recounted how the windows of his family's car were smashed in the driveway of their home in Davis. His response to the vandalism, which was preceded by an obscenity-laced threatening phone call, was outrage, while his father calmly swept up the shards. To his father, patiently enduring racism was part of the American dream tax. To Minhaj, the vandalism was an outrageous injustice that violated the core of America's purported values. The audacity of equality is central to the Asian American experience.

Esther's (second author) experiences growing up Korean American in Southern California bear similarities to Minhaj's story. One of her earliest childhood memories is of a neighbor smashing the window of her father's car with a hammer. Almost 30 years later and in a different city, another neighbor threw a brick at her family home, breaking the glass patio furniture. No one yelled racist slurs as they carried out their vandalism, but in both instances, hers was the only Asian American family in the neighborhood, and their Asianness felt like a target. The injustice and violation that were commonly felt by both Minhaj and Esther and the resigned acceptance by immigrant parents attest to their shared experiences as Asian Americans.

There are, however, differences between the two that must also be acknowledged. Being of East Asian descent, Esther is rarely perceived as a national threat based solely on the color of her skin or her religion. Even her name is a testament to a background more palatable to a culturally Christian America. In contrast, Minhaj and Noreen are often "marked" as threats due to their skin color and/or Muslim Arabic names, by strangers, the Transportation Security Administration, and the federal government via travel bans, among others. These differences are part of what make the banner of Asian American so complicated and why the teaching of Asian American (hi)stories is necessary *and* must reflect this complexity.

## The Sociopolitical Origins of the Term *Asian American*

*Asian American*, after all, was not an accidental term designed for simple categorization. In 1968, University of California, Berkeley, students Yuji Ichioka and Emma Gee deliberately chose the term *Asian American* to signal their desire to build a coalition of Chinese Americans, Japanese Americans, and Filipino Americans united by their political beliefs, grounded in anti-imperialism and antiracism (Maeda, 2012). At the time, there was no term that encompassed multiple nationalities of Asian origin. In fact, the diversity of immigrants from Asia was a relatively new phenomenon that resulted from the Immigration and Nationality Act of 1965. For Ichioka and Gee, forming a collective was essential: "We figured that if we rallied behind our own banner, behind an Asian American banner, we would have an effect on the larger public. We could extend the influence beyond ourselves, to other Asian Americans" (Ichioka in Maeda, 2012, p. 10). And so with the formation of the Asian American Political Alliance, the term *Asian American* was born.

Today, the activist vision that created *Asian American* is rarely known to those who have not taken an ethnic studies or Asian American history course. Instead, the term is one of several racial categories found on forms and surveys, a box checked off and often conflated with Asian, devoid of its sociopolitical history (Ishizuka, 2016; Philip, 2014). Moreover, the insidious model minority myth has led to the widespread perception of Asian Americans as apolitical and obedient while simultaneously masking the disenfranchisement experienced by many Asian Americans and recent immigrants. This chapter is written in the spirit of those early Asian American activists who took up the term *Asian American* as a rallying cry for solidarity and self-determination.

We are Asian Americans who did not learn about Asian American histories until we were in our doctoral program, after many years of teaching in K–12 schools. As we have detailed elsewhere, we rarely saw the stories of our families reflected in the curriculum of school (Rodríguez & Kim, 2019); for most of our lives, this absence led us to feel Othered and disconnected from the archetypal white American. K–12 curriculum has made little improvement regarding the inclusion of Asian Americans across U.S. history, despite substantial improvement in the representation of Asian Americans in children's literature over the last two decades (Rodríguez & Kim, 2018). In this chapter, rather than solely exploring Asian American histories, we complicate the problematic nature in which these histories are taught and told and explain the ways that Asian Americans are often excluded from educational topics and historical events directly related to their identities, experiences, and histories. We ground this work through Asian American critical race theory, which we explain in detail in the following section.

It is important to note that in this chapter we do not include the (hi)stories of Pacific Islanders. While Asian Americans and Pacific Islanders are often clustered as a single racial category and in demographic data, such a grouping is often to the severe detriment of Pacific Islander communities and their needs and interests, despite any common histories or experiences between the two groups. In fact, the very term *Pacific Islands* problematically situates them as "islands in a far sea" in contrast to the term *Oceania*, which denotes "a sea of islands" with their inhabitants, or "people from the sea" (Hau'ofa, 2008). As outsiders to this group, we will not attempt to tell their stories or describe their experiences and urge readers to learn more about the distinction between Asian Americans and Pacific Islanders from Pacific Islanders themselves (see Diaz, 2004, and Hau'ofa, 2008).

## Asian American Critical Race Theory

We frame our approach to Asian American histories, and Asian American education broadly, through Asian American critical race theory. Critical race theory (CRT) begins with the recognition that the United States is a nation in which racism abounds and is a normal part of society. CRT was first developed in legal studies (and later expanded to a wide range of disciplines, including education) and drew from both critical legal studies and traditional civil rights scholarship. The "critical" in CRT interrogates the way legal doctrine and legal institutions buttress and support oppressive systems and aims to expose normalizing processes to imagine more radical revisions of the world (Fitzpatrick & Hunt, 1987; Harris, 1994). However, critical legal scholarship failed to expose racism in legal reasoning and institutions, leading some scholars to demand a focus on the hegemonic roles of racism and white supremacy (Crenshaw, 1988).

Matsuda (1996) described the development of CRT as "a separate jurisprudential tradition of people of color" (p. 21) grounded in their social realities and experiences, and in particular, an understanding of "history from the bottom" (p. 22), alongside the need for the marginalized to be able to tell their own stories. However, legal scholar Robert Chang (1993) found that traditional civil rights work and CRT inadequately addressed the needs of Asian Americans, who face a unique form of discrimination and nativistic violence in addition to being viewed as a model minority. Chang (1993) proposed an Asian American legal scholarship that allowed Asian Americans "the opportunity to speak our oppression into existence" (p. 1314). Other scholars, including Matsuda (1996), Gotanda (1995), Teranishi (2002), Buenavista et al. (2009), and Park and Liu (2014), have examined the relationship between CRT and Asian American experiences and histories. Drawing from this interdisciplinary scholarship, Iftikar and Museus (2019) developed an Asian American CRT (AsianCrit) framework that explores how white supremacy uniquely shapes the experiences of Asian Americans.

In this chapter, we explore the AsianCrit tenets of Asianization, (re)constructive history, and strategic (anti-)essentialization as they relate to social studies education. Iftikar and Museus (2019) define *Asianization* as "the reality that people within the US only become 'Asian' because of White Supremacy and the racialization processes that it engenders" (p. 940). In particular, Iftikar and Museus (2019) point to the ways that white supremacy and nativistic racism have resulted in racialized constructions of Asian Americans as "perpetual foreigners, threatening yellow perils, model and deviant minorities, and sexually deviant emasculated men and hypersexualized women . . . vehicles through which White supremacy informs laws, policies, programs, and perspectives that dehumanize and exclude Asian Americans" (p. 940). We explore these constructions in detail in the following pages.

The tenet of (re)constructive history recognizes the invisibility of Asian Americans in U.S. history. While Iftikar and Museus (2019) describe Asian Americans as voiceless in the historical narrative, we contest this framing. Instead, we draw from Indian author and activist Arundhati Roy (2004), who insists, "there's really no such thing as the 'voiceless.' There are only the deliberately silenced, or the preferably unheard." It is important that social studies educators, in particular, are aware of the omissions and silences in the curriculum, but they must also be intentional about using Asian American voices and experiences to reconstruct the narratives that are missing rather than simply offering another history in service to the dominant, Eurocentric narrative.

Lowe (1996) insists on the necessity to organize, resist, and theorize as Asian Americans while also recognizing the immense differences within and among Asian Americans. Hence, any effort to include Asian American (hi)stories must engage with the heterogeneity, hybridity, and multiplicity inherent to this categorization. The tenet of strategic (anti-)essentialism attends to Lowe's concerns around how Asian American is understood and applied by recognizing and countering the ways that white supremacy racializes Asian Americans as a monolith while also emphasizing that Asian Americans can and do actively intervene in the racialization process (Iftikar & Museus, 2018). Thus, at times, Asian Americans must work against essentializing discourses, while other moments may call for strategic essentialism in order to attain political power and influence.

We argue that Asian Americans as a group have been racialized in particular ways across U.S. history that are often left unattended, much less complicated, in social studies curriculum. However, these racialization processes both overlap and deviate. For instance, the perception of the Chinese as a "Yellow Peril" in the 1800s has clear connections to contemporary anti-(East) Asian and Asian American racism during COVID-19. Yet the racialization of South Asian Americans and Arab Americans post-9/11 as terrorists is distinct (Grewal, 2003; Subedi, 2013) and stems from the Orientalist (Said, 1979) tradition of viewing those from "the East" as barbaric savages. Nonetheless, East, Southeast, and South Asian Americans are regularly considered foreigners, regardless of their place of birth or the number of generations they have lived in the United States. In this work, our lived experiences as a South/Southeast Asian American (Noreen) and East Asian American (Esther) are central in our positionalities and are important starting points for our research rather than identities we feel the need to confess and then disregard. *As* Asian Americans, we heed Lowe's (1996) call and demand that our colleagues and comrades in education do more to learn and share our (hi)stories.

## Interrogating Whiteness as a Pathway to Citizenship

Asian American history beyond the standard K–12 curriculum reveals a deliberate legal positioning of Asians as both non-white and noncitizen, illuminating how "two major elements of twentieth-century American racial ideology evolved from the genealogy of the racial requirement to citizenship: the legal definition of 'white' and the rule of racial unassimilability" (Ngai, 2004, p. 37). Such narratives fit within broader conversations of race in the United States. But they are also distinctly Asian American (hi)stories that are foundational to understanding the current ways that Asian Americans are racialized and strategically positioned and disregarded.

The Nationality Act of 1790 granted the right of naturalized citizenship to "free white persons" of good moral character. What legally constituted "white" was contested throughout the 19th century by Indigenous peoples, African Americans, and Asian immigrants. In 1868, the Fourteenth Amendment granted citizenship to all people in the United States not subject to a foreign power, thereby granting citizenship to African Americans but not necessarily to Indigenous peoples and certainly not to Asian Americans (Ngai, 2004). Two famous Supreme Court cases contesting these limitations on citizenship were brought by Asian immigrant defendants but are rarely taught in K–12 curriculum as essential to understanding both racial formation and citizenship. Here, we explore *Ozawa v. United States* (1922) and *United States v. Thind* (1923) to underscore their relevance in establishing white supremacy as part and parcel to citizenship and in constructing Asians as unassimilable others.

Takao Ozawa was born in Japan in 1875 and moved to California in 1894. In 1914, Ozawa applied for naturalization. At the time, the *United States v. Wong Kim Ark* decision of 1898 held that birthright citizenship applied "to children of foreigners present on American soil." However, for Asian immigrants, there existed no path to naturalization.

Ozawa based his case for naturalization on several arguments. The most notable argument relied on his skin color. As his skin was "whiter than the average Italian, Spaniard, or Portuguese" (*Ozawa v. United States*, 1922, at 71), he claimed to possess a white identity based on physical characteristics. The Supreme Court, however, did not agree that skin color correlated with racial identity, writing that "to adopt the color test alone would result in a confused overlapping of races and a gradual merging of one into the other, without any practical line of separation" (*Ozawa v. United States*, 1922, at 197). Ozawa's argument undermined the basic division of humans into racial categories that were supposedly based on science, but the Supreme Court ignored the implications of this argument by defining him as Mongolian due to his Japanese ancestry and therefore outside of the Caucasian race and ineligible for citizenship (López, 2006).

Months after the *Ozawa* decision, the Supreme Court took a different tack. Bhagat Singh Thind left India for the United States in 1913, served in the U.S. Army during World War I, and then sought naturalization in 1920. Thind relied on the anthropological classification of Indians as Caucasians, not Mongolians, in his naturalization petition to the state of Washington, which was granted in 1918, revoked, granted a second time, and finally appealed in a case sent to the Supreme Court for guidance on the question, "Is a high caste Hindu of full Indian blood, born at Amrit Sar, Punjab, India, a white person?" (*United States v. Thind*, 1923, at 206). As a "high caste Hindu," Thind would have been familiar with observing and benefiting from de facto and de jure rules (e.g. anti-miscegenation laws in the United States) that preserve an oppressive classification system such as caste in South Asia and race in the United States (Neogi, 2021).

The *Ozawa* case equated "white" and "Caucasian." Additionally, four lower courts had ruled that Indians were white. The odds, based on legal precedent, should have been in Thind's favor (López, 2006). However, while the Supreme Court did not dispute Thind's assertion that he was Caucasian, the court instead relied on common knowledge to reject the scientific argument that Thind was white:

> It may be true that the blond Scandinavian and the brown Hindu have a common ancestor in the dim reaches of antiquity, but the average man knows perfectly well that there are unmistakable and profound differences between them today; and it is not impossible, if that common ancestor could be materialized in the flesh, we should discover that he was himself sufficiently differentiated from both of his descendants to preclude his racial classification with either. (*United States v. Thind*, 1923, at 209)

The Supreme Court's decision invoked the intentions of the original framers of the law, who "intended to include only the type of man whom they knew to be white . . . bone of their bone and flesh of their flesh" (*United States v. Thind*,

1923, at 199). Furthermore, the court noted that "the words 'free white persons' are words of common speech, to be interpreted in accordance with the understanding of the common man, synonymous with the word 'Caucasian' only as that word is popularly understood" (*United States v. Thind*, 1923, at 214–215).

Together, the *Ozawa* and *Thind* cases illustrate the Supreme Court's insistence on making whiteness whatever it needed to be at any given time and thereby an unstable and highly contextual social construct subject to change. Therefore, as Ngai (2004) argues, the two decisions cast Japanese and Indians (along with Chinese, whose ineligibility to citizenship was included in the Exclusion Act of 1882) "as unassimilable aliens and helped constitute the racial category 'Asian.' The joining of Japanese and Asian Indians with Chinese . . . was the culmination of three decades of social, political, and judicial struggle over their status in America" (p. 38).

Common in this "joining" is the understanding that civic status is, and has always been, tied to whiteness. The cases of Ozawa and Thind can perhaps be viewed less as an attempt to claim whiteness than one of the only ways Asian immigrants could demand civic equality prior to 1943 (Repeal of Chinese Exclusion) and 1952 (McCarran–Walter Act) within a structure of white supremacy. Although attention must be given to problematic claims of privilege associated with whiteness, as well as the many socially constructed hierarchies from which many, past and present, Asian immigrants themselves benefited in their home countries and the diaspora, *Ozawa* and *Thind* show that they and others must also be framed within the particular ways that Asians and Asian Americans have been racialized in the United States. Whether labeled "not white" by skin color, ancestry, or common beliefs, Asianization is a reality across ethnicities and citizenship status historically and presently. Yet Asian racialization must be also complicated through strategic anti-essentialism. While many Asian American educators and activists are complicit in white supremacy through the trope of honorary whiteness, its application varies by time and community.

## The Complicated History of Honorary Whiteness

An aspect of racial hierarchies that often goes unquestioned in schooling spaces and popular discourse is the ascription of "honorary whiteness" to

Asian Americans. Honorary whiteness is the insistence that Asian Americans are "the most recent in a long procession of ethnic groups to have climbed up the social hierarchy" (Tuan, 1998, p. 30) as demonstrated by their/our positioning as a "model minority," an overgeneralization that Asian Americans achieve universal educational and occupational success (Yi et al., 2020), regardless or in spite of their race. What often is omitted from such conversations is the role of white supremacy in crafting the model minority myth in the first place (despite the breadth of scholarship about this problematic stereotype) and how the model minority myth has been leveraged in ways that harm Asian Americans *and* Black and Brown communities, as well as ways that disturbingly argue for Asian supremacy (Wu, 2014).

Asian American studies scholars consistently cite the mid-1900s for the emergence of the model minority stereotype, after the Watts riots and the release of Secretary of Labor Daniel Moynihan's controversial report pathologizing Black communities (Iftikar & Museus, 2018; Yi et al., 2020). Shortly after these events, articles in *U.S. News and World Report* and the *New York Times* (Petersen, 1966) uplifted the success of Chinese and Japanese Americans, which they attributed to ethnic assimilation and a "bootstrap" mentality that refused the support of social services. Robert G. Lee (2007) reminds us that World War II was an important prelude to the making of the model minority myth: The need for the United States to court wartime allies necessitated the end of the Chinese Exclusion Act, the first and only federal legislation to prohibit immigration on the basis of race. Likewise, Cold War competition and politics shaped U.S. government policies and discourse around Asians as model minorities in order to uphold an image of "American benevolence" while meeting practical economic needs, especially in the STEM (science, technology, engineering, and mathematics) fields (Hsu, 2015, p. 19).

Yet the end of Chinese exclusion must not be confused with Asian acceptance, as the perceived unassimilability of Japanese Americans on the West Coast resulted in their incarceration after the bombing of Pearl Harbor, demonstrating "the willingness of the U.S. government to invoke race as a category of subordination to achieve its goals" (Lee, 2007, p. 270). Anti-Asian sentiment, harassment, and violence continued during the Korean War and the Red Scare as they remained firmly tethered to white supremacist ideals. Therefore, the model minority myth entered popular discourse not because of Asian American success or excellence but as the result of a refusal to rely on social services from a government with a history of persecuting Asian American communities, Asian American political silence, and exclusionary immigration laws that privileged the entry of highly educated Asian professionals (Hsu, 2015).

The history and complexity around the emergence of the model minority stereotype is rarely addressed in K–12 curriculum and is overwhelmingly absent in popular media. What remains, however, is what C.J. Kim (1999) describes as racial triangulation, wherein Asian Americans are viewed as racially superior to Black and Brown communities while remaining limited in their racial positioning and political voice and are still viewed as inferior to whites. This often manifests in the exclusion of Asian Americans from conversations about race broadly, and educational, economic, and healthcare injustice specifically. Yet, when the inclusion of Asian Americans supports arguments grounded in white supremacy, like the dismantling of affirmative action, they are conveniently brought into the conversation and afforded honorary whiteness.

It is important to acknowledge that honorary whiteness is not universally applied to all Asian Americans, and is typically most relevant to East Asian populations even as anti-Asian rhetoric and violence during COVID-19 clearly exposes the Asianization of East Asian Americans. In this respect, the AsianCrit tenet of strategic (anti-)essentialism is useful in establishing ways in which the model minority can harm *all* Asian Americans *and* other communities. Anti-essentialism acknowledges that many Southeast Asian Americans arrived in the United States as refugees who escaped war and often did not have formal education in their home country (Uy, 2008), and that in some parts of the United States, Southeast Asian American youth are disproportionately involved in gang activity (Lam, 2015), upending notions of Asian American students as obedient and submissive and disrupting any elevation that these particular Asian Americans might have on the racial hierarchy. Two decades after 9/11, South Asian Americans continue to be viewed as terrorists and ridiculed as foreign Others. These regional distinctions notwithstanding, H1-B visas facilitate the entry of doctors, engineers, and tech workers, leading to a disproportionate number of immigrants from India, China, Korea, and the Philippines—immigrants who are highly educated, fluent in English, and whose representations abound in popular media, from *The Big Bang Theory* to *The Mindy Project*. Hence, the model minority stereotype, and honorary whiteness as a manifestation of this stereotype, must be understood as deeply and inextricably linked to white supremacy and an immigration system based on racism and exploitation.

## Expanding the Breadth and Depth of Asian American (Hi)Stories

As long as Asian American (hi)stories remain unexamined or disregarded in social studies, a more critical understanding of how race and racism function in and through historical narratives will be incomplete and therefore more vulnerable to distortions that divide communities of color and maintain white supremacy. We urge readers to examine when and how these (hi)stories are taught and to imagine a more iterative approach that embeds Asian American (hi)stories across time and place and weaves them with other struggles for justice and civic recognition. State standards largely limit Asian Americans to two topics: Chinese on the West Coast in the 1800s and Japanese American incarceration during World War II (An, 2016). This emphasis is also reflected in textbooks and curriculum, dismissing the contemporary Asian American experience as well as the ethnic diversity of Asian America and the many intersections within and across ethnicities. Moreover, limiting Asian American histories and experiences to these two topics reinforces the exclusionary conflation of Asian Americans solely with East Asian Americans (Lee & Ramakrishnan, 2019). Here we provide a brief overview of how "Asian American" can be (re)constructed and taught more expansively in social studies in ways that defy traditional add-on approaches.

Regarding citizenship and fights for civil rights, the *Wong Kim Ark*, *Thind*, and *Ozawa* cases described previously should be taught in addition to *Dred Scott v. Sandford*. However, legal battles were not the only pathways for Asian immigrants as they navigated a place in U.S. society. Looking beyond traditional views of significant historical moments, an examination of the seemingly ordinary yields intersections of communities that are almost always separated in history.

For example, in the late 19th and early 20th centuries, South Asian immigrants worked and married within Black communities in New Orleans and New York (Bald, 2013). Given anti-immigration and anti-miscegenation sentiments, a similar pattern emerged on the West Coast whereby Punjabi agricultural workers married Mexican American women (Prashad, 2000). Not only do these stories push beyond the dominant narratives that center East Asian Americans, but they also situate Asian American history within the long history of white supremacy in the United States and within communities of color who found ways to resist and thrive collectively.

Connections across continents must also be considered. Asian American narratives absent the context of Western imperialism preclude an interrogation of oppression and injustice. As historian Gary Okihiro (2015) argues, "Asians did not go to America; Americans went to Asia" (p. 9). When students respond to a lesson on the Chinese Exclusion Act with "They should have stayed in China," what becomes clear is that social studies education must include Asian American history beyond master narratives of U.S. liberalism and exceptionalism. When considering reasons for (im)migration, escaping poverty and tyranny in Asia and being lured by the freedom and economic opportunities in the United States (i.e., exceptionalism) are far too simplistic narratives. Instead, (im)migration ought to be situated within global patterns of Western imperialism and coerced, exploitative labor practices that continue today. The intense recruitment of Asian laborers by plantation owners and railroad companies (Takaki, 1998) is often omitted, as is the intentional strategy of importing Chinese laborers as trial replacements for enslaved Black people whose continued resistance alarmed enslavers and sympathetic government institutions (Jung, 2006; Lowe, 2015; Yun, 2008). That this shift did not take place on a large scale testifies both to coercive conditions and the agency of laborers.

Attention to Asian American history should likewise require that educators firmly situate U.S. imperialism within U.S. history curriculum. Although often relegated to world history, if mentioned at all, the history of the Philippines and Filipino Americans is one of several case studies that lays bare U.S. ambitions for world power. Acting within the ideas of white supremacy and manifest destiny (Ignacio et al., 2014), the U.S. government sought to colonize their "little Brown Brothers" (Takaki, 1998, p. 324), exploiting the land and people while taking measures to stem immigration and quell fears that "questioned the capacity of the nation's [U.S.] democratic institutions to absorb millions of newcomers of *suspect racial stock*" (Baldoz, 2011, p. 11, emphasis added). One answer to these fears was the designation of colonized peoples as U.S. nationals, not U.S. citizens, requiring the allegiance of Filipinos (and Native Hawaiians, Puerto Ricans, Chamorros in Guam, etc.)

without providing the benefit of civic rights. Such efforts spanned the Pacific as Filipinos immigrated to the United States and anti-miscegenation laws in California already targeting Asian men were extended to U.S. nationals from the Philippines. Furthermore, even after serving in the U.S. military during World Wars I and II with promises of citizenship and benefits, Filipino veterans often had to fight in courts to naturalize as citizens and were ultimately denied veteran benefits. Astonishingly, some veterans only *recently* received these benefits or have yet to receive them, such as 102-year-old Private Placido Laureta, who received his disability benefits and other compensation in 2020 (Sadongdong, 2020).

After Filipino independence from the United States in 1946, an examination of the Bell Trade Act reveals how the United States continued to plunder the Philippines and set up a post-independence relationship that benefited U.S. interests to the harm of the Filipino economy. Despite the expiration of such legal ties, the impact of U.S. colonialism remained with infrastructure that entrenched, as examples, education in the English language and, specifically, Western medicine. While one could argue that such legacies are to the benefit of development, the Philippines has also become a source for cheaper labor that the United States funneled into its own needs, draining the Philippines of professionals, such as nurses. Both in the Philippines and in the global diaspora, this pipeline has created and exacerbated inequities. For example, already suffering from a nurse shortage, COVID-19 has worsened access to medical care in the Philippines (Lopez & Jiao, 2020). In the United States, approximately 4% of nurses are Filipino, yet they also make up almost 33% of the nurses who have died from COVID-19 (Shoichet, 2020). Whether in the Philippines, the global diaspora, or the metropole, U.S. imperialism viewed through the lens of Asian American history is steeped in paternalistic racism/white supremacy and must be a part of U.S. history curriculum.

These examples illustrate the need to (re)construct and reorient Asian American (hi)stories to better attend to white supremacy, imperialism, and the long U.S. history of racist immigration policy. At the same time, Asian American (hi)stories should not only emphasize oppression and exploitation but must also offer students examples of innovation, resilience, joy, and solidarity with other historically marginalized groups. An important caveat to this work, however, is that educators must avoid teaching Asian American (hi)stories in ways that perpetuate the narrative template of U.S.

exceptionalism and progress (Rodríguez, 2020); white supremacy and the systems that uphold it must always be clearly identified and wrestled with when teaching about the histories and experiences of Black, Indigenous, and people of color (BIPOC).

## Taking Up a Pedagogy of Insurgency With Asian American (Hi)Stories

The (re)construction of Asian American histories requires a pedagogy of insurgency (Au, 2021) that attends to critical analyses of power, contradictions in schooling, and connection to broader social struggles and movements. Revisiting Chang's (1993) initial call for AsianCrit in legal studies, as Asian American educators, we argue for pedagogical opportunities "to speak our oppression into existence" (p. 1314). Although our experiences and oppressions are perhaps as diverse as our community, we are also bound politically and through common histories and diasporas shaped by Western imperialism. Hong (2020) argues that "our shared root is not the opportunity this nation has given us but how the capitalist accumulation of white supremacy has enriched itself off the blood of our countries. We cannot forget this" (p. 90).

Whether highlighting existing or weaving new Asian American narratives in social studies, educators must do so through lenses that have been developed by Asian American communities. To separate Asian American history from U.S. and Western imperialism obscures the role of Western avarice and racism in how and why *Asian* and *American* came together. To position Asian Americans within the diaspora without attending to *racial capitalism* (Robinson, 1983/2000) and the global exploitation of BIPOC, deliberately erases white supremacy and the struggles of people of color. To thread Asian Americans throughout U.S. history without deconstructing the model minority stereotype reifies a hierarchy of race that divides communities of color.

Merely adding Asian American narratives to the existing social studies curriculum is not enough. A celebration of Asian American Pacific Islander Heritage Month is not enough. Bringing in a guest speaker, attending a single professional development, and posting on social media are not enough. Teaching as an intellectual and insurgent act requires educators to deeply understand and contextualize historical narratives by doing the work of researching, listening to, and reflecting on the voices of the community.

Whether attending to organizations, such as Asian Americans Advancing Justice, Desis Rising Up and Moving, South Asian Americans Leading Together, AAPI Women Lead; activists, including Jose Antonio Vargas, Amanda Nguyen, Helen Zia, Yuri Kochiyama, and Grace Lee Boggs; scholars, such as Scott Kurashige, OiYan Poon, Jennifer Ho, Daryl Maeda, Mari Matsuda, Junaid Rana, Sunaina Maira, Dawn Bohulano Mabalon, Vivek Bald, Yen Le Espiritu, Judy Yung; social commentator Phil Yu; or institutional resources, such as the PBS series Asian Americans, the Smithsonian Asian Pacific American Center, Densho, and the Wing Luke Museum, what we have offered are initial steps in teaching Asian American (hi)stories that might enact change. If educators can bring these stories to the fore in their full complexity while recognizing the damage wrought by white supremacy throughout our history, we might continue the resistance and survival that will always accompany efforts to silence and erase.

## Note

1. *Desi* refers to anyone of South Asian ancestry.

## References

An, S. (2016). Asian Americans in American history: An AsianCrit perspective on Asian American inclusion in state US history curriculum standards. *Theory & Research in Social Education, 44*(2), 244–276. https://doi.org/10.1080/00933104.2016.1170646

Au, W. (2021). A pedagogy of insurgency: Teaching and organizing for radical racial justice in our schools. *Educational Studies.* Advanced online publication. https://doi.org/10.1080/00131946.2021.1878181

Bald, V. (2013). *Bengali Harlem and the lost histories of South Asian America.* Harvard University Press.

Baldoz, R. (2011). *The third Asiatic invasion: Empire and migration in Filipino America, 1898–1946.* New York University Press.

Buenavista, T. L., Jayakumar, U. M., & Misa-Escalante, K. (2009). Contextualizing Asian American education through critical race theory: An example of US Pilipino college student experiences. *New Directions for Institutional Research, 142*, 69–81. https://doi.org/10.1002/ir.297

Chang, R. S. (1993). Toward an Asian American legal scholarship: Critical race theory, post-structuralism, and narrative space. *California Law Review, 81*(5), 1241–1314. https://doi.org/10.2307/3480919

Crenshaw, K. W. (1988). Race, reform, and retrenchment: Transformation and legitimation in antidiscrimination law. *Harvard Law Review, 101*(7), 1331–1387. https://doi.org/10.2307/1341398

Diaz, V. M. (2004). "To 'P' or not to 'P'?": Marking the territory between Pacific Islander and Asian American Studies. *Journal of Asian American Studies, 7*(3), 183–208. https://doi.org/10.1353/jaas.2005.0019

Fitzpatrick, P., & Hunt, A. (1987). *Critical legal studies*. Blackwell.

Gotanda, N. (1995). Critical legal studies, critical race theory and Asian American studies. *Amerasia Journal, 21*(1–2), 127–136. https://doi.org/10.17953/amer.21.1-2.2j46202k85658662

Grewal, I. (2003). Transnational America: Race, gender, and citizenship after 9/11. *Social Identities, 9*(4), 535–561. https://doi.org/10.1080/1350463032000174669

Harris, A. P. (1994). The jurisprudence of reconstruction. *California Law Review, 82*, 741–785.

Hau'ofa, E. (2008). *We are the ocean: Selected works*. University of Hawai'i Press.

Hong, C. P. (2020). *Minor feelings: An Asian American reckoning*. One World.

Hsu, M. Y. (2015). *The good immigrants: How the yellow peril became the model minority*. Princeton University Press.

Iftikar, J. S., & Museus, S. D. (2018). On the utility of Asian critical (AsianCrit) theory in the field of education. *International Journal of Qualitative Studies in Education, 31*(10), 935–949. https//doi.org/10.1080/09518398.2018.1522008

Ignacio, A., de la Cruz, E., Emmanuel, J., & Toribio, H. (2014). *The forbidden book: The Philippine–American War in political cartoons*. Eastwind Books of Berkeley.

Ishizuka, K. L. (2016). *Serve the people: Making Asian America in the long sixties*. Verso Books.

Jung, M. (2006). *Coolies and cane: Race, labor, and sugar in the age of emancipation*. Johns Hopkins University Press.

Kim, C. J. (1999). The racial triangulation of Asian Americans. *Politics & Society, 27*, 105–138. https://doi.org/10.1177/0032329299027001005

Lam, K. D. (2015). *Youth gangs, racism, and schooling: Vietnamese American youth in a postcolonial context*. Springer.

Lee, J., & Ramakrishnan, K. (2019). Who counts as Asian. *Ethnic and Racial Studies, 43*(10), 1733–1756. https://doi.org/10.1080/01419870.2019.1671600

Lee, R. G. (2007). The Cold War construction of the model minority myth. In M. Zhou & J. V. Gatewood (Eds.), *Contemporary Asian America: A multidisciplinary reader* (pp. 852–882). New York University Press.

Lopez, D. B., & Jiao, C. (2020, April 23). *Supplier of world's nurses struggles to fight virus at home*. Bloomberg. https://www.bloomberg.com/news/articles/2020-04-23/philippines-sends-nurses-around-the-world-but-lacks-them-at-home

López, K. (2013). *Chinese Cubans: A transnational history*. University of North Carolina Press.

Lowe, L. (1996). *Immigrant acts: On Asian American cultural politics*. Duke University Press.

Lowe, L. (2015). *The intimacies of four continents*. Duke University Press.

Maeda, D. J. (2012). *Rethinking the Asian American movement*. Routledge.

Matsuda, M. J. (1997). *Where is your body? And other essays on race, gender and the law*. Beacon Press.

Minhaj, H., & Storer, C. (Directors). (2017). *Homecoming king* [Film]. Netflix.

National Center for Educational Statistics. (2019). *Number and percentage distribution of teachers in public and private elementary and secondary schools, by selected teacher characteristics: Selected years, 1987–88 through 2017–18. Table 209.10.* U.S. Department of Education. https://nces.ed.gov/programs/digest/d19/tables/dt19_209.10.asp

Neogi, A. (2021). How does it feel to be a solution?: How South Asian migration from 1885 to 1923 created a modern South Asian "other" used to promote conservative rhetoric. *Hastings Constitutional Law Quarterly, 48*(3), 508–533.

Ngai, M. M. (2004). *Impossible subjects: Illegal aliens and the making of modern America—updated edition.* Princeton University Press.

Okihiro, G. (2015). *American history unbound: Asians and Pacific Islanders.* University of California Press.

*Ozawa v. United States*, 260 U.S. 178 (1922).

Park, J. J., & Liu, A. (2014). Interest convergence or divergence? A critical race analysis of Asian Americans, meritocracy, and critical mass in the affirmative action debate. *Journal of Higher Education, 85*(1), 36–64. https://doi.org/10.1080/00221546.2014.11777318

Petersen, W. (1966, January 9). Success story: Japanese-American style. *New York Times*, V1–20. https://www.nytimes.com/1966/01/09/archives/success-story-japaneseamerican-style-success-story-japaneseamerican.html

Philip, T. M. (2014). Asian American as a political–racial identity: Implications for teacher education. *Race Ethnicity and Education, 17*(2), 219–241. https://doi.org/10.1080/13613324.2012.674024

Prashad, V. (2000). *The karma of Brown folk.* University of Minnesota Press.

Robinson, C. J. (2000). *Black Marxism: The making of the Black radical tradition.* University of North Carolina Press. (Original work published in 1983)

Rodríguez, N. N. (2018). From margins to center: Developing cultural citizenship education through the teaching of Asian American history. *Theory & Research in Social Education, 46*(4), 528–573. https://doi.org/10.1080.00933104.2018.1432432

Rodríguez, N. N. (2020). "Invisibility is not a natural state for anyone": (Re)Constructing narratives of Japanese American incarceration in elementary classrooms. *Curriculum Inquiry, 50*(4), 309–329. https://doi.org/10.1080/03626784.2020.1831369

Rodríguez, N. N., & Kim, E. J. (2018). In search of mirrors: An Asian critical race theory content analysis of Asian American picturebooks from 2007 to 2017. *Journal of Children's Literature, 44*(2), 17–30.

Rodríguez, N. N., & Kim, E. J. (2019). Asian and American and always becoming: The (mis) education of two Asian American teacher educators. *Oregon Journal of the Social Studies, 7*(1), 67–81. https://drive.google.com/file/d/1nu7Cba5ruZKiXMsbij8ZU2QEo1GQYp_h/view

Roy, A. (2004). *Peace & the new corporate liberation theology. 2004 City of Sydney Peace Prize Lecture* (CPCS Occasional Paper No. 04/2). Center for Peace and Conflict Studies.

Sadongdong, M. (2020, October 5). Centenarian Filipino WW2 veteran gets P435K benefit after 11 years. *Manila Bulletin*. https://mb.com.ph/2020/10/05/centenarian-filipino-ww2-veteran-gets-p435k-benefit-after-11-years/

Said, E. W. (1979). *Orientalism*. Vintage.

Shoichet, C. E. (2020, December 11). *COVID-19 is taking a devastating toll on Filipino American nurses*. CNN. https://www.cnn.com/2020/11/24/health/filipino-nurse-deaths/index.html

Subedi, B. (2013). The racialization of South Asian Americans in a post-9/11 era. In M. Lynn & A. D. Dixson (Eds.), *Handbook of critical race theory in education* (pp. 167–180). Routledge.

Takaki, R. (1998). *Strangers from a different shore: A history of Asian Americans*. Little, Brown.

*Takao Ozawa v. United States*, 260 U.S. 178 (1922).

Teranishi, R. T. (2002). Asian Pacific Americans and critical race theory: An examination of school racial climate. *Equity & Excellence in Education, 35*(2), 144–154. https://doi.org/10.1080/713845281

Tuan, M. (1998). *Forever foreigners or honorary Whites?: The Asian ethnic experience today*. Rutgers University Press.

*United States v. Bhagat Singh Thind*, 261 U.S. 204 (1923).

*United States v. Wong Kim Ark*, 169 U.S. 649 (1898).

Uy, P. S. (2008). How the American Community Survey informs our understanding of the Southeast Asian community: One teacher's perspective. *Journal of Southeast Asian American Education and Advancement, 3*(1), 44–48. https://doi.org/10.7771/2153-8999.1108

Wu, F. H. (2014). The moral dilemma of honorary whiteness: A comment on Asian Americans and affirmative action. *Asian Pacific American Law Journal, 20*, 25–30. https://doi.org/10.5070/P3201031946

Yi, V., Mac, J., Na, V. S., Venturanza, R. J., Museus, S. D., Buenavista, T. L., & Pendakur, S. L. (2020). Toward an anti-imperialistic critical race analysis of the model minority myth. *Review of Educational Research, 90*(4), 542–579. https://doi.org/10.3102/0034654320933532

Yun, L. (2008). *The coolie speaks: Chinese indentured laborers and African slaves in Cuba*. Temple University Press.

FOUR

# "Existence Is Resistance": Palestine and Palestinians in Social Studies Education

*Hanadi Shatara*

> Are we not allowed to be Palestinian on Instagram? This, to me, is bullying. You can't erase history by silencing people.
>
> —*Bella Hadid*

IN JULY 2020, INSTAGRAM FLAGGED Bella Hadid's post of her father's passport photo as violating community guidelines that regulate content for harassment and nudity, as examples (Mahdawi, 2020; O'Malley, 2020). Hadid responded to this censorship by writing a new post: "Are we not allowed to be Palestinian on Instagram? This, to me, is bullying. You can't erase history by silencing people" (O'Malley, 2020, para. 1). This incident is not the only instance of censorship of Palestinian identities and experiences (Salaita, 2016). In May 2021, Palestinian activists were censored in their social media resistance on several platforms when using #SaveSheikhJarrah, #FreePalestine, and #GazaUnderAttack, calling on the global community to spread awareness and action (Alsaafin, 2021). Despite obstacles of censorship, harassment, and constant need to validate Palestinian identity, academic scholars and activists continue to push for recognition and legitimacy of Palestine and Palestinians, combating the erasure of our heritage, culture, and existence (Abu El-Haj, 2007, 2015; Erakat, 2019; Khalidi, 2010, 2020; Said, 1992; Tamari, 2009).

The mere existence of Palestinians and the connection to the land of Palestine is insurgent as our existence continues to be questioned and doubted by governments, academia, the media, and individuals. With the erasure of our identities both in academic spaces and on social platforms like the preceding example, Palestinians continue to resist and have agency in the injustice that has plagued them since British colonialism and the Nakba (النكبة)[1] in 1948 (Khalidi, 2020). Palestinians come together throughout the diaspora to resist. Yet, other Arab countries continue to neglect Palestinian existence for their own betterment. In August and September 2020, the leaders of the

United Arab Emirates and Bahrain, respectively, decided to normalize relations with Israel without the inclusion of Palestinian approval or opinion (Erakat, 2020). These deals prioritize the economic and geopolitical interests of Arab countries, Israel, and the United States even as Israel continues to enact a blockade on Gaza, de facto "annex" Palestinian land, and enforce the illegal occupation and building of settlements throughout the West Bank (Erakat, 2020). These settlements which have bright lights, paved roads, and resources that were stripped from Palestinians are evidence of a prior "annexation" that began without announcement. Take for instance Figure 4.1, which shows the progression of appropriated land. An examination of the last map reveals the immense growth of illegal settlements surrounding present-day Palestine.

This chapter tackles the ways in which Palestine and Palestinians are reduced and/or erased within social studies education and what educators can do to combat these notions. I break up this chapter into two parts. First, I begin by looking at the ways *Theory and Research in Social Education*, the

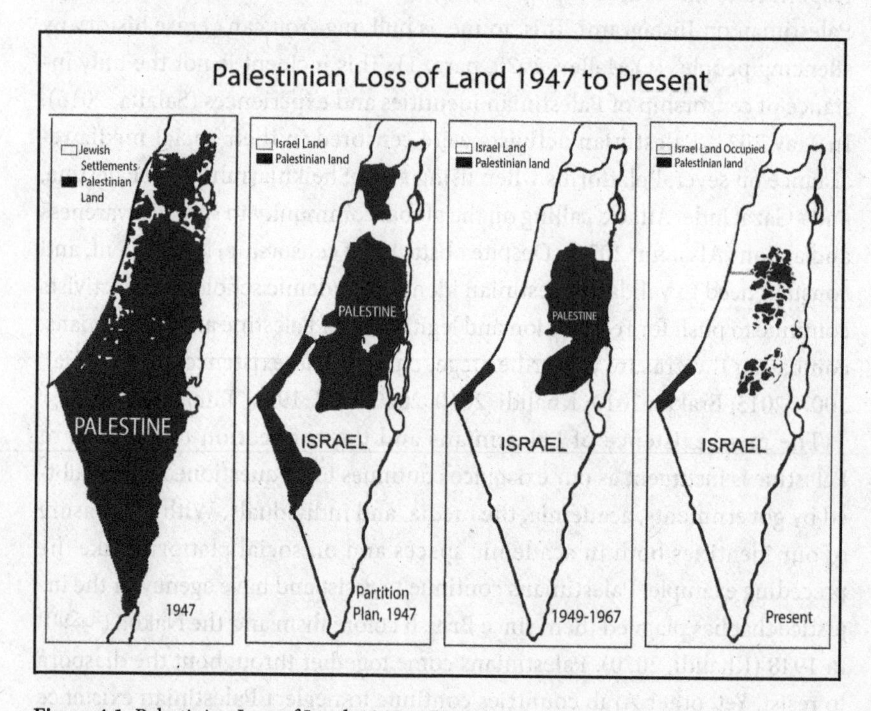


**Figure 4.1.** Palestinian Loss of Land, 1947 to Present

leading journal on social studies education, uses the words *Palestine* and *Palestinians* within its publications. In the second part, I offer ways teacher educators and researchers in social studies education should discuss Palestine and Palestinians in their teaching and research.

## My Positionality

My positionality plays a major role in how I discuss Palestine. As a Palestinian American and the child of Palestinian Christian immigrants, my Palestinian identity was instilled in me since my birth. Living with my parents, paternal grandmother, and great-grandmother, along with the intimate presence of my maternal grandmother, I grew up hearing and speaking Palestinian Arabic while trying to navigate my Americanness that I encountered in school and the outside world. From the food to the decor at home to the family gatherings, I was surrounded by my Palestinian culture and identity.

The events on and after 9/11 would further solidify my identity as a Palestinian, as I experienced blatant anti-Arab and anti-Palestinian sentiments at school and the conflation of Islam with Arabs and terrorism within representations in the media. Although this discrimination has left a lasting impression, I want to acknowledge my privilege of being born in the United States, being a Christian, and having access and ease of mobility to travel with a U.S. passport and without a Palestinian identity card. Palestinians' mobility is restricted and regulated every day. Because of this and the diversity of Palestinians, I do not represent all Palestinians. Instead, I present ways social studies educators and researchers can raise awareness of authentic narratives and disrupt the continued minimization, misrepresentation, and erasure of Palestine.

## Palestine in Social Studies Education Today[2]

### *In Publications*

A keyword search in the leading social studies journal, *Theory and Research in Social Education* (*TRSE*), yielded 11 articles for *Palestine* and 26 for *Palestinians* out of more than 500 articles since 1973. The first instance of Palestine and Palestinians in the articles was in 1985. However, I chose 2000 to begin my analysis as that was the beginning of the Second Intifada, an uprising within Palestine against Israeli military occupation and Israel's approval of building the apartheid wall on Palestinian ancestral land (Al Jazeera Media Network, 2015).[3] I organized the articles by alphabetical order by last name before I began reading, as that was my organizational preference. Although I did not have an initial coding scheme, I read and developed descriptive codes (Saldaña, 2009).

The field of social studies teaching and research as represented by *TRSE* neglected including Palestine and Palestinians given the number of mentions. When the journal tried to include them, beginning in the 2000s, the publication, for the most part, disregarded how they represented Palestine and Palestinians. I noticed three patterns within the articles: (1) the brief mention of Palestinians without context, (2) the connection of Palestinians to (the) conflict, and, conversely, (3) the intention of scholars to represent Palestine as a country and Palestinians as a people.

Several authors briefly mentioned Palestinians as an example in their articles to support their arguments or reference examples of Palestine and Palestinians (Crocco, 2002; Houser, 2005; Lévesque, 2003; Levy, 2018). The authors minimized Palestine and Palestinians within their arguments or briefly summarized a referenced article about Palestinians that connected to their work, without connecting to the context of occupation and oppression of Palestinians. For example, connecting peace education with gender, Crocco (2002) refers to Palestinians once at the end of the article, indirectly referring to the events of the Second Intifada in the early 2000s. In her attempt to connect peace education to current events but without context, she reduces the teenagers she described as "offer[ing] their lives as sacrifices to the Palestinian cause" (Crocco, 2002, p. 468) without acknowledging the devastating consequences of occupation and apartheid on the psyche, especially for children. Many of the Palestinian teenagers she referenced were encountering soldiers who had machine guns, protective gear, and tanks. And yet, there was no acknowledgment of who was perpetuating this "violence" on Palestinians, an oppressed people experiencing settler colonialism. The call for peace in a context of extreme imbalance of power, where one group has the resources (natural, economic, military) and allyship of the most powerful countries in the world and continues to kill, occupy, appropriate land, and break international law, is a call for the status quo, a call that invites complicity. Briefly mentioning Palestinians in an article on peace education without a context of their lives, especially during the Second Intifada, denies both the reality of power and the lived realities of Palestinians.

The majority of the articles connected Palestine and Palestinians to (the) conflict within curriculum and teaching (Brkich & Newkirk, 2015; Goldberg, 2017; Honig & Porat, 2019; Jacobs, 2009; King, 2009; Sheppard et al., 2015; Wansink et al., 2018; Werner, 2002). Examples of this included the centering of Israel when referring to Palestine or Palestinians (Honig & Porat, 2019; Jacobs, 2009; Werner, 2002), the referencing of the backlash experienced by educators teaching about the conflict (Brkich & Newkirk, 2015; King, 2009; Sheppard et al., 2015), and the teaching of Palestine as inherently a controversial issue (King, 2009; Sheppard et al., 2015). Controversial issues are highly politicized in social studies, allowing teachers and students to question the validation of a group's humanity, particularly in relation to conflict. In one example, Goldberg (2017) researched Israeli teachers' instruction on the Holocaust and the "Palestinian refugee problem" (p. 349). He noted that Israeli teachers were more willing to teach the Holocaust but dismissed the teaching of the "Palestinian refugee problem" to students (with the exception of a few teachers). Although there was an acknowledgment that Israel created the problem of displacement and continued to cause atrocities, the phrase "Palestinian refugee problem" centered the conflict or the problem rather than humanizing Palestinians who were experiencing settler colonialism, occupation, and oppression. Palestinians are conveyed as a distant problem that was prescribed by education institutions as a way to incorporate the teaching of Palestinians without tarnishing Israel's image. This approach strips Palestinians of their nationalities and identities and solidifies the Us-versus-Them binary (Said, 1978) that continues to Other the people who live(d) on the land.

The last pattern I noticed among the articles discussed Palestine and Palestinians in ways that affirmed their humanity. Although their arguments and research were not about Palestine, these scholars were intentional in what they wrote through their choice of citation and wording. Saada (2013), a Palestinian, and Yoder (2020) referenced Thea Abu El-Haj's (2007, 2015) work on Palestinian youth identities in the post-9/11 era in conversation to their work with teachers' and youths' perspectives on Islam, respectively. Hahn (2020) discussed the countries of origin of the immigrant students of European teachers and her table explicitly says Palestine, not Palestinian territories, legitimizing Palestine as a specific place. Additionally, Díaz and Deroo (2020) were intentional about how they referenced Palestine in their article. In a paragraph in their literature review that discusses how textbooks present conflicts, they referenced Bickerton and Kausner (2018) as an example that shows the "contention between Palestine and Israel" (p. 5). When I looked up the publication's title in their references, that book was called *A History of the Arab–Israeli Conflict*. There was no mention of Palestine or Palestinians in the book's title. Although this example connects to conflict, Díaz and Deroo (2020) intended to write Palestine in their article as a way to show its existence and legitimacy as opposed to erasure.

*In Social Studies Education*

There is a lack of representation of Palestine and Palestinians in curricula as well as standards and other education policies. Abu El-Haj (2007, 2015) wrote about the tensions between teachers and Palestinian students when students became insurgents in the classroom and corrected teachers. She pointed out an instance from a student, Lamia, who argued with her teacher on the erasure of Palestine on the world map. In another instance, a Palestinian teacher, Layla, recalled her experience as a middle school student when a social studies teacher assigned her as the role of the Palestinian Liberation Organization in an Arab–Israeli conflict simulation activity (Shatara, 2020). Layla felt tokenized, and the activity was void of the larger context of the oppression and dehumanization of Palestinians. These instances of minimizing the existence and experiences of Palestinians are similar in the ways Black, Indigenous, and people of color are largely minimized in social studies education (King & Simmons, 2018; Merchant, 2016; Rodríguez, 2018; Sabzalian, 2019; Shear et al., 2015).

Standards also play a role in the erasure of Palestine and Palestinians in social studies education. There are seven states in which teachers are asked to incorporate Israel and its conflict with the Arab states into their teaching, while 12 states explicitly want teachers to discuss the creation of Israel (Marino & Bolgatz, 2010). Yet, there is no explicit mention of Palestine or Palestinians. For example, New York state's social studies framework uses language that favors Israel with deliberate erasure of Palestine and Palestinians, using the term *Arab* instead. The following is an example of this erasure in one New York standard.

> 10.7c Nationalism in the Middle East was often influenced by factors such as religious beliefs and secularism.
>
> - Students will investigate Zionism, the mandates created at the end of World War I, and Arab nationalism.
> - Students will examine the creation of the State of Israel and the Arab-Israeli conflict. (New York State Education Department, 2015, p. 25)

This standard explicitly asks for students to examine the creation of Israel and lacks any mention of the people who already lived on this land. In another standard, you will notice the erasure of Palestine *and* the designation the standards give to Palestinians:

> 11.9c American strategic interests in the Middle East grew with the Cold War, the creation of the State of Israel, and the increased United States dependence on Middle Eastern oil. The continuing nature of the Arab-Israeli dispute has helped to define the contours of American policy in the Middle East.
>
> - Students will examine United States foreign policy toward the Middle East, including the recognition of and support for the State of Israel, the Camp David Accords, and the interaction with radical groups in the region. (New York State Education Department, 2015, p. 42)

In this U.S. history standard, the United States is centered in the conflict and involved in supporting Israel with some type of diplomacy between Israel and the "radical groups in the region." This standard commodifies any group against Israel as radical. Not only are Palestinians erased from this narrative, but they are also indirectly designated as a radical group. As if the will to live with freedom and recognition is radical!

In California, where there is activism around requiring Ethnic Studies for all ninth-grade students, the governor blocked the requirement due to pressure to eliminate Arab American studies from the curriculum because conservative pro-Israeli organizations deemed the inclusion of Palestine and Palestinians as anti-Semitic (Arab Resource & Organizing Center, 2020; Morrar, 2020). The California Department of Education then placed Arab American Studies in the appendix of the curriculum, negating Arab American Studies as an essential part of Ethnic Studies (MPower Change, 2020). The Arab Resource and

Organizing Center (2020), along with other activists from MPower Change (2020) and CAIR-San Francisco Bay Area, continue to advocate for Palestine and Palestinians into Arab American Studies and as integral to the Ethnic Studies curriculum.

How do social studies teachers, teacher educators, and researchers approach the discussion and teachings of Palestine and Palestinians in a humanizing way? Rather than write some instructional strategies, I focus the next section on key actions and resources when engaging with this content and evaluating resources on Palestine and Palestinians. It is important to note that there are resources through organizations and online that lean toward Israel and promote dehumanizing and essentializing perspectives of Palestinians. By instilling the specific actions that follow, educators will be able to critique what is available and center content knowledge and awareness on Palestine and Palestinians.

## Recommendations for Learning, Teaching, and Discussing Palestine and Palestinians

### *Say Palestine and Palestinians*

It is important to say Palestine and Palestinians. Recognizing Palestine on a map is significant in that the erasure of the name affects how others view and remember it. For example, Google has never labeled Palestine on Google Maps (Cresci, 2016). The application designated certain areas as the West Bank and Gaza. Although these are significant areas to Palestinians, this reduces Palestine to two areas, and it separates them from each other as if they are not connected. Many texts refer to the areas as Palestinian territories, with territories connoting an inherent lack of autonomy or authority. Palestine is either referred to as a historical place (similar to Persia, Byzantium, etc.; e.g., Bickerton & Kausner, 2018; Honig & Porat, 2019; Institute for Curriculum Services, n.d.; Jacobs, 2009) or within governmental/political language such as Palestinian Liberation Organization or Palestinian Authority (e.g., Bickerton & Kausner, 2018; Institute for Curriculum Services, n.d.). Most countries in Western Europe, North America, and Oceania do not recognize Palestine as a state (Al Jazeera Media Network, n.d.).

Curricula focused on Palestine and its history will refer to the topic as the Arab–Israeli conflict, representing Arabs as a homogeneous people and not distinguishing the various nationalities and cultures within the area. During the Ottoman Empire and British rule, Arabs identified with their region (Doumani, 2017; Tamari, 2009). As the Zionist[4] motto read, "a land without people for a people without land" (Khalidi, 2020, p. 11; Said, 1992, p. 9), Zionists equated Palestinians with Arabs, and one less Arab state would not matter (Khalidi, 2020). By including Palestinians as just Arabs, Zionists and the state of Israel tried to erase Palestinian identities. Palestinians who live in the state of Israel, often called "Arab citizens of Israel," are treated as second-class citizens (Erakat, 2019). Some scholars have chosen to refer to these Palestinians as 48 Palestinians (Maira & Shihade, 2012) or Palestinian citizens of Israel (Institute of Middle East Understanding, n.d.; Institute for Palestine Studies, n.d.), naming the Palestinians who remained on their ancestral land after 1948. By using these designations, there is a recognition of Palestinians as a people and their lived experiences. It is also important to recognize the displacement of many Palestinians living outside of Israel, or "in exile" (Bazian, 2020), and their desire to return to their homeland (Khalidi, 2020). We are and always will be Palestinians.

### *Remember That Although We Are Connected as Palestinians, We Are Not a Monolith*

Often, Palestinians are generalized as a monolith. Teachers need to actively become aware of and teach the diversity of different communities (Subedi, 2013), including Palestinians. Even as our identity and experiences as Palestinians connect us, Palestinians are diverse.

Many cities and villages within Palestine have their own culture and heritage. For example, people from the city of Ramallah have different cuisines and embroidery designs than the city of Nablus and Gaza. Racially, there are Black and Brown Palestinians. Given the history of different empires ruling over the area, Palestinians have a variety of physical attributes. Palestinians are also diverse religiously. The majority are Sunni Muslims, with secularists and many sects of Palestinian Christians such as Greek Orthodox, Eastern Catholic, Roman Catholic, Quakers, and Protestants, along with others of different religions (Khalidi, 2010).

Some diversity among Palestinians was the result of the Israeli government preventing the physical movement of Palestinians, thus creating physical and experiential divisions. Palestinians, human rights activists, and organizations regard the Israeli government as a settler-colonial government that engages in apartheid (Erakat, 2019; Institute for Middle East Understanding, 2013; Khalidi, 2020). The physical divisions created Palestinian refugees, those fleeing to neighboring Arab countries, and the creation of refugee camps during and after the Nakba. Many Palestinians keep their keys from their ancestral homeland, with hopes of returning. Within Palestine, there are four divisions that Israel inflicted onto Palestinians: Palestinians in Gaza, Palestinians in the West Bank, Palestinians in East Jerusalem, and 48 Palestinians. These divisions give restrictions and certain privileges to each group and are constantly changing. For example, Gazan Palestinians are rarely allowed to travel to the West Bank, while Palestinians in the West Bank have to apply for a permit in order to go to Jerusalem (Berda, 2018; Erakat, 2019; Gross, 2017; Laub & Daraghmeh, 2018). These permits are difficult to obtain, and even after they are, Palestinians must go through checkpoints and searches.

The apartheid wall further divides Palestine and Palestinians from each other. It was approved to be built in 2000 at the beginning of the Second Intifada as a form of security for Israel and segregating Palestinians. It separates Jerusalem from Palestinians in the West Bank and families from each other by running through neighborhoods. Israel enforces the wall with checkpoints and military presence. Travel can be very difficult for Palestinians who work and holiday in East Jerusalem and the Old City. Those who have vehicles with Israeli license plates (yellow) are able to travel between the West Bank and Israel while Palestinians, with white-colored license plates, issued from the Palestinian Authority, are restricted from traveling outside the West Bank (B'Tselem, 2004; Visualizing Palestine, 2012). Roads are also segregated based on license plates (B'Tselem, 2004; Visualizing Palestine, 2012). Despite the UN Security Council (2016) adopting Resolution 2334,[5] Israel continues to divide Palestinians from each other. While Palestinians are not a monolith in their identities and experiences, each group continues to identify as Palestinian and connect to our ancestral home in Palestine.

*Include Everyday Palestinians and Palestinian Culture and Joy Into Your Learning and Teaching*

As Bettina Love (2019) wrote, it is important to showcase Black joy within the narrative of Black people. It is essential to go beyond conflict and include

Palestinian joy into learning and teaching. Palestinians take great pride in our culture as it continues to sustain who we are. Preserving and passing down our culture to the next generation is an insurgent act when Zionists strive for ethnic cleansing (Pappe, 2006). The following are some of the many aspects of Palestinian culture.

Traditional artwork is embedded into every aspect of Palestinian life. *Tatriz* (تطريز), Palestinian embroidery, represents different areas, towns, and villages of Palestine. This embroidery can be found on a number of items, such as pillows cases, purses, bags, and *thwab* (ثَوب, *thob* in singular), which was notably worn by Congresswoman Rashida Tlaib in 2019 at her swearing-in ceremony. Ceramics are also known within traditional Palestinian artwork. For example, the Fakhoury family in Hebron creates and exports many Palestinian ceramics and pottery that represent traditional Palestinian artwork using techniques that date back to the Ottoman empire (Deprez, 2019).

Olive trees are one of the symbols of Palestine. Printed on T-shirts and shaped for jewelry, the olive tree represents the longevity of the Palestinian people (with the oldest olive trees in the world currently in Palestine) and their steadfastness. Olive wood becomes a part of artwork with wood carvings of the Dome of the Rock in Jerusalem and the nativity scene as just some of the creations. Olive oil is also a major staple within Palestinian cuisine along with olive soap, specifically from Nablus, thus furthering the olive tree as a Palestinian symbol.

With the establishment of Israel, Palestinian culture became and continues to be appropriated by Israel. Most notably, Israelis "Columbused" our cuisine and branded it as theirs. Many Palestinian chefs and writers, such as Reem Assil and Laila El-Hadad, have resisted the erasure of Palestine and Palestinians from popular foods such as hummus and falafel. As Reem Kassis (2020) stated, "food, after all, is an expression of history, culture, and tradition. By this token, presenting dishes of Palestinian provenance as 'Israeli' not only denies the Palestinian contribution to Israeli cuisine, but it erases our very history and existence" (para. 5). Palestinians once again preserve our culture and heritage from erasure by passing down recipes and continuing to struggle for our identity and culture through food.

Palestinian contemporary art continues to flourish in history and today. Notable writers contribute to the rich culture of Palestine; these include Mahmood Darwish's poems, Edward Said's academic work, and Susan

Abulhawa's novels. Music artists such as the Arab idol winner Muhammad Asaf and hip hop group DAM sing for Palestine. Traditional folk and *dabke* (دبكة, Palestinian folk dance) songs are preserved and sung throughout weddings and celebrations. Fine artists and filmmakers showcase their connection to the land and culture through their work. Some artists have been featured in exhibits at the Museum of the Palestinian People and films showcased at the Palestine Film Festival in Washington, D.C. present diverse stories and narratives. Some films to watch are *Five Broken Cameras, Rana's Wedding*, and *Omar*, among hundreds of others. These are just a few of the numerous names and places to engage with Palestinian art. These aspects of Palestinian culture showcase our joy in who we are and what we create.

### *Read and Follow Palestinian Scholars, Organizations, and Activists and Their Allies*

In August 2020, Gazans, Palestinian news networks, and organizations supporting Palestine and Palestinians went to social media to report and raise awareness of the attacks on Gaza (Al Jazeera, 2020b; Institute for Middle East Understanding, 2020). The Institute for Middle East Understanding reported that Gaza was attacked by Israel for 12 consecutive days in August during the COVID-19 pandemic. This was completely ignored by mainstream media. Rather, the media focused on the relationship between Israel and the United Arab Emirates. This is just one of many times that the media, particularly in the United States, neglected reporting these attacks as well as many of the other atrocities from the Israeli government to the Palestinians. And if there are news reports on Palestine, journalists center Israel and often ignore the perspectives and counternarratives from Palestinians. How can teachers, teacher educators, and researchers learn information that is authentic and gives a range of narratives from Palestinians themselves? Who do educators and researchers need to read and engage with in order to begin to learn about Palestine and Palestinians?

Before tackling these questions, we need to acknowledge that the dominant narrative is focused on Israel, Israelis, and Zionists and that any criticism against Israel is too often misrepresented as anti-Semitic. This is ingrained within the consciousness of academia and social studies education. By enacting an analysis through "contrapuntal reading" (Said, 1993, p. 62; Subedi, 2013) on this dominant knowledge, scholars must target their reading of this knowledge through the lens of colonialism and imperialism. Contrapuntal reading is a way to analyze and critique the mainstream "with an effort to draw out, extend, give emphasis and voice to what is silent or marginally present or ideologically represented" (Said, 1993, p. 66). If scholars and teachers encounter a news article from Western outlets such as the Associated Press, the BBC, the *New York Times*, and National Public Radio, they will need to enact a contrapuntal reading of the text to analyze if Palestine and Palestinians have voice and agency. This process can be implemented in published research and curricula. Questions that can be asked during this analysis are:

- What language is being used? Are *Palestine* and *Palestinians* included in the text?
- If so, how are they included? Are they discussed in active or passive voice? Does Palestine have an acknowledged existence? Do Palestinians have agency?
- Who is centered in the text? Where and from whom are the resources and references?
- Is conflict only discussed or does the text also include other dimensions of Palestinian existence?
- Is the context of occupation and settler colonialism discussed?
- Who is being silenced, erased, and neglected?
- What are the counternarratives from Palestinians?

To tackle this last question, it is imperative to engage with knowledge coming from Palestinians who discuss their experiences, their scholarship, and their identities. There are a variety of ways to engage and learn from news media to activists and educators. Following are some organizations in support of Palestine and Palestinians and allies to follow on social media and support their scholarship. This ensures the spread of accurate and often-ignored information on Palestine and Palestinians. It is important to recognize that the people and outlets produce and share content predominantly in English as a way to reach English-speaking populations. All handles are for Twitter unless specified for Instagram.

- Adalah, the Legal Center for Arab Minority Rights in Israel: Adalah (عدالة), meaning justice in Arabic, is an independent human rights organization and legal center working to advocate for the rights of Palestinians living in Israel. There is a chapter in New York. Follow them at @AdalahNY and @adalahjusticeproject on Instagram.
- AJ+ and Dena Takruri: an online news and current events media organization from Al Jazeera Media Network. While their reporting and content include a wide range of topics and critical perspectives, they do include stories and content on Palestine and Palestinians. Dena Takruri, one of their journalists and producers, a Palestinian from the United States, continues to produce content centered on Palestine. Follow AJ+ at @ajplus and Dena at @Dena.
- Dr. Hanan Ashrawi: a Palestinian feminist, activist, and scholar. Follow her at @DrHananAshrawi.
- Dr. Sa'ed Atshan: an associate professor of Anthropology at Emory University. Dr. Atshan has published notable works including *Queer Palestine and the Empire of Critique* and *The Moral Triangle: Germans, Israelis, Palestinians*, coauthored with Katharina Galor. Follow him at @Dr_Atshan.
- Center for Palestinian Studies at Columbia University: This center promotes and supports research, teaching, and collaboration for Palestine. This center sponsors various events, projects, and resources for those engaged in learning and teaching about Palestine and Palestinians. Visit its website at palestine.mei.columbia.edu.
- Institute for Middle East Understanding and *This Is Palestine* podcast: an independent, nonprofit organization whose mission is to provide information and sources on Palestine and Palestinians to increase public awareness and understanding. Follow the institute at @theIMEU and subscribe to its podcast, *This Is Palestine*.
- Institute for Palestinian Studies and *Journal of Palestine Studies*: an independent nonprofit organization that promotes research and scholarship concerning the question of Palestine. They have various publications including the *Journal of Palestine Studies*. Follow at @PalStudies.
- Jewish Voices for Peace: a U.S. activist organization that seeks to end the illegal occupation of Palestine, foster a just solution for Palestinian

refugees, and promote peace through opposing "anti-Jewish, anti-Muslim and anti-Arab bigotry." Its work utilizes grassroots organization, solidarity, respect for humanity, and tenacity. Follow at @ jvplive.

- Dr. Rashid Khalidi: a Palestinian historian who is the Edward Said Professor of Modern Arab Studies at Columbia University and editor of the *Journal of Palestine Studies*. He has written many notable books about Palestine, Palestinians, and Palestinian identity. His latest book, *The Hundred Years' War on Palestine: A History of Settler Colonialism and Resistance, 1917–2017*, traces the history of modern Palestine in the 20th and 21st centuries. Check out his books at your local library.
- Noura Erakat: a Palestinian human rights attorney, legal scholar, assistant professor at Rutgers University, and cofounding editor of *Jadaliyya*, a website that promotes scholarship and analysis on historical and current events of the Middle East. Her latest award-winning book, *Justice for Some: Law and the Question of Palestine*, centers on the relationship of politics and law of Palestine through its history, diplomacy, and foreign relations. Follow her at @4noura.
- Museum of the Palestinian People: a museum in Washington, D.C., solely focused on the history and culture of Palestine. The museum provides both in-person and virtual tours. Visit the website for information about tours at mpp-dc.org and follow at @MPPDC
- *Palestinians Podcast*: a podcast dedicated to showcasing the everyday stories of Palestinians from around the world. Subscribe to this podcast and follow at @PalestiniansPod.
- Palestinian Youth Movement: a grassroots organization of Palestinian young people in Palestine and in exile promoting activism for Palestine and Palestinians. There are chapters throughout the world that engage in organizing, protests, and other events for justice in Palestine. Follow at @palestinianyouthmovement on Instagram.
- Ilan Pappe: an Israeli historian, activist, and professor of history and the director of the European Centre for Palestine Studies at the University of Exeter in the United Kingdom. He has several publications critical of Israel, including *The Ethnic Cleansing of Palestine*. Follow at @pappe54.
- Linda Sarsour: a Palestinian Muslim American organizer and activist from Brooklyn who promotes equity and justice not just for

Palestinians but for other marginalized groups in the United States as well. Follow at @lsarsour.

- U.S. Campaign for Palestinian Rights: a U.S. network of activists and organizations committed to justice, freedom, and equality for Palestine. This organization calls to end U.S. complacency and complicity in the oppression of Palestinians and promoted the Black-Palestinian Solidarity Movement. Follow at @USCPR_.
- Visualizing Palestine: website by the organization Visualizing Palestine that uses data from researchers, designers, technologists, and communication specialists to create visuals and infographics with information to "advance a factual, rights-based narrative of the Palestinian-Israeli issue." Visit the site at visualizingpalestine.org and follow at @visualizingpal.

These are just a sliver of the many activists and organizations that are spreading awareness of Palestine and Palestinians in humanizing and authentic ways.

*Resist*

Palestinians are participating in resistance against Zionism, settler colonialism, and apartheid. Internationally, one way for Palestinians and allies to resist is through the BDS movement (Barghouti, 2010), which stands for Boycott, Divest, and Sanctions. BDS is a Palestinian-led global movement that was inspired by the nonviolent antiapartheid movement in South Africa. This movement is for "freedom, justice, and equality [for Palestinians as they] . . . are entitled to the same rights as the rest of humanity" (BDS Movement, n.d., para. 1). The movement calls for boycotts to cultural, sporting, and academic events in Israel, on products from Israeli corporations, and on international companies that support Israel. BDS also calls for divestment from banks, councils, universities, and other moneymaking entities from Israel and companies that support Israel, and promotes sanctions on Israel by putting pressure on governments throughout the world. BDS's nonviolent movement has three demands: "[1] ending its occupation and colonization of all Arab lands and dismantling the Wall . . . [2] recognizing the fundamental rights of the Arab-Palestinian citizens of Israel to full equality . . . [and 3] respecting, protecting and promoting the rights of Palestinian refugees to return to their homes and properties as stipulated in U.N. Resolution 194" (BDS Movement, n.d., para. 10–12). The BDS website presents different ways to get involved with actions. For example, there is a list of companies to boycott due to their contribution of profits to the Israeli government.

It is important to note that BDS comes with much controversy. Zionists believe the BDS movement is a threat to the state of Israel and paint it as anti-Semitic. Zionist organizations have created lists that advertise and target scholars, activists, educators, and other people who support BDS. Their goals are to ostracize these people and hope for consequences, such as losing their jobs and credibility.

Zionists are also threatened by the BDS movement entering the space of social studies education. In 2016, Rethinking Schools had a booth at the National Council for the Social Studies conference offering an issue of their journal that had an article supporting the BDS movement. Their representative noticed that there were people who came to the booth and took every copy of the magazine at once. In our conversations at the time, we both assumed that these people did not want teachers and conference-goers to read and engage with the BDS movement. Read *Boycotting Occupation: Educators and Palestine* written by the editors of Rethinking Schools (2016) and learn about the nonviolent movement for Palestine and Palestinians. Additionally, follow BDS on Twitter at @bdsmovement.

## Conclusion

As I write this chapter during the escalation of attacks on Palestinians in Palestine during a pandemic, buildings, businesses, residences, offices, schools, hospitals, and COVID-19 testing centers were destroyed by Israeli military forces in Gaza, along with the murder of more than 200 Palestinians and displacing about 91,000 Palestinians in just 11 days in May 2021 (al-Hajjar, 2021; Al Jazeera, 2020b; Hashem, 2021; Institute for Middle East Understanding, 2020; Krauss, 2021; Rasgon, 2021). Palestinian worshippers and civilians are tormented and attacked while residences are stolen and demolished by Israeli forces in Jerusalem and other parts of Palestine (Abdellatif, 2021; Andrews, 2021; B'Tselem, 2020a, 2020b, 2020c; Masarwa & Abu Sneineh, 2021; Middle East Monitor, 2020). Israeli settlers are threatening and killing unarmed protesters and Palestinians in the occupied West Bank (Frykberg, 2021).

The Israeli military has already killed many unarmed Palestinians, such as Eyad El Hallaq and Ahmed Erekat in 2020 (Al Jazeera, 2020a; Alsaafin, 2020; Federman, 2020; Jadaliyya, 2020; Trew, 2020). These are just some of the many atrocities faced by Palestinians every day for the past 73 years. Social studies teachers, researchers, and teacher educators have the responsibility to combat the hateful language of erasure used to represent Palestine and Palestinians. This chapter has brought to the forefront some of the ways in which educators can practice insurgency by taking a critical perspective with the mainstream media and curriculum and engage with those who disrupt the inauthentic and inaccurate depictions and narratives of Palestinians. If Palestine and Palestinians were taught in humanizing ways, the world could stand in solidarity with our struggle for freedom and the freedoms of all peoples living and experiencing oppression. Our existence is resistance and allies can contribute to that resistance through their work.

## Acknowledgments

I would like to thank Hanya Shatara, Muna Saleh, Sa'ed Atshan, Esther Kim, Amanda Najib, and Lara Hovsepian for their time reading and providing feedback on this chapter.

## Notes

1. The *Nakba*, the Arabic word for "catastrophe," is the name used for the start of land appropriation, expulsion of Palestinians, and creation of the state of Israel in 1948.
2. Although this is not an extensive and exhaustive representation of Palestine in social studies teaching and research in the United States, I show general examples of how Palestine and Palestinians are discussed and minimized in these areas that are typically encountered by researchers, teacher educators, and teachers.
3. The wall separates the West Bank from Israel. Many Palestinians and human rights activists and organizations named it the apartheid wall, while Israelis call it a separation wall and a security fence (Al Jazeera Media Network, 2015).
4. Zionism is a national movement and ideology for a Jewish state. This movement began in the 19th century in central and eastern Europe due to the "growing pressure on Jews in those regions either to assimilate totally or risk continuing persecution" (Pappe, 2006, p. 10). By the beginning of the 20th century, Zionists eyed Palestine as the site for a Jewish state (Khalidi, 2020; Pappe, 2006).

5. UN Resolution 2334 stated that Israel violates international law by displacing Palestinians and building illegal settlements.

## References

Abdellatif, L. (2021, May 21). Al-Aqsa Mosque: Israel police storm the complex following Gaza ceasefire. *Middle East Eye*. https://www.middleeasteye.net/news/israel-palestine-aqsa-police-raid-ceasefire

Abu El-Haj, T. R. (2007). "I was born here, but my home, it's not here": Educating for democratic citizenship in an era of transnational migration and global conflict. *Harvard Educational Review, 77*(3), 285–316. https://doi.org/10.17763/haer.77.3.412l7m737q114h5m

Abu El-Haj, T. R. (2015). *Unsettled belonging: Educating Palestinian American youth after 9/11*. University of Chicago Press.

al Hajjar, M. (2021, May 21). In pictures: Palestinians return to piles of rubble following Gaza ceasefire. *Middle East Eye*. https://www.middleeasteye.net/news/pictures-israel-gaza-palestine-return-demolished-homes

Al Jazeera Media Network. (2015). *Separation Wall*. Palestine Remix. https://interactive.aljazeera.com/aje/palestineremix/wall.html

Al Jazeera Media Network. (2020a, June 23). *Israeli forces kill Palestinian at occupied West Bank checkpoint*. https://www.aljazeera.com/news/2020/6/23/israeli-forces-kill-palestinian-at-occupied-west-bank-checkpoint

Al Jazeera Media Network. (2020b, August 24). *Israeli warplanes carry out more attacks on Gaza*. https://www.aljazeera.com/news/2020/8/24/israeli-warplanes-carry-out-more-attacks-on-gaza

Al Jazeera Media Network. (n.d.). *Palestine and Israel: Mapping an annexation*. https://www.aljazeera.com/indepth/interactive/2020/06/palestine-israel-mapping-annexation-200604200224100.html#palestinetoday

Alsaafin, L. (2020, June 3). Family of slain autistic Palestinian not optimistic over inquiry. *Al Jazeera*.https://www.aljazeera.com/news/2020/6/3/family-of-slain-autistic-palestinian-not-optimistic-over-inquiry

Alsaafin, L. (2021, May 11). Palestinians criticise social media censorship over Sheikh Jarrah. *Al Jazeera*. https://www.aljazeera.com/news/2021/5/7/palestinians-criticise-social-media-censorship-over-sheikh-jarrah

Andrews, F. (2021, May 12). Al-Aqsa under attack: How Israel turned holy site into a battleground. *Middle East Eye*. https://www.middleeasteye.net/news/israel-palestine-aqsa-attacks-how-violence-unfolded

Arab Resource & Organizing Center. (2020). *Action*. http://araborganizing.org/actionalerts/

Barghouti, O. (2010). *BDS: A global movement for freedom and justice* (Al-Shabaka Policy Brief). Al-Shabaka. https://al-shabaka.org/briefs/bds-global-movement-freedom-justice/

Bazian, H. (2020, July 23). *Dr. Hatem Bazian Conversation with Dr. Hanan Ashrawi on occupation, annexation and the unfolding consequences for Palestine.* https://www.facebook.com/dr.bazian/videos/10111060900977583/

BDS Movement. (n.d.). *What is BDS?* https://bdsmovement.net/what-is-bds

Berda, Y. (2018). *Living emergency: Israel's permit regime in the occupied west bank.* Stanford University Press.

Bickerton, I. J., & Klausner, C. L. (2018). *A history of the Arab–Israeli conflict.* Routledge.

Brkich, C. A., & Newkirk, A. C. (2015). Interacting with upset parents/guardians: Defending justice-oriented social studies lessons in parent–teacher conference simulations. *Theory & Research in Social Education, 43*(4), 528–559. https://doi.org/10.1080/00933104.2015.1099485

B'Tselem. (2004). *Forbidden roads: Israel's discriminatory road regime in the West Bank.* https://www.btselem.org/download/200408_forbidden_roads_eng.pdf

B'Tselem. (2020a, July 6). *Despite coronavirus outbreak: Israel ramps up demolition of West Bank Palestinian homes in June* [Press release]. https://www.btselem.org/press_releases/20200706_israel_ramps_up_demolitions_despite_coronavirus_outbreak

B'Tselem. (2020b, September 6). *Statistics on demolition of houses built without permits in the West Bank (not including East Jerusalem).* https://www.btselem.org/planning_and_building/statistics

B'Tselem. (2020c, September 6). *Statistics on demolition of houses built without permits in East Jerusalem.* https://www.btselem.org/planning_and_building/east_jerusalem_statistics

Cresci, E. (2016, August 10). Google Maps accused of deleting Palestine – but the truth is more complicated. *The Guardian.* https://www.theguardian.com/technology/2016/aug/10/google-maps-accused-remove-palestine

Crocco, M. S. (2002). Peace education: What's gender got to do with it? [Book review]. *Theory & Research in Social Education, 30*(3), 462–469. https://doi.org/10.1080/00933104.2002.10473206

Deprez, M. (2019, June 10). *Fakhoury family keeps Ottoman-era pottery techniques alive in Hebron.* Mondoweiss. https://mondoweiss.net/2019/06/fakhoury-ottoman-techniques/

Díaz, E., & Deroo, M. R. (2020, February 21). Latinxs in contention: A systemic functional linguistic analysis of 11th-grade US history textbooks. *Theory & Research in Social Education.* Advanced online publication. https://doi.org/10.1080/00933104.2020.1731637

Doumani, B. B. (2017). *Family life in the Ottoman Mediterranean: A social history.* Cambridge University Press.

Editors of Rethinking Schools. (2016, Spring). Boycotting occupation: Educators and Palestine. *Rethinking Schools, 30*(3). https://rethinkingschools.org/articles/editorial-boycotting-occupation-educators-and-palestine/

Erakat, N. (2019). *Justice for some: Law and the question of Palestine.* Stanford University Press.

Erakat, N. (2020, September 15). *Trump "peace" deals for Israel, UAE and Bahrain are shams. They boost oppression, not amity.* NBC News. https://www.nbcnews.com/think/opinion/trump-peace-deals-israel-uae-bahrain-are-shams-they-boost-ncna1240085

Federman, J. (2020, June 4). *Killing of Palestinian man with autism draws Floyd parallel.* Associated Press. https://apnews.com/article/cacec6c902909685f4da88c5a6311143

Frykberg, M. (2021, May 18). Israeli forces kill Palestinian protester in occupied West Bank. *Al Jazeera.* https://www.aljazeera.com/news/2021/5/18/palestinian-fighters-engage-israel-soldiers-in-west-bank-gunfire

Goldberg, T. (2017). Between trauma and perpetration: Psychoanalytical and social psychological perspectives on difficult histories in the Israeli context. *Theory & Research in Social Education, 45*(3), 349–377. https://doi.org/10.1080/00933104.2016.1270866

Gross, A. (2017). *The writing on the wall: Rethinking the international law of occupation.* Cambridge University Press.

Hahn, C. L. (2020). Educating citizens in an age of globalization, migration, and transnationalism: A study in four European democracies. *Theory & Research in Social Education, 48*(2), 244–284. https://doi.org/10.1080/00933104.2019.1707139

Hashem, M. (2021, May 15). Sheikh Jarrah: Settler colonialism, media coverage, and forced expulsions. *Middle East Eye.* https://www.middleeasteye.net/video/sheikh-jarrah-settler-colonialism-media-coverage-and-forced-expulsions

Honig, M., & Porat, D. (2019). The British, the tank, and that Czech: How teachers talk about people in history lessons. *Theory & Research in Social Education, 47*(4), 526–547. https://doi.org/10.1080/00933104.2019.1577196

Houser, N. O. (2005). Arts, aesthetics, and citizenship education: Democracy as experience in a postmodern world. *Theory & Research in Social Education, 33*(1), 45–72. https://doi.org/10.1080.00933104.2005.10473271

Institute for Curriculum Studies. (n.d.). *Curriculum.* https://icsresources.org/curriculum/

Institute for Middle East Understanding. (2013). Is Israel an apartheid state? https://imeu.org/article/is-israel-an-apartheid-state

Institute for Middle East Understanding [@theIMEU]. (2020, August 25). *Gaza is under attack and continues to suffocate under Israel's 13 years of blockade.* [Tweet]. Twitter. https://twitter.com/theIMEU/status/1298299902011813888?s=20

Institute for Palestine Studies. (n.d.). *Palestinian citizens of Israel.* https://oldwebsite.palestine-studies.org/resources/special-focus/palestinian-citizens-israel

Jacobs, B. M. (2009). Affordances and constraints in social studies curriculum-making: The case of "Jewish Social Studies" in the early 20th century. *Theory & Research in Social Education, 37*(4), 515–542. https://doi.org/10.1080/00933104.2009.10473409

Jadaliyya. (2020, June 24). Palestinian scholar Noura Erakat: Israeli forces killed my cousin on his sister's wedding day (on Democracy Now!). *Jadaliyya.* https://www.jadaliyya.com/Details/41333/Palestinian-Scholar-Noura-Erakat-Israeli-Forces-Killed-My-Cousin-on-His-Sister%E2%80%99s-Wedding-Day

Kassis, R. (2020, February 18). Here's why Palestinians object to the term "Israeli food": It erases us from history. *Washington Post.* https://www.washingtonpost.com/lifestyle/food/heres-why-palestinians-object-to-the-term-israeli-food-it-erases-us-from-history/2020/02/14/96974a74-4d25-11ea-bf44-f5043eb3918a_story.html

Khalidi, R. (2010). *Palestinian identity: The construction of modern national consciousness.* Columbia University Press.

Khalidi, R. (2020). *The hundred years' war on Palestine: A history of settler colonialism and resistance, 1917–2017.* Metropolitan Books.

King, J. T. (2009). Teaching and learning about controversial issues: Lessons from Northern Ireland. *Theory & Research in Social Education, 37*(2), 215–246. https://doi.org/10.1080/00933104.2009.10473395

King, L. J., & Simmons, C. (2018). Narratives of Black history in textbooks: Canada and the United States. In S. A. Metzger & L. M. Harris (Eds.), *The Wiley international handbook of history teaching and learning* (pp. 93–116). John Wiley & Sons.

Krauss, J. (2021, May 10). *Palestinians fear loss of family homes as evictions loom.* Associated Press. https://apnews.com/article/middle-east-religion-2ba6f064df3964ceafb6e2ff02303d41

Laub, K., & Daraghmeh, M. (2018, April 30). *For Palestinians, Israeli permits a complex tool of control.* Associated Press. https://apnews.com/article/7cfac1e5441747da841e51fdf3851460

Lévesque, S. (2003). "Bin Laden is responsible; it was shown on tape": Canadian high school students' historical understanding of terrorism. *Theory & Research in Social Education, 31*(2), 174–202. https://doi.org/10.1080/00933104.2003.10473221

Levy, B. L. M. (2018). Youth developing political efficacy through social learning experiences: Becoming active participants in a supportive model United Nations club. *Theory & Research in Social Education, 46*(3), 410–448. https://doi.org/10.1080/00933104.2003.10473221

Love, B. L. (2019). *We want to do more than survive: Abolitionist teaching and the pursuit of educational freedom.* Beacon Press.

Mahdawi, A. (2020, July 15). Bella Hadid's deleted Instagram post shows how Palestinians are silenced. *The Guardian.* https://www.theguardian.com/commentisfree/2020/jul/15/bella-hadid-deleted-instagram-post-palestinians-silenced

Maira, S., & Shihade, M. (2012). Hip hop from '48 Palestine: Youth, music, and the present/absent. *Social Text, 30*(3/112), 1–26.

Marino, M., & Bolgatz, J. (2010). Weaving a fabric of world history? An analysis of US state high school world history standards. *Theory & Research in Social Education, 38*(3), 366–394. https://doi.org/10.1080/00933104.2010.10473431

Masawra, L., & Abu Sneideh, M. (2021, May 5). Sheikh Jarrah: Israeli police storm Palestinian protest over Jerusalem evictions. *Middle East Eye.* https://www.middleeasteye.net/news/israel-palestine-sheikh-jarrah-jerusalem-police-storm-protest

Merchant, N. H. (2016). Responses to Islam in the classroom: A case of Muslim girls from minority communities of interpretation. *International Journal of Multicultural Education, 18*(1), 183–199. https://doi.org/10.18251/ijme.v18i1.1087

Middle East Monitor. (2020, August 7). *Report: Israel demolished 313 Palestine homes in West Bank, East Jerusalem in 2020.* https://www.middleeastmonitor.com/20200807-report-israel-demolished-313-palestine-homes-in-west-bank-east-jerusalem-in-2020/

Morrar, S. (2020, November 6). *Changes to ethnic studies in California include expansion on Asian American lessons. The Sacramento Bee.* https://www.sacbee.com/news/local/education/article247016937.html

MPower Change. (2020, December 18). *Defend ethnic studies*. https://act.newmode.net/action/mpower-change/take-action-save-ethnic-studies

New York State Education Department. (2015). *New York state Grades 9–12 social studies framework*. http://www.nysed.gov/common/nysed/files/programs/curriculum-instruction/ss-framework-9-12.pdf

O'Malley, K. (2020, August 7). Bella Hadid accuses Instagram of "bullying" after "removing" photo of father's Palestinian passport. *Elle*. https://www.elle.com/uk/life-and-culture/culture/a33244063/bella-hadid-accuses-instagram-censorship-palestinian-passport/

Pappe, I. (2006). *The ethnic cleansing of Palestine*. One World.

Rasgon, A. (2021, May 18). An Israeli airstrike damaged Gaza's only lab for processing coronavirus tests, officials said. *New York Times*. https://www.nytimes.com/2021/05/18/world/middleeast/israel-gaza-covid-lab.html

Rodríguez, N. N. (2018). From margins to center: Developing cultural citizenship education through the teaching of Asian American history. *Theory & Research in Social Education, 46*(4), 528–573. https://doi.org/10.1080*00933104.2018.1432432

Saada, N. L. (2013). Teachers' perspectives on citizenship education in Islamic schools in Michigan. *Theory & Research in Social Education, 41*(2), 247–273. https://doi.org/10.1080/00933104.2013.782528

Sabzalian, L. (2019). The tensions between Indigenous sovereignty and multicultural citizenship education: Toward an anticolonial approach to civic education. *Theory & Research in Social Education, 47*(3), 311–346. https://doi.org/10.1080/00933104.2019.1639572

Said, E. W. (1978). *Orientalism*. Vintage.

Said, E. W. (1992). *The question of Palestine*. Vintage.

Said, E. W. (1993). *Culture and imperialism*. Vintage.

Salaita, S. (2016). *Inter/nationalism: Decolonizing Native America and Palestine*. University of Minnesota Press.

Saldaña, J. (2009). *The coding manual for qualitative researchers*. SAGE.

Shatara, H. (2020). *The influence of globally oriented teachers' positionalities in world history classrooms* [Doctoral dissertation]. Columbia University.

Shear, S. B., Knowles, R. T., Soden, G. J., & Castro, A. J. (2015). Manifesting destiny: Re/presentations of Indigenous peoples in K–12 US history standards. *Theory & Research in Social Education, 43*(1), 68–101. https://doi.org/10.1080/00933104.2014.999849

Sheppard, M., Katz, D., & Grosland, T. (2015). Conceptualizing emotions in social studies education. *Theory & Research in Social Education, 43*(2), 147–178. https://doi.org/10.1080/00933104.2015.1034391

Subedi, B. (2013). Decolonizing the curriculum for global perspectives. *Educational Theory, 63*(6), 621–638. https://doi.org/10.1111/edth.12045

Tamari, S. (2009). *Mountain against the sea: Essays on Palestinian society and culture*. University of California Press.

Trew, B. (2020, June 25). Israeli forces kill relative of top Palestinian negotiator accused of ramming checkpoint. *The Independent*. https://www.independent.co.uk/news/world/middle-east/israel-ahmad-moustafa-shot-erekat-saeb-checkpoint-video-a9584951.html

United Nations Security Council. (2016, December 23). *Resolution 2334*. http://www.un.org/webcast/pdfs/SRES2334-2016.pdf

Visualizing Palestine. (2012, May). *Imagine a segregated road system where the color of your license plate dictates which roads you can drive on*. https://visualizingpalestine.org/visuals/segregated-roads-west-bank

Wansink, B., Akkerman, S., Zuiker, I., & Wubbels, T. (2018). Where does teaching multiperspectivity in history education begin and end? An analysis of the uses of temporality. *Theory & Research in Social Education, 46*(4), 495–527.

Werner, W. (2002). Reading visual texts. *Theory & Research in Social Education, 30*(3), 401–428. https://doi.org/10.1080/00933104.2002.10473203

Yoder, P. J. (2020, June 12). "He wants to get rid of all the Muslims": Mexican American and Muslim students' use of history regarding candidate Trump. *Theory & Research in Social Education*. Advanced online publication. https://doi.org/10.1080/00933104.2020.1773364

FIVE

# Insurgente: A Familia in Conversation About Latinx Voices in the Field of Social Studies

*La Familia Aponte-Safe Tirado Díaz Beltrán Ender Busey Christ*[1]

WE ARE WRITING THIS CHAPTER as a conversation. To help you, the reader, through it, we think there are a few characteristics that we should tell you about. First of all, this is an *ongoing* and *extended* conversation. It has been happening, and we're giving you the opportunity to be a fly on the wall.[2] We are mindful that these are our voices, and we are centering these voices that are usually on the margin. This is our chance to talk. You're hearing us talk. This is not the time to "what about" or center yourself. In some ways, we are not inviting you *into* the conversation. Rather, we invite you to listen and to learn and to respond, but first you should listen.

The second thing is that the writing can be a bit circular. It's presented in the way we talk. We talk from, like, different themes, and we bring them up, you know, as ideas come up. We love the organic flows of our conversations, but we felt it important to let you know that: No, we didn't organize our writing by themes or sections such as in a "talk about social media all together" and "talk about performativity all together" kind of way. That's just not how people talk, or at least, that's not how *we* talk. Concepts and ideas come up time and time again, sometimes much later in the conversation. So, we are letting you know about that ahead of time.

And then, this is a *conversation*—with individuals who are multilingual and use whichever language comes to mind,[3] and it will look like a conversation when people stop and switch directions or that the flow is like . . . "That made us think about how . . ." So, when you read it, it might look *odd* because this is not (intended as) a written piece, and we are trying to be intentional about that. This is not *written*. We love how Tommy starts us out with talking about breaking up that Western notion of writing. Sort of like, *No*! We are trying to replicate an *oral* tradition—or we are trying to *foster* an oral tradition. Unfortunately, it has to be written down because that's what our academic world expects, but it's an oral tradition, and we are maintaining it as such (as much as we can).

Finally (and relatedly), we particularly like the way the chapter starts with Tommy: "My tension is, and I hate to keep doing this, but for me how do we get this down into the chapter itself?" We think that captures the tenor of our conversations every time. We are disrupting the way academia typically wants you to write. We do not just *get to the point*. I mean, *look at the authors of this piece*. You expect *any of us* to get to the point quickly?! That is *not* how we talk, that is not how we *learn*. So we are asking you to listen to the point *in* the flow of the conversation. That's the insurgency of our writing. So, um, here we go . . .

---

**Tommy:** My tension is, and I hate to keep doing this, but for me, how do we get this down into the chapter itself?

**Gerardo:** Actually, I was just thinking we've been practicing different forms of writing for our chapter. There's something really beautiful about our conversation today and the way that it flowed and the concepts that were brought up, the references to literature that were also brought up. In some ways, I almost think that writing a transcript of this conversation with some minor editing, that's plenty. There's a lot of things that we've shared, and we've gone back and forth between concepts and theory and experiences and anecdotes and how we come to the conversation. So again, based on the writing that Ana, Becky, and I have been doing, where we think about this idea that we're inviting people into a conversation, a conversation that has been going on for a long time. If we frame the chapter in this way that, literally, you all get to read our conversation, right? It's just sort of this flowy, not necessarily like a play, but something of that sort that I think it emphasizes the focus on story, right? That many of these things come from our lived experiences. And so, we get to capture that voice when people are able to see who's talking. So, weaving that in, and then it lets the reader sort of see the threads that each of us is trying to make, not only in response to each other but also in response to what is informing us. Because all of us, when we speak, we'll say something like, "I was driving and this is what I saw, and it's making me feel this way." So, we contextualize where our ideas are coming from, and so the reader is able to follow a little bit from that thread by seeing us talking to each other but just in the written form.

**Ana:** Yes. So, Becky has suggested this before, and I think today, just because we all kind of started with this idea of insurgency and what it meant; it can be the beginning of that conversation. So, it would be a matter of transcribing our conversations. And then trying to arrange what makes sense.

**Tommy:** And then as a side note, I think also this is another example of our insurgency: We are capturing testimonios.[4] Think about it. The Western canon is based on the written word, but Indigenous sources have always been oral-based, and that is insurgent right there, and I love that.

**Chris:** I've been thinking about the process that we've engaged in over the years and how often times we can center our critiques around a particular condition, and rightfully so. But I think what this chapter does and what we've been doing collectively opens itself up to write about process and what it means to engage in this work, in particular, in contrast to the discipline and to the field. I went back to thinking, and that's kind of where many of these thoughts germinate from, was the idea of collective and that the collective is not honored in academia. Social studies education is a discipline within academia, where the collective is not honored. The collective is, in fact, the one thing that summons caution, caution from those in leadership positions. People of Color moving in collective typically signals a threat for those in power. The fear of having these systems and these processes known, for example, the process that we've been engaged in, is that it becomes co-opted and done so against our will. If we're not careful, efforts at insurgency end up becoming taken up and adopted to fit either a liberal frame, or to move a right-moderate frame closer to the center. It's almost like what we were seeing with Black Lives Matter now. Every institution is now doing something, and this isn't what Black Lives Matter has asked for. They haven't asked for inclusion. It is an insurgent, Black, antiracist, intersectional movement, but it's been co-opted.

**Tommy:** You mean Gatorade doesn't really care about racism in the U.S.?!

**Chris:** Hell, no. Gatorade. You already know; you already know. So yeah, my thinking was insurgency isn't asking for something. I don't think it is so much about demanding something either, as much as it is about asserting one's humanity. So, the theories that we work with are more about assertion than inclusion. And I think so many times we work with the spaces given rather than working to create our own spaces.

**Jesús:** I was thinking about how we do our work in the "crevices." I feel like there's been a push at every conference for the past, I don't know, at least 3 years, maybe longer, of the "unconferenced spaces." They're trying to make those crevices official. Every time I go to an unconferenced space, it's about as empty as anything else. It's almost like they know that there's important work happening in these unofficial spaces that they're trying to colonize them. I do think if we name the spaces, if we allow them to put their epistemological lens on what really is, I think we're all talking about ontological work and being that we're moving through. They'll put that epistemological lens, and they'll go, "Oh no. This is this. This is that. This is what you're doing and this is how it should look." They just love to do that. The whole time I was thinking, when you were talking, Chris, is the whole reason why it's needed is because every time Western epistemologies look at marginalized people, they're like, "No, you're either X or Y. You can't be both." God forbid, you're three at once. If you're AfroLatino, that's just going to make them run scared. I want an insurgency against naming and, instead, for being. I don't necessarily know if they'll do that, because they're going to want names. To quote the Unamerican Activities Committee, "they want names."

**Tommy:** And so, yes. You have to resist from within. I mean that's the whole thing. If you ever study social movement theory, you have to look at it from different perspectives and how those different perspectives feed into what the argument is for the movement itself. Because oftentimes movements will then simplify the message or become very narrow-minded, and that's how they fail. But if you have a community of different thoughts, like us folks in this Zoom image right now, we can advance something spectacular and significant, and sometimes folks don't want to hear that.

**Gerardo:** Okay, so that was a lot of really good stuff!

**Tommy:** It's the Colombian coffee that's now kicking in.

**Gerardo:** And resistance from within, right? Those are three things that my brain was like, "Boom." So, I've been thinking a lot about social media. I had to go on a social media fast because I get so angry, right? Just angry. And I know that there's a lot of things to be angry about, but not in the righteous indignation, Jesus-is-turning-the-tables-in-the-temple type of thing, but just like . . . I think for many of us, it's leading to a performativity of social justice something or other, that it's like, "I'm more woke than you. And I'm showing you just how woke I am." And so, I'm like, "Wait, wait, wait, wait, I want to take a step back from that." Because I want to be woke—if I'm going to be "awaked"—in my classroom, right? Where I'm with the students, sort of saying, "Hmm, let's rethink that problematic thing you're saying." And I think those are much more valuable than only putting stuff on Facebook.

But I struggle, right? Because of the second part, the idea of how we engage in the resistance that, for me in my experience, it's been more of a silencing, right? Like I'm going to silence my gut reaction in order to maintain the peace or in order to not offend. . . . And so, I struggle with the tension of, well, disruption and resistance are disruptive, right? They will disrupt the peace. But at the same time, we have to be strategic. So, there are moments that need to be disrupted, and there's discomfort in that, but there are moments where an aggressive stance is not helping people grow. I think as an educator, the layer of what we do for resistance is different than an activist, right? I see the leaders of the Black Lives Matter movement, the different people who are leaders, and they have to be provocative, right? That's part of their job as activists. As an educator, I have to be provocative sometimes, but my goal is not that this system will change. I need to change the heart, right? I need to foster growth in the young people. And me ranting on a soapbox about the government isn't necessarily going to help them grow as individuals and toward the movement.

**Tommy:** Hot damn, Gerardo. That was quite the soliloquy.

**Gerardo:** It was what you said! [laughs]

**Tommy:** No, yeah, the performativity that is associated with social media is starting to weigh me down because I've talked to folks. I've seen it on Twitter especially where they'll cite Bettina Love.[5] And the thing is, yeah, that's some good shit she's putting out, but it's becoming more of like, "Oh, well, Bettina Love said X, Y, and Z here," and therefore, "I'm woke." But then they'll post something that contradicts what Bettina Love's talking about. And it just racks my brain. That's why I'm like, you know what, I should be done with social media. But these are folks that are within our spheres of influence. These are folks that, if you do the Kevin Bacon Six Degrees of Separation, they're close by, and it's like, I don't know them well enough to challenge them. But at the same time, I want to challenge them because they're contradicting themselves on social media.

**Ana:** The other thing that I was thinking about is insurgence in terms of how Third World Feminists of Color[6] or Chicana feminists of color talk about labels and contesting others in power who try to define who they were, to redefine the terms that have been used to name you. Like, "¿Quieres que sea una mujer tercer mundista? So, I'm going to tell you what a third world woman is, and a scholar is, and this is what it means. And these are the experiences we come from. I'm not going to let you put that label on me that just diminishes me." So, talking about the meaning of insurgency—and I did the same as Becky, which is just to look it up, although I did it in Spanish, is *insurgente*: "Que se levanta o se subleva contra la autoridad."[7] So it's against authority, right? And so insurgent as bringing to that definition that has been put on you, what you know, what you've lived, what your family and people around you have told you about life, and how you navigate spaces that have not been created for you. And then to create them when they don't exist. Right? Just to imagine them and create them despite the order that exists already there. That's why I was bringing on Third World feminists because, you're put in a box as a Woman of Color in the academy, like, "Okay, you're going to belong to the multicultural program, and I'm just going to let you talk when you talk about culturally relevant teaching. That's when you can speak." And I'm going to tell you no, because how I see it is an epistemological framework to think about education, a locus of enunciation,[8] where I'm going to tell you that this order that exists doesn't work for me, right? So that's what I thought when I thought about insurgency.

**Chris:** I think, Ana and Tommy, the points that you brought up, though, would be critical to how we frame the chapter, just in the sense that we operate from these multiple loci of enunciation so that bearing witness that we speak from is an opportunity to map a more insurgent frame onto what we traditionally conceive of as social studies education. On the flip side, as critical scholars, you're also reflective. Then you look at your positionality and your loci in the world and then your local context and then you're hypercritical of that, which is why I think critical scholars honestly die early. To be blunt, you look at Fanon,[9] yo, you look at damn near any critical scholar, we grapple with this work here [points to the heart], and shit, man, we all fall early out here, because while we're trying to critique the field, we're being critical of ourselves, at least perhaps publicly in this sense, but we are being critical of ourselves on a personal level, and it just keeps us in this cycle of incompleteness.

**Ana:** Gerardo was talking about how he was both conscious of how he accommodated more than he disrupted sometimes, and how he tried to navigate dominant spaces without stirring the pot but then, at the same time, feeling conflicted and becoming very conscious of having an internalized oppression or being naïve or ignorant but then also growing into this person that wanted to push back more and do critical work. I think it's just the contradictions of navigating this space that I think is also what Chris is talking about.

**Chris:** It's so personal, though, because there's almost like a level of betrayal—I don't know if betrayal's the right word—that white scholars on the average just don't have to sit with. There's that privilege of sitting in discomfort and sitting in unknowing and then leaving, whereas for us our complicitness in some of these systems of dominance, in some ways, it feels like a matter of life and death. It just feels so much deeper and far-reaching. I wrote a piece in 2009. It was like, "I wrote this shit, man. Oh, I hate this." I don't know. It was for one of my doc classes. I took a class discussion I had with my students on colorism and borderism in the Black community. Anyways, I wrote this piece for the class. I was told, "Oh, you should write this up into an article," and I'm like, "Yeah, I'll do it." I write this shit up into an article. It gets published. I felt really uneasy about it at the time. I swear to you, yo, to this day, that piece, it sat with me more than any other shit that I've written because I'm like, one, I took a conversation. It was anecdotal, so it wasn't interviews. It was a teaching experience. I took a conversation that should've sat in confidentiality with my students. Then two, I just talked about it in a really unnuanced, irresponsible way. There's going to be some white researcher who's going to be like, "Look, Black folk discriminate against each other." That shit, when I tell you that piece, it eats at me, yo, to this day. I've been thinking about writing a rejoinder to myself. I've been jotting down notes to write back.

**Tommy:** When I think about the notion of labels, and we're all guilty of using labels, but I think also at the same time, it forms our identities on how we look at the world. So, it's kind of like that complex tension that we all are struggling. I'm going to situate myself since I can't speak to any of your other experiences, but the fact that I grew up having an Indigenous Colombian woman and a white European father and the battles that went on between both sets of families to essentially claim me. And I deal with that. And now my kids are like dealing with those identities and those labels, and Zed1, in particular, now that she's 14, she's asking all sorts of questions. And I'm like, "I can't tell you what your identities are. You will figure that out." And I think that's what we run into, especially with the social media aspect, is these folks that are doing these performative social media jobs are implying through their posts that "You have to find this identity that corresponds to what I'm thinking about," and that's the problem that I really have. Cuéntame, Jesús!

**Jesús:** And I was thinking about that as everyone was saying all these brilliant things. It reminded me of, like, how social media acts just like the textbook, in the sense that it simplifies media, it simplifies identity. Civil Rights, too, thinking about insurgency. We tell the story of Dr. Martin Luther King, Jr., which is totally valuable, totally amazing, but we don't share the story about Fannie Lou Hamer. We don't tell the story about CORE [Congress for Racial Equality][10]; we don't tell the story about the SNCC [Student Nonviolent Coordinating Committee]. We just talk about this blunt incident and it's like this one man, and we don't even talk about his life going forward, we don't talk about that insurgency as a communal act or as a complicated act; it can only be a simplistic act, you know? And the story of Dr. King is put in the mold fitting of an epistemology of civic identity. He gave a speech, he created an action, and now we're done. It's the scientific process of civic action, like there was no complication, there was no pushback, you know? Oh, and then anyone who hasn't followed our side is his enemy. I'm trying to think like, the one time you'll see him in opposition to someone is Malcolm X, but they wrote letters to each other. They were not these fatal enemies that like, "Oh, Dr. King said we should all love each other," and "Malcolm X said burn it all down," and like, "Never the twain shall meet," following Rudyard Kipling.[11] And it's complicated, the story needs to be complicated to come back to social media. We should all have the tags, and social media doesn't allow you to actually have a conversation. You kind of, like, drop your thing and move on, and so you don't actually get to engage with people. But you get the illusion of engaging and being with people, but you're really just staring at a screen once again. And some people get satisfaction out of that because they've only seen that. . . . It's sort of like a binary epistemological view of like how things work. Like, "Oh, I shared this on Facebook and now I'm woke." No, that's not how it works. That's not how any of this works.

**Ana:** And there's a pressure to be there—present in social media, and also if you're silent—because social media is not isolated from power and network—you become invisible. And then having high visibility also means "Oh, she shares some good material." You know what I'm saying? It seems simple, but at the same time, it's being present on social media 24/7. I'm in social studies 24/7. And yeah, it's not only individual engagement. It's like, I don't know how to say that, but it's both in terms of identity as a scholar, as Tommy was talking about, and it is also about networking and the pressure of that.

**Gerardo:** So, I want to go back to Ana, when you were talking about sort of the . . . I heard references of living, which is connected to our Nepantlera paper, right?[12] Like the idea that Nepantlera women are resisting,[13] not because they're doing something that can be seen as resistant but just in the course of living and being in that space, right? In their bodies, they literally embody that resistance. That "I am not doing things the way that I'm expected to." Like, you're expected to stay in your country, right? Or you're expected to follow the law in these ways that have been imposed specifically to marginalize you, right? I guess what I'm going back to is the notion of living. Not to somehow take away the importance of acting, of doing something purposefully or as a counter to the performativity, to the way that acting can just be performative. Because I know that for some people, posting on social media is their action. They have a lot of followers, and when they speak, people hear them. And their ideas influence others. I mean, technically that's why we write a lot, right? We're supposed to influence others with our brilliantness [just kidding!]. So, I don't want to take away from that, but I want to elevate the importance of, when you are living, when you are engaging in being the person that disrupts—sometimes just by your very being in a space. And you speak the English and you speak the Spanish and that's what you do. And no matter how they tell you, like, "Oh, you can't speak English, speak right," or whatever, you continue. You're not necessarily caring what people are saying on social media. You're just speaking your language, and you pray to the Virgin, and you continue to blend the cultures, and you continue to fight for your kids, and make sure you learn English so that you can have a better life. Well, like these are the ways that the resistance happens in living, not necessarily at a very visible "making waves," even though that's also a part of it.

**Ana:** So, going back to what you're saying, the writing on social media, the finding sources, etc., seems to be an intellectual exercise, right? And the other thing is talking, as you're saying, the living of it. So, going back to what you're saying, Gerardo, the insurgency comes from constantly creating, from waking up and making tortillas after you just experienced a killing last night, and just holding onto what you've learned from your family and what people have told you about navigating spaces you don't necessarily feel you belong to all the time. There are safe spaces, and then there are parts of the city where you feel pretty unsafe. Not because you feel threatened by people but because you feel like you don't belong, and you might be attacked because you don't belong in those spaces. But I think it is really central highlighting that divide of having an intellectual tension and energy and adrenaline as you are in social media, and that tension and energy, very subtle in theory, in the everyday living, of creating worlds that may not seem as insurgent.

**Becky:** I just want to echo Ana's saying, like, there's a world I need to create because it doesn't exist for me. That's the insurgency. I think that that's just really key and really beautifully stated. Devastatingly beautiful and beautifully devastating.

**Gerardo:** But not even that it's a new world that is different, but it's a world within. It's the cracks, right? Like it's cracking open within that world that was created to exclude you or to marginalize you, I would add.

**Ana:** Also, the collective spaces that we've created to talk to each other and to think through the past CUFA [College and University Faculty Assembly] meetings that I've attended, not just the speakers but also the spaces that were there made it a bearable space. I'm just going back to that idea, Chris, that you were talking about, about collective learning or collective work or just going through this process where we are not just going for the publication and all these things that are stimulated by the field, but also what are the things that we're trying to do in these spaces that I don't think they existed before? At least I didn't know about them. I don't know, I guess what we need to think about is, what is it that this chapter can do? Because there's so much that the chapter can do. Of course, we cannot do everything, but what is it that we want to say in the collective voice, I guess?

**Chris:** I keep going back to *The Undercommons*, that Moten and Harney book,[14] because we were talking about cultivating the collective. Me, personally, I think things are going to come to a head next year. When I think about what our chapter could potentially do, it lays the grounds for understanding the undercurrents. Then when people do write about the undercurrents, when Crenshaw[15] writes about the undercurrents, when Dalton[16] writes about the undercurrents, like we talked about before, it's conversations that exist at the bar after conference sessions, in the corner of the conference, the crevices of the space. I think we may have an opportunity though to bear witness to those crevices, to those cracks, and perhaps, I don't know, maybe offer a template.

**Jesús:** I'm thinking about the creation of worlds and stories and how it's valuable, but it's also very easy for people to not know how to distinguish between story and fiction sometimes, or like, life story and fiction. As we're thinking about these stories of survival, which are extremely powerful, it's also easy for someone to put on the mask of the insurgent and to completely come up the space and make it about them. And that's not what this is about. How do we get people to engage with other people's life stories, know and listen to them and not co-opt them, or confuse them with fiction? I don't have a brilliant point; what does it mean for us when we're in spaces, like Gerardo said, and we want to change people's hearts? That really resonated with me, but then I'm also wondering, how do we change people's hearts and then teach them to guard those hearts at the same time?

**Ana:** And you're making me think about helping students, especially white students. Helping students understand that the only position possible is not to compare yourself to that story about people who have been marginalized or to become that story of how you have been oppressed too in order to not be the oppressor, I guess, is the thing. I think there's an exercise that needs to happen in order to find a position that is not in either one or the other, but what is your role here? A different position, I guess.

**Gerardo:** That's making me think about Jeanine Cummins's *American Dirt*.[17] There was this big criticism of this person coming in to tell these stories, and the critique was something that I took to heart, or rather that I thought carefully about, because I only lived in the Texas Rio Grande Valley for 2 years, and I'm not from there, that's not my experience, and this is something, Ana, you and I have had conversations about, like, how do we bring these stories, some of which are not ours, and how we do honor to them but also use them? We use them in order to help others understand but also recognize when this is a story we cannot tell. And I wrestle with that. So, last year I went to the American Indian Studies Institute in Wisconsin, and one of the facilitators . . . we were in the Ho-Chunk Nation, and I don't believe she was Ho-Chunk, her husband was Ho-Chunk, but she's from a different Native nation. And I asked her a couple of questions, and she said, "I can't tell you. That's not knowledge that I'm allowed to have." Not even that she's not allowed to share it; that was knowledge she wasn't allowed to have because she was a woman. And it was kind of interesting, this notion that there's knowledge, and there are stories that are not for us to know, or for us to have, was something that I sort of wrestled with. As an academic, our whole thing is curiosity—you want to know everything, right? And it's like, "No, there might be limits." And so how do we navigate those limits? Acknowledge them, honor that they exist and that they should be sacred in the separation of "This is not something to be known." So, am I totally off base?

**Jesús:** I think that's particularly a quagmire for us as social studies teachers/ teacher educators, because we have so many encounters with so many stories, and how do we navigate those that have been co-opted? How do we navigate our own co-opting of stories? How do we build a curriculum while being mindful of co-option? I'm always trying to open the black box of what we're doing with our students, because I want them to know that I'm having the same struggles they are. I don't want them to think that there's a difference between us, they're mostly white and I'm not white.

**Gerardo:** Well, for example, if we take just an example of a teaching situation, right? Most of us in this group are Latinos, from different parts of Latin America, and as social studies teachers, we have to share about some of the experiences of Middle Eastern cultures, some of those tensions, right? What are things that we can share? And then what are things that "Actually this is not for me to teach because I'm not Israeli or Palestinian or Saudi or Egyptian," right? "I will do more harm than good by trying to explain this to you, or I will do more harm than good by giving you this knowledge when you might not be at a good space for this to be edifying." Even though we teach with a lot of nuance, trying to explain Israel–Palestine, the various conflicts that are involved, the student sort of takes what they can understand and might just sort of say, "Well, they're fighting, and they've been fighting for a long time." And that's it. And sort of like, "Well, would it have been better not to teach that . . . ?" Does that make sense? Because it's like our positionality differs from that experience.

**Jesús:** It's different. I think for us, and I feel this teaching—I was just talking about this yesterday, with a master's student teaching the Mexican–American War and adding in some ethical questions. But it's different doing that with someone else's history, because you don't want students to get the message that, "Oh, you should just stay clear of teaching complicated history." You actually want to give them the tools to do it. But those are very complicated tools, and I think if we don't do it well, the student gets scared and runs away, and they're only going to teach the version of history that's in the textbook and "safe." That's what we've seen in a lot of the classrooms that we find ourselves visiting—the teaching of the safe version of history because it's easiest. We see things in only two sides or versions, but there are actually 15 sides!

**Gerardo:** And they are *not* all equally valid.

**Jesús:** Right! People get uncomfortable criticizing that. But why do we only stick to this binary of like, "Are you pro-Israel, or are you pro-terrorism? Those are the two sides." That's not at all how this works. You could be pro- a lot of things. So, I am grappling with how do we teach and invite students into those conversations, into the complex realities of how the world is, how the world works, how the world has come to be and have those questions emanating from them. Do we have to teach them to be insurgents first? Teach them to look for those worlds within worlds that are being built? Because, for at least some of our white students, they're taught that these worlds don't exist and that they're invalid. Or that they're not invited to learn or even ask questions about those worlds and find out if they are. And then our Students of Color, our marginalized students, have a variety of worlds. Whatever is marginalizing them, they have to learn to safeguard those spaces too, because now we've got people who are faking everything and anything to get into those spaces so that they can be "woke."

**Gerardo:** For example, in my global education class, we're using Subedi's decolonizing curriculum,[18] right? So, like, anti-essentialism, contrapuntal readings, building solidarity, etc. And so, teacher education students need to have those skills. And they're not just skills, because there's also dispositions involved, like, affective dispositions and attitudes. Because then you'll be able to sort of navigate in and out the parts of the stories that you can engage with and the parts of the stories you have to honor and not engage with. Right? So, like, when your disposition is toward anti-essentialism, when your disposition is toward building solidarity, then you are mindful where your limitations might be. And you might choose to not engage with some topics, not because they're not important, but because it's not your place, or your knowledge is limited to do it justice, through those attitudes and dispositions. So the insurgency might be more about your attitudes and dispositions than the actual topics that you're familiar with and that you're talking about, right?

**Ana:** I am just thinking that there is an important aspect of recovering this idea of the teacher as an intellectual, in the sense that there's so much focus on the skill and professionalism of the teacher, but in reality, how we now think about things in complex ways has taken us 20 years of reading, you know? And so, I'm not going to ask my 20-year-olds to think the same way as I do or to have read the same things that I have, but yes, to understand that there's complexity as you have talked about. Also, to acknowledge, as we were talking about before, the lived experiences of people. Not everything's going to be in a book, and knowledge is not always going to look like a rationale about a topic. There's knowledge about how you navigate circumstances of life, that might be ajeno, foreign, to preservice teachers. And so, I think sometimes it is hard to recognize in their relationship with students and students' families that because they're not talking in the same language as you are, it doesn't mean that there's no knowledge.

**Jesús:** Insurgency comes from the heart. It's not finished. It's an act of love. Those things aren't finished, not finite, and we can't describe it. We can't attach enough force to that. To resist the overarching narrative of this nation, that seeks to obscure our empire, we have to engage in unfinished work, recognize that there are networks in the city that are not visible, recognize the invisible and the visible. Because we have these negotiated positions from where we think about empire and the influences around us. Empire asks for our heart, soul, and blood. The Aztecs did that literally, but the American empire is more invisible and has more invisible costs.

**Gerardo:** So that has been a space of learning for me, and so to me, this is what this work of insurgency has meant: how it pushes my thinking, how it helps me reframe things that I've learned in the past, or things that I've thought of in a certain way. So, for example, "This is how my people show up in the curriculum and only like this." So, I, even as a teacher, didn't always feel like I could question or push back to show the things that I knew, because I was born in Puerto Rico and then I grew up in Latin America. I didn't grow up in the U.S. So, things that I learned from different perspectives, I was like, "Oh, this is what the textbook says about Peru; this is what the textbook says about Mexico." But I didn't necessarily push it; I hid back the ways that I could counter those narratives, even though I knew different. I knew better. I didn't always do that. So, I think that in this space, in this work, I've been able to start reclaiming those things that, "Oh, I knew a counternarrative, I knew something different that I could have used, and I didn't realize that I could do that." So, it's connecting with what some of you were saying earlier about the idea of validating and feeling validated for being able to take that space and the empowerment of saying like, "No, this is messed up, and I'm going to tell you, here's a different way. This is the right way or a better way or whatever," depending on the situation. Okay, I ranted enough.

**Jesús:** That made me think of how I rarely saw myself in the social studies classroom. I am Mexican, and I only saw ancient versions of myself. I remember very vividly in fifth grade learning about ancient Mexicans, and it was a snapshot that basically said, "They had a big empire, and they killed lots of people. Move on." It's stuffed in that chapter with other ancient civilizations, and the real learning occurred when I got home, and I remember telling my parents like, "Hey, we learned about the Aztecs. Did you know they killed people?" My dad was like, "They did more than that, let's dive into it." We had this whole huge book full of images, stories, and pictures of buildings, and we just tore through it. I want to bring that out more in the classroom and not just the textbook version.

**Becky:** Something that keeps coming to mind, and it's not a full thought yet, so bear with me, but I think part of this conversation is also, at least in this particular iteration of this conversation, is the fact that we are coming at it from all these various backgrounds. In my case, I'm not Latina. I'm not Hispanic. I don't identify as such. And we've talked before about how we have a variety of racial, ethnic, national lineages, and I think that that's an interesting part of what we have going on in this group. I don't know how to go about unpacking that, if it's even necessary to unpack that right now, but I think it's something that's different about this iteration of the conversation than in some others. But I'm not ignorant to the fact that my experiences are very different than each of yours are—individually, and perhaps collectively, right? And that I am in a space that I honor very much being a part of. Hopefully my actions on the outside of this group speak to that as well, right? But there are navigations that are happening, and I just want to recognize that and thank you all for sharing the pieces of you that you have shared with me along the way, across these years of friendship and familia, but also right now, in this process of writing this chapter. And I think that I just want to open the space for unpacking that if we need to say anything about that, if we need to.

**Gerardo:** I tried to capture what you said in our notes document, but do you mind checking if this is accurate? I know what you're discussing and saying is very personal, so if you wouldn't mind just looking at what I wrote.

**Becky:** But that's the thing, everything y'all are sharing has been personal too, right? This is all very personal. And I think that that conversation about what stories do we share outside of this space, who gets to know these stories, who gets to be let into these spaces is really important to think about. And in moving forward for, like, what it is that we actually publish in this chapter, right? Some of this is not going to be shared. And I know I made comments before, like, I think these conversations are really powerful, and I would love for others to see them, but also recognize that that's not for me to say, right?

**Ana:** And a way in which I personally am thinking about it is in my experience as doing research for my dissertation. There's a big, complicated painful understanding of the difference of what it means to be a Latina raised in Colombia who came here as an adult, who went through private education back in Colombia, light-skinned Mestiza, and coming here and working with second-, third-generation Latino immigrant students who have been moving around the country. Just very different kinds of people, right? Even in terms of language, do you share it? Is there a conflicted experience with language? Do you think you can connect because you can speak some Spanish? And then, well, no. I'm just trying to bring that personal experience as a very complicated one in terms of ethics, but in terms of . . . I almost feel like I came into that research with a colorblind ideology that I brought from Colombia, right? Now I'm here, a Person of Color in the U.S., doing this kind of research. I'm just trying to move that experience of researcher in a conference—CUFA—how do we affect, how would we say this work touches classrooms and kids' experiences, I guess, is the kind of very long path that I'm trying to build in a way. I'm bringing that in.

**Tommy:** Ana, you reminded me of that piece that you wrote for *Curriculum Inquiry*[19] that I read three or four times. After each time I was like, I never thought about that Ana. I never saw that point. Every time I read it, something new came out of it. When you were writing that piece, what was your process like? I think that's also part of the conversation: what are the processes that we each use to put something together in writing? For you, what was it like when you put that piece together?

**Ana:** I didn't know you had read it. Thank you for reading it.

**Chris:** I also read the piece.

**Ana:** Initially, I was trying to write about my biography, if you want to say something like that. But I didn't know what I needed to put in there until I started understanding the racial and class tensions that came in my own experience, the intention to separate myself from Indigenous and Black people in Colombia. You grow up anti-Black even though you might not see that, right? It was a long process, but I think also the editors from *Curriculum Inquiry* helped me a lot because they started asking the complicated questions. It's like when you go on Instagram and read a thread of AfroLatinos, and they're asking, stop calling yourself mestizas, you are white, you don't experience racism—you experience xenophobia, if anything. These are very strong stances that make you question things, and it's true, it's painful, but you need to realize that when you come here, you're called a Person of Color. You say that you are in solidarity with everybody. But honestly, my experience with racism is completely different from a person who grew up in the U.S., right? I feel like my experiences with racism and xenophobia happened when I left, when I went out of the country, which is a privileged position already, because who travels outside Colombia? Then that's when you are colombiana, prostituta, narcotraficante, all of those come in. But before that, you're the majority, and you are in a very good position of power that also came from education. I just think it's a very slow process, but it also is asking yourself painful questions. You could be very comfortable here thinking that you're just a Person of Color in solidarity, and say that you go through the same experiences, painful experiences Black people go through, and you don't. I don't know if that answers that question, but . . .

**Gerardo:** No, it's okay. What you were sharing is part of what we have discussed in other conversations in preparation for sessions, right? About the way we come to this work, which is so expansive! We're talking about stories of becoming, and being, and growing, especially through moments of having to deconstruct parts of ourselves. At least that was in my experience. Similarly, I had a process of unlearning and changing my perspective and having to see differently. Those are really important parts of our narrative, which this work facilitated in many ways—the work, the people, the spaces facilitated that.

**Chris:** As I was listening to you talk, I was thinking about the idea of locating ourselves in empire, right. I think we can sometimes use empire as singular and not as something plural. When I think about what I've learned from many of you, it's been a process of unpacking over the past four to five years. My interest in AfroLatinidad, the work that I do in Colombia and a lot of it has been just that very similar to you, locating myself in empire. How in one empire, I'm on the margins of the empire, with the privilege to travel and be in conversation with AfroColombians, right? About their position on the margins of empire in Colombia and negotiating that as a U.S. Black American who has an interest in global Black lives. That has brought me to this work on AfroLatinidad, in addition to raising two beautiful AfroLatina girls, who are AfroLatina through a biracial, bicultural marriage union or relationship. I'll go back to what I was saying last week: locating yourself and finding yourself in empire again, I think requires an undisciplined approach. You will never get there through a narrow look at yourself or your scholarship. You'll never accomplish that. You'll never find yourself if that's the case. I don't think I would have arrived at this understanding through that narrow process either.

**Tommy:** Right. It's not narrow. And like, at the conference, I have all these white dudes, and they're all saying, "What are the next steps? What can we do?" I'm thinking, well, it's not that easy; there isn't "next steps." I don't know.

**Becky:** Right. There's no clear-cut, single answer.

**Gerardo:** All these things come together and just because we can't wrap a nice bow around it, it doesn't mean that that's not the work of insurgency. Insurgency is not done.

**Becky:** Without conclusion, but a pause perhaps because—

**Tommy:** A great way to end the chapter.

**Becky:** Yeah.

**Tommy:** We are just . . .

**Becky:** Just pausing.

---

In lieu of a conclusion—again, we do not *end* the (ongoing, nonlinear, complex, full of multiplicities) conversation, but we *pause* it here in writing—for now. There is so much more that we couldn't share with you this time around. Luckily, this familia has plans to continue/extend this conversation into new space(s), but for now, we need to close. So, we bring in a quote that is critical race theory (CRT)–specific, but that we think speaks to the overall ethos of our conversation(s). It says,

> For CRT, theory is not a matter of abstraction, but a way to make intelligible the lived dimensions of race. . . . CRT guards against theoreticism, or what Leonardo and Porter call intellectualism. While not *anti-intellectual*, CRTheorists reject an intellectualist approach that reduces racism to an idea and prefer to testify to its brutal reality. (Leonardo, 2013, p. 24)

Our conversations are also not a matter of abstraction, but a way to (attempt to) make intelligible the lived dimensions of (our) insurgency(ies). In our conversations, we talk often about this tension of insurgency: having intellectual conversations vs. the living. Or said another way, insurgency as *living* as opposed to just within an intellectual conversation. We continuously asked ourselves (and now ask you):

> What does it mean to talk about (*and do*) insurgency as scholars?
> As teacher educators?
> As (former) teachers?
> As humans in this world?
> In all these senses?

And, similar to what Busey et al. (2019) argue, scholars have often dealt with race within an ideological sphere, but not so much within its material domain in social studies education and race scholarship in social studies. Busey, Duncan, and Dowie-Chin (2019) ask, what do we lose when we fail to deal with the material domains of racism? With the material realities? Similarly, we wanted to make sure that our insurgency (here and beyond) dealt within the material domains, the material realities of ourselves, our colleagues, our students, our fellow beings. And we find Michael Dumas's (2014) work in education to be most profound because, when he talks about "losing an arm," when he talks about spirit murdering, there's something about that work that we think communicates the disembodiment that happens—the *literal* pulling apart of *our bodies*, and of children's bodies, families, and so forth, in this work. This work is personal (and more-than-personal), and the work has evolved each time we come to it—together, collectively and individually. Thus, we're mapping ourselves onto these conversations of the field—which is important work. But when we talk *insurgency*, we're talking insurgency against something larger. We're talking insurgency against something greater—that has a material impact on people's lives, that shapes people's social condition(s).

## Notes

1. The following individuals contributed equally to the thinking/writing of this manuscript: Gerardo J. Aponte-Safe (University of Wisconsin-La Crosse), Jesús Tirado (Auburn University), Ana C. Díaz Beltrán (Texas A&M University), Tommy Ender (Rhode Island College), Christopher L. Busey (University of Florida), and Rebecca C. Christ (Florida International University).

2. A note on our process: This is a compilation of transcripts from conversations that took place over several months (and in some cases, with connections to conversations that took place over years). Multiple transcripts have been collapsed into one, and the resulting conversation has been edited for clarity, flow, and comfort for us, individually and collectively. We say "comfort" because these conversations are personal and vulnerable, so we were mindful in our compiling and editing process to hold space for the sacredness of our stories and to be respectful to them and to ourselves as sharers in/of those stories.

3. Please note that Spanish-language terms will not be italicized or translated in most cases within the writing of this chapter.

4. *Testimonios*, as defined by Cervantes-Soon (2012), allow individuals to position difficult experiences in a new way that encourages consciousness and action.

5. See, for example, Love (2019).

6. If you are unfamiliar with the work of Feminists of Color that both contest and reappropriate the terms *Third World* and *Third World woman* in the 1990s and 2000s, we encourage you to check out the work by *Third World feminists of Color* Chandra Mohanty (2003) and Uma Narayan (1997).

7. Oxford Languages (n.d.).

8. Foucault (1972); Mignolo (1994).

9. See, for example, Fanon (1952).

10. If you are unfamiliar with the history of the CORE and of the SNCC and their role in the civil rights movement, take a moment to reflect on why that might be the case. To learn more about this history we recommend Charles Payne's (2007) *I've Got the Light of Freedom*.

11. Kipling (1889).

12. Aponte-Safe, Díaz Beltrán, and Christ (in press).

13. Anzaldúa (2015).

14. Moten and Harney (2013).

15. See, for example, Crenshaw (2011).

16. See, for example, Dalton (1995).

17. See Martin (2020).

18. Subedi (2013).

19. Díaz Beltrán (2018).

## References

Aponte-Safe, G. J., Díaz Beltrán, A. C., & Christ, R. C. (in press). Aspiring nepantleras: Conceptualizing social studies education from the rupture/la herida abierta. *Theory and Research in Social Education*.

Anzaldúa, G. (2015). Geographies of selves—Reimagining identity: Nos/otras (us/other), las Nepantleras, and the new tribalism. In A. Keating (Ed.), *Light in the dark/Luz en lo oscuro: Rewriting identity, spirituality, reality* (pp. 65–94). Duke University Press.

Busey, C. L., Duncan, K. E., & Dowie-Chin, T. (2019 April). *CRT ain't for everybody: The current status and dilemma of CRT in social studies education research* [Paper presentation]. American Educational Research Association annual meeting, Toronto, Canada.

Cervantes-Soon, C. (2012). Testimonios of life and learning in the borderlands: Subaltern Juárez girls speak. *Equity & Excellence in Education, 45*(3), 373–391. https://doi.org/10.1080/10665684.2012.698182

Crenshaw, K. W. (2011). Twenty years of critical race theory: Looking back to move forward. *Connecticut Law Review, 43*(5), 1256–1300. https://opencommons.uconn.edu/law_review/117/

Dalton, H. L. (1995). The clouded prism: Minority critique of the critical legal studies movement. In K. Crenshaw, N. Gotanda, G. Peller, & K. Thomas (Eds.), *Critical race theory: The key writings that formed the movement* (pp. 80–84). New Press.

Díaz Beltrán, A. C. (2018). The nowhere of global curriculum. *Curriculum Inquiry, 48*(3), 273–292. https://doi.org/10.1080/03626784.2018.1474712

Dumas, M. J. (2014). "Losing an arm": Schooling as a site of Black suffering. *Race Ethnicity and Education, 17*(1), 1–29. https://doi.org/10.1080/13613324.2013.850412

Fanon, F. (1952). *Black skin, white masks*. Grove Press.

Foucault, M. (1972). *Archaeology of knowledge*. Pantheon Books.

Harney, S., & Moten, F. (2013). *The undercommons: Fugitive planning and Black study*. Wivenhoe.

Kipling, R. (1889). *The ballad of East and West*. http://www.kiplingsociety.co.uk/poems_eastwest.htm

Leonardo, Z. (2013). *Race frameworks: A multidimensional theory of race*. Teachers College Press.

Love, B. L. (2019). *We want to do more than survive: Abolitionist teaching and the pursuit of education freedom*. Beacon Press.

Martin, R. (2020, January 24). *Latinx critics speak out against "American Dirt"; Jeanine Cummins responds*. National Public Radio. https://www.npr.org/2020/01/24/798894249/latinx-critics-speak-out-against-american-dirt-jeanine-cummins-responds

Mignolo, W. (1994). Editor's introduction. Loci of enunciation and imaginary constructions: The case of (Latin) America. *Poetics Today, 1*, 505–521. https://www.jstor.org/stable/1773098

Mohanty, C. T. (2003). *Feminism without borders*. Duke University Press.

Narayan, U. (2013). *Dislocating cultures: Identities, traditions, and Third World feminism*. Routledge.

Oxford Languages. (n.d.). Insurgente. Retrieved October 27, 2020, from www.google.com

Payne, C. M. (2007). *I've got the light of freedom: The organizing tradition and the Mississippi freedom struggle*. University of California Press.

Subedi, B. (2013). Decolonizing the curriculum for global perspectives: Decolonizing the curriculum for global perspectives. *Educational Theory, 63*(6), 621–638. https://doi.org/10.1111/edth.12045

SIX

# Unsatisfied: The Conceptual Terrain of De-Essentializing Islam in Social Studies

*Natasha Hakimali Merchant*

A DECADE AGO, WHILE STILL IN graduate school, I was invited to deliver a short presentation on my research to a group of public-school teachers concerned about anti-Muslim bias and interested in progressing their own understandings about Islam. This workshop had two primary goals: (1) to dispel Islamophobic precepts about Muslims and Islam and (2) to substitute those myths with basic education about what Islam is and who Muslims are. When I walked into the room, I saw marked-up quizzes where each question asked about the Five Pillars of Islam. I became increasingly anxious as my planned presentation, which was based on preliminary data from Muslim high school students' impressions of curricula on Islam, intended to challenge the teaching of this very set of practices. After all, I thought to myself, I am a practicing Muslim, and this framework had very little to do with how I (or my community) practiced or defined Islam. In fact, this framework has been used against me and so many others as a purity test for who counts as "Muslim" and who doesn't. The narrowing definition of who is Muslim has widespread implications in various parts of the world through economic and social oppression as well as through bodily violence and loss of life.

Moments of cringing at what gets taught as "Islam" are always accompanied by internal anxieties that my identities, experiences, and knowledge are far too marginal and niche to matter or influence what is covered about Islam in classrooms. These anxieties are perhaps the reason why I approach my critiques of how Islam is taught by highlighting the curricular experiences of Muslim students from minority communities of interpretation. Much of my work in social studies thus far has been exploring the impact on Muslim students who learn about themselves as subjects while not recognizing what they learn. Highlighting the disjuncture between lived experience and curricular representation therefore creates a justification for why curricular approaches to teaching about Islam must avoid essentialism at all costs. In this chapter, I do not seek to justify why essentialism must be avoided. Instead, I assume that the readers of a volume on insurgent social studies are not in need of being convinced of curricular honoring of human complexity.

While this chapter discusses a conceptual mapping of various curricular approaches which specifically attempt to be anti-essentialist, it does not evaluate approaches to teaching about Islam through examining actual teacher practice. The fact is that much of the scholarship on pedagogical and curricular approaches to Islam has occurred through examination of teacher practice in higher education contexts (Asani, 2011b; Ramey, 2014), specialized programs atypical to most public high school social studies course offerings (Klepper, 2014; Moore, 2007), through the lens of Islam as a public controversy (Jackson, 2014; Moore, 2012), or through a review of secondary curricular materials and standards (Douglass & Dunn, 2003). While materials like textbooks and standards are crucial pieces of the pedagogical puzzle, there is also a largely untold story of public school, insurgent social studies teachers who queer, flip, and subvert texts and standards in order to teach about Islam such that what they teach aligns with justice-oriented political commitments. By way of example, I pull from a previous study (Merchant, 2018) to demonstrate the significance of teacher agency in mediating curriculum. Mr. Corder, a high school world history teacher, found ways to challenge a Eurocentric narrative of Islam by reorganizing the chapters in the textbook. He explained that the "Christian chapter talks about the Crusades and makes Islam seem very like *other* because you have the Europeans encountering Islam and so I put Islam in front so that we can have a little bit of an understanding of what Islam is before we talk about Crusades" (Merchant, 2018, p. 184). Mr. Corder's critical considerations to ways in which the narrative of Islam sits in relation to Christianity is a hint into the most subtle ways critical educators intervene and interrupt normative understandings. Insurgent educators' teaching practice about Islam is something that needs more careful study and exploration and I acknowledge that the absence of research stemming from actual teacher practice is not indicative of what happens in a classroom.

By acknowledging the lack of knowledge based in teacher practice I not only critique the social studies field, I also speak to the limitations of this chapter. It is critically important to mention this gap because thus far, much of the scholarship on teacher practice in relation to lessons on Islam frame teachers as ill-informed about the right to teach about religion (Douglass & Dunn, 2003) or simply avoidant of teaching lessons about Islam for fear of controversy (Jackson, 2014). What of the insurgent practitioners who fight white supremacy in its various avatars, be they anti-Blackness, myths of meritocracy, anti-Semitism, Islamophobia, and so on? I hold this question as a placeholder and invitation for further opportunities to learn from insurgent teacher practice.

This chapter does not explore the wisdom stemming from insurgent teacher practice. Instead, the conceptual map I draw of various pathways to teaching about Islam is based on the landscape of scholarship on anti-essentialist approaches to teaching about Islam. Through navigating the terrain of possibilities and pitfalls within each approach (pathway), I hope to think alongside insurgent practitioners as they teach about Islam in social studies classrooms. Ultimately through this traversing, I am not seeking a curriculum on Islam that strives to soothe the anxieties of those who aren't Muslim; I am searching for a curriculum on Islam that, at once, centers the Muslim experience of Islam while not essentializing *the* (singular) Muslim experience of Islam. Although there is a plethora of approaches to teaching about Islam in the K–12 context (Asani, 2011a; Merchant, 2018; Moore, 2007), in this chapter I describe only those paths which I feel deliberately combat essentialist perceptions about Islam.

## Path 1: Centering Islamophobia

Teaching about Islam has received particular attention over the last two decades largely due to anti-Muslim sentiment and the rise in discriminatory acts toward those perceived as Muslim. The urgency to dismantle Islamophobia is often discussed as the impetus driving scholarship around approaches to teaching about Islam in classroom settings. This is reflected in my own work as well. Due to its overwhelming prominence, tackling Islamophobia through teaching about Islam is the curricular path where I find myself beginning.

While delving into a discussion about the multiple meanings and manifestations of Islamophobia is beyond the scope of this chapter, it is important to be precise about how I conceptualize Islamophobia in what follows. Islamophobia is cultivated as a tool of cultural and epistemic dominance

(Grosfoguel, 2012); it goes beyond individual anti-Muslim bias out of a lack of exposure and acknowledges that anti-Muslim bias is curated through an infrastructure bending to economic ambitions (Tamdgidi, 2012). Yet, the idea that Islamophobia is a phenomenon based in a lack of knowledge or understanding about what Islam is has been a prevalent assumption undergirding many organizations, individuals, and programs striving to address anti-Muslim sentiment. The connection between education and anti-Muslim prejudice is made explicit in the companion document for the National Council for the Social Studies (NCSS, 2017) C3 framework, which states that "the study of religion from an academic, non-devotional perspective in primary, middle, and secondary school is critical for decreasing religious illiteracy and the bigotry and prejudice it fuels" (p. 92). The emphasis on decreasing bigotry as an impetus for teaching about religion in schools is echoed throughout the social studies.

However, on closer examination, one might notice that fomented hatred toward Muslims has been a long-standing technology for imperial powers to wage war, occupy land, and control resources. The well-worn anti-Islam and anti-Muslim discourses find new resonance in a post-9/11 world, but their utility in furthering imperial projects across the world remains steadfast. Anti-Muslim ideologies, particularly in the post-9/11 era, not only have fueled economic and political agendas abroad but have also heavily funded and bolstered domestic surveillance programs and military technologies largely used against Black and Brown bodies in the United States (Bittle, 2020). In the last several years, with the modest broadening of the Counter Violent Extremism (CVE) framework explicitly including "right-wing terrorism," abolitionists caution that the expansion of focus on counterterrorism efforts will once again strengthen inherently white supremacist institutions and make deeper the coffers for fighting terrorism, but the focus of the so-called war will continue to land disproportionately on people of color (Nguyen & Zahzah, n.d.). Without addressing white supremacy at all its levels (not simply in responses to attempted insurrections or mass hate acts of violence), white supremacy will still continue to define the threat while also implementing its remedy. I take this diversion in topic to demonstrate that Islamophobia as an ideology has a wide reach and utility in further threatening the civil liberties for Black and Brown communities (Ali, 2016) and relegating Islamophobia to individual bias is insufficient.

Conflating Islamophobia with a lack of understanding about Islam is tantamount to ignoring the roots of what one might term *Islamophobia* and focusing instead on a naive assumption that understanding one's beliefs and practices will inoculate from the deluge of well-funded, manufactured misinformation campaigns. My critique does not suggest that educators should not attempt to address Islamophobia in the social studies classroom. On the contrary, I believe the study of Islamophobia, as well as other manifestations of oppression, should be taught in the context of their histories and their functions. Instead, my objection rests with attempting to undermine Islamophobia through teaching about Islam.

Centering Islamophobia as part of teaching about Islam often motivates educators to teach lessons addressing stereotypes about Muslims and Islam. One such popular lesson asks students to brainstorm stereotypes they've heard about Muslims and Islam (Moore, 2007, p. 114). Although this exercise is in service of ultimately "debunking" stereotypes, the assumption that Muslim students will survive such an exercise unscathed is a risky bargain. Tara, a 10th-grade student who participated in my 2015 study centering Muslim girls, discussed her experience during a myth-busting brainstorm exercise in which the teacher asked students to list what they associated with Islam. She reported,

> People would say that most people think that they're (Muslims) all terrorists, all of them. It's a violent religion, and stuff like that. It was kind of like . . . every time it comes up, I feel like everyone's turning to look at me. It doesn't really happen, but it just feels like that. (Merchant, 2015, p. 104)

Despite the potential anxiety and embarrassment this type of lesson may cause to Muslim students, if the well-meaning teacher executes the lesson as intended, students may come away with a sense that Islam is a religion of peace and Muslims are peaceful. In some cases, students may even understand that Muslims are diverse and not a monolith; not *all* of them have objectionable views. Depending on the iteration of this lesson, some students might even glean the message that Muslims are "just like us." Scales that measure interventions toward reducing Islamophobia are focused on shifts of individual affective dimensions (Lee et al., 2009). Therefore, even if myth-busting exercises and drawing commonalities between Muslims and Christians might actually shift individual affective perceptions about Muslims and Islam, these strategies rely on centering the anxieties of those who are not Muslim without having to ever question the social conditions which cultivated those anxieties to begin with.

Although in principle, teaching against Islamophobia is a worthy curricular goal, doing so by trying to claim Islam as a "good religion" or Muslims as mostly "moderate" serves to frame Islam and Muslims in terms that make non-Muslims comfortable (Mamdani, 2002). The understanding of the "good Muslim" may also cause a psychic endearment toward Islam and Muslims, understood as "Islamophilia," which commits the same grave sin central to Islamophobia itself, specifically the essentializing of an entire group of people or its practice without room for nuance (Shryock, 2010).

While I would agree that in today's context it is irresponsible to teach about Islam or Muslims without the broader political context of what is called Islamophobia, I do wonder about the pedagogical implications of prioritizing an anti-Islamophobic agenda as a driving force for teaching about Islam. Questioning the shape of Islamophobia, Shryock (2010) admits skepticism about the proposition that mis/understandings of Islam have much at all to do with Islamophobia. Instead, he postulates,

> perhaps it [Islamophobia] is better explained in relation to ideas adapted from Cold War polemics, in which formerly Red scares are now Green. Perhaps it depends for its imagery and appeal on ideological residue from much older contests between European and Ottoman powers. It is also obvious that Islamophobia draws its symbolism more from European and American models of race, empire, and human progress than it does from political symbolism dominant among Muslims, past or present. (Shylock, 2010, p. 3)

The assumption that teaching about Islam will address Islamophobia is unreliable because Islam (the faith of those who call themselves Muslims) is not relevant to Islamophobia. Being disgusted by anti-Muslim vitriol, one might find it difficult to disentangle teaching about Islam from the larger goal of disassembling Islamophobia. However, Islam and Muslims exist/ed in a multitude of ways outside of Islamophobia. By attaching a goal of undoing Islamophobia through the teaching of Islam, what might be missed in understanding aspects of Islam and Muslims?

## Path 2: Dynamic and Lived Islam

The undergirded longing in delinking Islamophobia from the study of Islam is one of understanding Islam on its own terms. Instead of learning about Islam as a means to make Islam or Muslims more palatable for the dominant, why not center Islam in order to understand it properly? This path, too, leads to a fast-approaching dead-end. After all, Islam does not speak for itself, nor does it "do" anything agentive. Rather, Islam (or any religion) is imagined by individuals who associate with a religion "in ways that relate to their particular context and the range of interests that enliven that context" (Ramey, 2014, p. 109). To desire a religion to speak for itself would be to accept a sense of conceptual unity or essence of any given religion. In such a *sui generis* model, "the category of religion names a specific and stable set of things in the world set apart from all others" (Cotter & Robertson, 2016, p. 9). The essentialist pitfall awaits those who call on Islam hoping for an answer.

So, the next obvious path to a greater understanding of Islam is to understand it through its adherents. However, before too long, the pitfalls on the road once again appear. The most glaring challenge here is the question, *Whose Islam*? If one is learning about Islam through the practices and self-reported beliefs of its adherents, what is selected and what isn't selected as making it under the banner of Islam? This is an internal problem within Muslim spaces too. In "the real world" as in the world of curricula, differently powered groups experience disproportionate access to voice and representation and this leads to what Diane Moore (2007) has discussed as a sectarian approach (intentional or unintentional) to teaching about religion.

After reviewing several approaches to studying religion, Moore (2007) posits a cultural studies approach as one that both avoids essentialist understandings of a religion and opts for a lived-religion perspective with the ever-important critical lens. According to Moore, a cultural studies approach to religion includes the following six features: (1) the approach be multidisciplinary to reflect the various ways in which religion influences numerous spheres of life; (2) disciplinary lenses cannot be removed from one another when studying a phenomenon so one cannot consider a political dimension of a certain event without considering the influence of a religious dimension; (3) all claims to knowledge are situated and cannot be considered as objective; (4) acknowledging that, in addition to knowledge, the interpreter is also situated in their positionality; (5) a power analysis, exploring dominant and marginalized perspectives, is necessary; and (6) that education is inherently political and that individuals and structures have motivations that need to be made transparent.

While it is a challenge to imagine a cultural studies approach to teaching about Islam in the K–12 classroom, where constraints on time and coverage abound (Douglass & Dunn, 2003; Jackson, 2014), theoretically, the approach offers it all. Moore (2007) builds her approach on certain premises about the way religion is typically taught about and understood. One such premise is that religion is often taught from a sectarian perspective (intentionally or unintentionally). With little knowledge of religion, it is no wonder that dominant, singular narratives are generalized across an entire faith. Utilizing Haraway's notions of "situated knowledges," Moore (2007) argues that

> a cultural studies approach that affirms all knowledge claims as situated provides an especially useful foundation upon which to study religion in a way that exposes both the internal complexity of any given tradition as well as the multiple ways that religion is woven into the fabric of human experience and utilized to justify a full range of ideological convictions. (p. 81)

As someone who has often felt invisible in curricula on Islam, the multiplicity of representation as well as the situated nature of truth claims resonates and brings relief. However, as I think about the implementation of a cultural studies approach one question continues to nag. Assuming that multiple and situated examples of Islam are presented, what constitutes as legitimate under the umbrella of "Islam"? The boundaries of what counts and what doesn't count as Islam comes into focus in James Moore's (2008) operating premises:

> Religious traditions are often represented inaccurately by individuals who define themselves as "religious" as well as those who self-define as "non-religious." For those who define themselves as "religious," this inaccuracy often manifests itself in relationship to their own traditions as well as the faith traditions of others. (para. 5)

As Diane Moore (2007) states, situating religious expressions and manifestations within a particular historical and cultural context will include a "full range of ideological convictions" (p. 81). In considering religion as something dynamic across time and space, is there anything then that would not be contextualized to fit into the fold of Islam or be deemed as "inaccurate"? Moreover, who decides accuracy or legitimacy? These questions call for a more intricate analysis of the categories within which this investigation takes place.

## Path 3: Decolonial Deconstructions of Religion

The need to revisit and rethink the categories and classifications that organize the topic of this chapter, namely, "Islam" and "religion," goes beyond an academic exercise. The examination of rethinking these categories is a personal reckoning with the colonial imprinting on my ancestors and its impact on the communal division and religious definition today. From the start of my life, I have been surrounded by melodic, devotional poetry called *ginans*, a "term . . . derived from the Sanskrit word for 'knowledge', in the sense of esoteric truth or wisdom" (Asani, 2011b, p. 99). These poems, dating back at least to the 12th century, used references and stories that I recognized as Quranic and as Hindu. When I inquired about this seeming contradiction, I was told that in precolonial South Asia, the Shi'i Ismaili community (an anachronistic term in that time and geography) were all Hindus and in order to convert to Islam, a slow transition was necessary, and therefore, Hindu registers were used to entice people to convert to Islam. It wasn't until I was well into adulthood that I began to read and understand that this narrative was constructed through colonial logics of the time that could not fathom how such diverse discourses (Hindu and Muslim) might exist as coherent esoteric wisdom (Shodhan, 1995).

The multivalent (seemingly contradictory) lyrics of the *ginans* recited over the centuries by my ancestral community, read today as both "Hindu" and "Muslim" and "Shi'i" and "Sunni," were commonplace in pre-colonial South Asia (Asani, 2011b). Beyond *ginans*, other religious practice was conducted through local expressions and guided by wise sages, many of whom did not affiliate strongly with a categorized religious social identity. It was the colonial encounter, "in which notions of religious identity and the categories 'Hindu' and 'Muslim' were contested and also rigidly and narrowly demarcated" (Asani, 2011b, p. 97). Giving primacy to practices and doctrines as constitutive of religious identity, the British used their own assumptions about the anatomy of religion to "learn" about their subjects despite the fact that for many, religion was not a primary identity marker (Asani, 2011b). Given the significance of religious division in postcolonial South Asia today, it is remarkable to note that

> the idea of religion as a distinct and separate category of practices arose in part and initially as a tool of the Christian administration of colonized subjects, and became increasingly entrenched through the emergence of new class interests as a way of legitimating not only scientific knowledge but also new concepts of ownership, new forms of labour and productivity, and new concepts of rationality. (Fitzgerald, 2011, p. 9)

Despite the success of proliferating a uniform definition of religion (as coherent and apart from "the secular"), it is important to note that multivalent practices and understandings still live today throughout local contexts.

In reflecting upon the role the British colonial encounter had on the ways in which I form my religious identity today, I am reminded of how powerful yet facile these seemingly universal categories are. As Foucault (1973) states, "the criteria by which such distinctions are made do not describe reality, but rather the assumptions of those making them" (p. xxii). The curricular question then of what is classified as a "legitimate" manifestation of a particular religion is only robust if a serious deconstruction of the categories "Islam" and indeed "religion" are explored.

Before reflecting on the category of Islam, it is essential to understand how religion itself is a contested category, one that critical religious studies scholars have been deconstructing for over two decades. While the term *religious* (especially in contrast to *secular*) first appears in the medieval period, "the dawn of the Enlightenment period, and the beginning of the colonial encounter" is when the term "religion" is given the shape we recognize today (Cotter & Robertson, 2016, p. 3). Notably, an essential attribute of religion becomes its definition in contrast to its constructed binary—the secular (Ahmed, 2016; Cotter & Robertson, 2016; Fitzgerald, 2011; Tayob, 2018). The domain of what is religious is also bifurcated in Enlightenment thought as either the domain of institutions or in the domain or a personal, private matter of the heart and conviction (Ahmed, 2016; Cotter & Robertson, 2016). As such, the set elements that constitute what was/is defined as "religion" (according to a particular Christian episteme) was based in the

> paces of the Church and of the private, personal conscience of the individual members of the communion of the Church. The remainder of liberated thought-territory becomes the public space of the non-religious or secular in which other epistemic claims hold sway: these secular claims *ipso facto* are (understood to be) non-scriptural, non-pious, non-spiritual, non-sacred, and engaged with the rational or empirically-verifiable. (Ahmed, 2016, p. 180)

In the 19th century, as the expansion of colonial empires grew, so did the many exotic "items," ripe for religious classification. Ultimately, it was through colonial impulses and encounters that "world religions" were cemented (Cotter & Robertson, 2016). Narrow conceptions of religion, largely based on a Protestant algorithm, not only read other "religions" through a specific formulation, but these classifications also created a hierarchy of religions and indeed boundaries for what counts as a legitimate religion and what does not (Cotter & Robertson, 2016; Tayob, 2018). The ideas of coherent, ready-to-wear religions legible to the Protestant imagination is what (from the earlier example) frustrated "British officials who lamented the lack of 'pure Moslems in India'" (Asani, 2011b, p. 102).

While Diane Moore's (2007) cultural studies approach does speak of the interaction between religion and other dimensions of social life, the coherence of "religion" as a distinct category is not meaningfully challenged nor are its historical antecedents. Similarly, the Religious Studies Companion Document for the C3 Framework (NCSS, 2017) calls for educators to adhere to an academic study of religion versus a devotional study but it does not challenge, or even acknowledge, the construction of "religion" itself. Instead, the document takes religion for granted as a coherent and universal category and states that religious traditions and expressions "continue to shape and to be shaped by particular social, historical and cultural contexts" (NCSS, 2017, p. 94) without ever questioning the distinctness or construction of the category "religion" itself.

Seeing religion as a distinct category from what counts as "secular" (political, cultural, economic, etc.) has many implications beyond the narrowness with which non-Christian "religions" are viewed. For instance, Enlightenment logics have constructed the so-called secular domain of capitalism alongside the category of religion itself. In his work, Fitzgerald (2011) argues that the commonsense myths of capitalism resemble the logics of religion:

> The invention of religions has facilitated the invention of natural reason that transforms modern rhetorical constructs like the rationality and inevitability of capitalism and "politics" into common sense. The mythological nature of our belief in self-regulating markets, self-maximizing individuals and private property has been mystically transformed into the inherent nature of things, the real world of facts and rational-decision making. (p. 10)

Critiquing the arbitrary nature of what is classified as self-evident "religion" and what is contrasted as "secular," many critical scholars of religious studies uncover how Western and Christian hegemony permeate seamlessly through civil and political life without detection (Ahmed, 2016; Bellah, 2005; Fitzgerald, 1997; Smith, 1991).

As is the case with dominant frames that become commonsense conceptualizations, it is difficult for even the "insider" to question and recognize what is being left out, misunderstood, or twisted. My entire life I kept hearing from my elders and religious educators that "Islam is a way of life." It wasn't until I allowed myself to recognize the Christian dominance of religious frames that this common saying came into focus. While many equate and translate the Arabic word *dīn* as "religion" (Esposito, 2003), a deeper look into the term reveals that the meaning is closer to an entire conscious way of life, including aspects of life considered in hegemonic terms as "secular." In the Qur'ān, the term *dīn* is used several times. One such use is in *Sūrah* (chapter) *Al ʿImrān*, *Āyah* (verse) 19, "The *dīn* in the sight of God is submission" (Nasr et al., 2015, p. 135). Interpreting *dīn* as religion makes this statement very exclusive and narrow, given the modern meaning of *religion* as innately distinct from "the secular."

Moreover, interpreting the term *Islam* itself as the coherent conception of a "religion," as defined by a Protestant template, limits the possibility of other potential definitions of Islam. For example, with the first revelation to Muhammed in 632 CE, the message was addressed to a variety of audiences. Some revelations were addressed to humanity, other messages were addressed to believers, and others to "the people of the book." Taken literally, "*Islam* is derived from the Arabic root s-l-m, which means 'submission' or 'peace'" (Esposito, 2003), and some argue that this definition should not be conflated with how Islam is conceptualized today as a codified and coherent religion characterized by a particular set of rituals and beliefs (Asani, 2011a).

Furthermore, the word *Muslim* was used in the Qur'ān to refer to individuals such as Prophet Abraham and Prophet Moses, who were active before the revelations of the Qur'ān, ipso facto predating the "religion" of Islam. While a deep study into these foundational terms is outside the scope of this chapter, I raise these questions to demonstrate the imaginative possibilities of what Islam could be (conceptually) outside of a Protestant frame.

The path of examining the Western, indeed Protestant, conception of religion as universal and self-evident raises important questions about power and meaning-making. Walking a path that uncovers the enmeshment of religion within the colonial project leads to the question, "Is the study of religion a rotten fruit of the poisoned tree of colonialism?" (Nye, 2019, p. 2). Said differently, to what extent does the academic study of religion need to change? Are the very categories we use no longer reasonable? From a desire to reject colonial conceptions of religion while also not wanting to disavow the idea of something that might be identifiable as Islam, many Muslim scholars have gone back to the drawing board to ask, *What is Islam*?

## Path 4: What Is Islam?

With incredible diversity across time and space, the question in search for a coherent conceptualization of Islam or "the Islamic" is an ongoing area of thought and debate, of which "Muslims have long been well aware" (Ahmed, 2016, p. 147). Some thinkers have approached this by shifting the focus away from Islam as a coherent religion and instead employing "the islams approach" which stresses not simply the diversity of lived Islam but also resists a reductive "ahistorical Islamic 'essence'" (Eickelman, 1982, p. 1). Locating Islam exclusively in its multiple manifestations (islams) challenges a coherent analytic understanding of Islam. Vanquishing the possibility of a coherent Islam poses a problem for those who utilize anthropological methods to understand lived Islam because those who enact Islam are themselves likely to affiliate with a sense of a coherent Islam. In other words, those who profess to believe in Islam, while they may differ from other Muslims in a variety of beliefs and practices (Karamustafa, 2003), are likely to agree that Islam is a coherent reality (Ahmed, 2016; Eickelman, 1982; Roff, 1987).

Scholars like Karamustafa (2003) and Ahmed (2016) assert that one can avoid understanding Islam through an essentialist framework while also avoiding relativizing Islam such that there is no possibility of coherence. However, both agree that what is typically presented as a common foundation is anything but. The most proliferated sense of common, definitional tenets is the ubiquitous five pillar formula that "do[es] not form a good and accurate measure of being a Muslim, historically, sociologically, or theologically" (Karamustafa, 2003, p. 107). Without going into too much detail, which the work of Karamustafa (2003) and Ahmed (2016) approach with beautiful nuance, it is evident that though the canonization of the five-pillar framework is understood as essential, millions upon millions of Muslims do not theologically adhere to this framework while many others may choose to "emphasize beliefs over acts" (Karamustafa, 2003, p. 107) in their approach to Islam, making the pillars not as foundational in defining religion.

This reality is contrasted by what many texts and teachers refer to as "the basics" of Islam (Merchant, 2018, p. 189). Pennington and Kahn's (2018) recent publication, which addresses representations of Islam and Muslims in the media, utilizes the last third of the text, titled "Crash Course in Islam" (p. 146), to provide basic information about Islam. Unsurprisingly, the first of these encyclopedic entries is called "The Five Pillars of Islam." With definitive language, the first sentence begins, "The Five Pillars of Islam are the foundation of the entire faith. Without the pillars there is no Islam" (Pennington & Kahn, 2018, p. 147). The schism between the lived experiences of Islam for millions of Muslims and what is distilled, bottled, and sold as Islam is vast. Although in reality there are many communities who do not theologically adhere to a five-pillar framework, in the modern period, the Five Pillars have become a purity test of *muslimness* that is subjected by Muslims onto other Muslims. The impulse of Muslims "who regard their interpretations of Islam as definitive, ironically and unintentionally provides a conceptual end product which likewise reduces Islamic tradition to a single essentialist set of principles" (Eickelman, 1982, p. 1). The five-pillar framework focuses primarily on actions performed by Muslims, but the same danger of generalization can be extended to beliefs/doctrines. After all, one's community of interpretation along with the ways in which one's self-understanding of particular concepts like "the unicity of God" or "the omniscience of God" or, for that matter, "God" is developed and evolved in one's particular context. If bulleted lists of beliefs and practices cannot be relied on as Islam, then what can?

## The Uncharted Path

The terrain consisting of arterial paths leading to a wide expanse, narrow paths leading to dead-ends, and unknown paths left uncharted place me back where I began. Considering the colonial frameworks of "religion" and "Islam," the hyper-focus on responding to Islamophobia, and the incomplete and inaccurate notions of cross-cutting tenets, how might Islam meaningfully be taught? Accompanying my larger inquiry is a set of wonderings that I raise for the reader's genuine engagement. I wonder:

> *What knowledge and understanding are lost when specific classifications based on a Protestant model are utilized to study "the other"; how can Islam be understood locally and particularly without vanquishing it as an analytic category altogether; how can Islam be taught as a way of life without falling into the trap of classification that demands a conformity to the secular/religious binary?*

Added to these wonderings is the anxiety of how K–12 curricula on Islam could possibly honor and represent a complex sense of Islam given the time/coverage constraints in social studies classes (Douglass & Dunn, 2003; Jackson, 2014).

Although the perfect curriculum on Islam is beyond my imagination at this time, I am reminded that perfection itself is a register of white supremacy (Jones & Okun, 2001). Given how deeply embedded the Protestant episteme is around the conception of "religion," the possibilities of a decolonial K–12 curriculum on Islam will take time to conceptualize, implement, and iterate upon. Yet, there are curricular interruptions to the standard curricula on Islam that might lay the groundwork toward a more robust and complex understanding of Islam. In what follows, I outline three curricular strategies to interrupt the ways in which Islam is taught in most classrooms today.

### *Deconstructing Religion, Unearthing the Colonial Impulse*

The vast majority of K–12 classrooms, as well as courses in higher education that cover Islam, do so through what is called the World Religions Paradigm (WRP; Baldrick-Morrone et al., 2016; Taira, 2016). As mentioned earlier in this chapter, the WRP is credited to European thinkers in the late 1800s interested in classification as an integral process of the colonial project (Cotter & Robertson, 2016). However, critical scholars in religious studies departments are implementing subversive pedagogical strategies to rethink religious classifications in their university courses on religion. One of the greatest challenges facing these educators is the ever-prominent Introduction to World Religions course that heavily relies on a "comprehensive" textbook and curricula that "all too easily becomes 'death-by-e.g.,' a forced march through a variety of pre-selected 'ism'" (Baldrick-Morrone et al., 2016). Given the structural constraints of these courses, which continue as a mainstay of liberal education (Fitzgerald, 2011), critical religious studies scholars subvert the WRP by utilizing the curriculum itself as data on which to critically study how and why particular classifications were/are constructed (Baldrick-Morrone et al., 2016; Ramey, 2016; Taira, 2016).

Before students can adequately critique the standard world history or world civilizations curriculum, which encompasses coverage of Islam, lessons that focus on deconstructing classifications like "religion" are essential. Deconstructing with students how and why the binary between secular and religious exists today is a case study in critiquing the dominance of Western epistemologies which cut across the curriculum. A conceptual appreciation for the construction of what seem like natural classifications is most effectively understood through examples. It wasn't until I learned about my own ancestry that I was able to grasp the politics behind certain classifications. Consequently, this learning has shifted my entire perspective on theological boundaries and identity, which holds particular power for someone who comes from a region of the world whose identity is mired in narratives of religious division and notions of religious purity.

Beyond deconstructing the categories that exist through historical lessons, it is also illuminating to pull from students' real-life experiences about the nature of what we call "religion." Questions like *What makes someone part of a religion? What role does a declaration of religion play in classifying someone in a particular religious group? Can you be a cultural Muslim? What about a cultural Christian? Is there a difference between being spiritual and religious?* and *How do you know?* are the kinds of questions that open the window to considering what religion might mean (or not mean) in everyday life. The lived complexity within each of our experiences acts as a counterbalance to the overly simplistic representations awaiting us in the widely used textbooks.

### *Unreading the Text*

In addition to teaching about classifications and their history, introducing critiques of the approaches to studying religion is also important. This is where textbooks, as they are, can be of tremendous use. In utilizing the textbook as an artifact, educators can lead an inquiry into how the textbook is organized, the ways in which religions are divided up, what is emphasized about each religion, and what is left out. The textbook itself, along with other curricular resources, acts as data of dominance. Setting up and familiarizing critical frameworks for students ensures that students

> learn much more than "facts" and history relevant to the so-called religions. They also explore the arbitrary and contested nature of representation itself. They learn that any given source—including textbooks and other academic sources—is not a simple representation of a thing that exists a priori; rather, they learn to question the contingent nature of all authenticity claims. (Baldrick-Morrone et al., 2016, p. 42)

While certain observations about power and perspective require only a critical mindset, other learning necessitates a deeper exposure to manifestations of a particular religion. To supplement this, the study of multiple, seemingly contradictory sources is helpful.

### *Embracing Contradictions*

Utilizing interdisciplinary and popular media sources as contrary texts to the standard textbook allows students to appreciate the breadth of experience in religion. This strategy is one already emphasized by scholars writing about religious literacy in the K–12 context (Asani, 2011a; Moore, 2007). Allowing for well-chosen examples that provide the greatest range in the experience of/with Islam emphasizes the limitations of current narrow constructions of religion, in general, as well as Islam, in particular. Including examples of Islam that are diverse in geography and time-period is essential as these examples will help counter the predominant focus of Islam during and immediately after the life of Prophet Muhammed (Ahmed, 2016). Including popular-culture sources (historic and contemporary) allows for the focus on everyday experiences of Muslims rather than grand narratives of empire through what is often called in textbooks "the spread of Islam."

## Conclusion

While teaching about religion is seen as "necessary for effective and engaged citizenship in a diverse nation and world" (NCSS, 2014), there remains a lack of engagement around how the project of knowing "the diverse other" can create more harm when done without accompanying questions and analyses of power. The call to teach about religion as "objective" (NCSS, 2019) continues to reinforce ideas that religion is a separate category from "the secular" and that each religion can be encapsulated by a set of coherent beliefs and practices. Exploring what I think of as some of the most critical paths to teaching about religion still leaves me unsatisfied. Even after living the complexity and contradictions of my own religious life, and even feeling heard and seen through the work of critical religious studies scholars, like the late Shahab Ahmed, what blocks my vision is my inability to imagine Islam outside of a narrow WRP model. For example, when I learned about Omar Ibn Said, a man subjected to enslavement in what is now called the United States, I am in awe of the fact that in the 1800s, he wrote an autobiography in Arabic that, along with details of his capture, enslavement, and freedom, included verses from the Qur'ān. I wondered to myself: *Where in the curriculum might his story get covered? Is it a story of U.S. history? Is it a story in the realm of religious studies? Is it a story of religion at all?* I think about how Omar Ibn Said's autobiography, written in a language the oppressor couldn't read, didn't separate out the events of his life from his Islam. I ask myself, In what ways might curriculum honor the wholeness of his life?

The exercise of adding in more complex and varied examples on Islam and Muslims throughout the standard world history and world civilizations curricula will not disturb the hegemonic framework of "religion," which is informed by white supremacy and the colonial impulse. Reimagining a curriculum that does more than offer interruptions to what exists currently will surely take collaborative work, expansive imagination, and iteration. This process, which many educators are currently engaged in will, Inshallah, lead to a more robust (multivalent) and dignified path to teaching about Islam.

## References


Ahmed, S. (2016). *What is Islam? The importance of being Islamic*. Princeton University Press.

Ali, A. I. (2016). Citizens under suspicion: Responsive research with community under surveillance. *Anthropology & Education, 47*(1), 78–95. https://doi.org/10.1111/aeq.12136

Asani, A. S. (2011a). From Satpanthi to Ismaili Muslim: The articulation of Ismaili Khoja identity in South Asia. In F. Daftary (Ed.), *A modern history of the Ismailis: Continuity and change in a Muslim community* (pp. 95–128). I. B. Tauris.

Asani, A. S. (2011b). Enhancing religious literacy in a liberal arts education through the study of Islam and Muslim societies. In J. M. Shephard, S. M. Kosslyn, & E. M. Hammonds (Eds.), *The Harvard sampler: Liberal education for the twenty-first century* (pp. 1–31). Harvard University Press.

Baldrick-Morrone, T., Graziano, M. & Stoddard, B. (2016) Graduate instructors and critical theory in the world religions classroom. In C. R. Cotter & D. G. Robertson (Eds.), *After world religions: Reconstructing religious studies* (pp. 37–47). Routledge.

Bellah, R. N. (2005). Civil religion in America. *Daedalus, 134*(4), 40–55. http://www.jstor.org/stable/20028013

Bittle, J. (2020, June 5). The NYPD sees coordination in protests. It's incentivized to. *Foreign Policy*. https://foreignpolicy.com/2020/06/05/nypd-sees-coordination-protests-counterintelligence-police-brutality/

Cotter, C. R., & Robertson, D. G. (2016). Introduction: The world religions paradigm in contemporary religious studies. In C. R. Cotter & D. G. Robertson (Eds.), *After world religions: Reconstructing religious studies* (pp. 75–91). Routledge.

Douglass, S. L., & Dunn, R. E. (2003). Interpreting Islam in American schools. *The Annals of the American Academy of Political and Social Science, 588*(1), 52–72. https://doi.org/10.1177/0002716203588001005

Eickelman, D. F. (1982). The study of Islam in local contexts. *Contributions to Asian Studies, 17*, 1–16.

Esposito, J. (2003). *Oxford dictionary of Islam*. Oxford University Press.

Fitzgerald, T. (1997). A critique of "religion" as a cross-cultural category. *Method & Theory in the Study of Religion, 9*(2), 91–110. http://www.jstor.org/stable/23549638

Fitzgerald, T. (2011). *Religion and politics in international relations: The modern myth*. Bloomsbury.

Foucault, M. (1973). *The order of things: An archaeology of human sciences*. Random House.

Grosfoguel, R. (2012). The multiple faces of Islamophobia. *Islamophobia Studies Journal, 1*(1), 9–33. https://doi.org/10.13169/islastudj.1.1.0009

Haynes, C. C. (2019). *Teaching about religion in the social studies classrooms* (NCSS Bulletin, 117). National Council for the Social Studies.

Jackson, L. (2014). *Muslims and Islam in U.S. education: Reconsidering multiculturalism*. Routledge.

Jones, K., & Okun, T. (2001). The characteristics of white supremacy culture. In *Dismantling racism: A workbook for social change groups*. https://www.showingupforracialjustice.org/white-supremacy-culture-characteristics.html

Karamustafa, A. (2003). Islam: A civilizational project in progress. In O. Safi. (Ed.), *Progressive Muslims: On justice, gender and pluralism* (pp. 98–110). One World.

Klepper, A. (2014). High School Students' Attitudes toward Islam and Muslims: Can a Social Studies Course Make a Difference? *The Social Studies, 105*(3), 113–123.

Lee, S. A., Gibbons, J. A., Thompson, J. M., & Timani, H. S. (2009). The Islamophobia scale: Instrument development and initial validation. *International Journal for the Psychology of Religion, 19*(2), 92–105. https://doi.org/10.1080/10508610802711137

Mamdani, M. (2002). Good Muslim, bad Muslim: A political perspective on culture and terrorism. *American Anthropologist, 104*(3), 766–775. https://doi.org/10.1525/aa.2002.104.3.766

Merchant, N. H. (2015). *Unflattening the Muslim-other in social studies: Student perspectives and curricular approaches* [Doctoral dissertation]. University of Washington.

Merchant, N. H. (2018). Critical considerations in teaching about the Muslim-other in social studies teacher education. In C. C. Martell (Ed.), *Social studies teacher education: Critical issues and current perspectives* (pp. 175–191). Information Age.

Moore, D. L. (2007). *Overcoming religious illiteracy: A cultural studies approach to the study of religion in secondary education*. Palgrave Macmillan US.

Moore, J. R. (2012). A challenge for social studies educators: Teaching about Islam. *Jihād*, and *Shari'ah* Law. *The Social Studies, 103*(5), 179–187. https://doi.org/10.1080/00377996.2011.601357

Nasr, S. H., Dagli, C. K., Dakake, M. M., Lumbard, J. E. B., & Mohammed, R. (Eds.). (2015). *The study Quran: A new translation and commentary*. HarperCollins.

National Council for the Social Studies. (2017). *College, career, and civic life: C3 framework for social studies state standards*. https://www.socialstudies.org/sites/default/files/c3/c3-framework-for-social-studies-rev0617.pdf

Nguyen, N., & Zahzah, Y. (n.d.). *Why treating white supremacy as domestic terrorism won't work and how to not fall for it: A toolkit for social justice advocates*. https://static1.squarespace.com/static/593f2dbaebbd1a0b706908ea/t/5fa0518556b08d66e6c5d4e8/1604342152141/white_supremacy_toolkit.pdf

Nye, M. (2019). Decolonizing the study of religion. *Open Library of Humanities, 5*(1), 1–45. https://doi.org/10.16995/olh.421

Pennington, R., & Kahn, H. E. (2018). The five pillars of Islam. In R. Pennington & H. E. Kahn (Eds.), *On Islam: Muslims and the media* (p. 147). Indiana University Press.

Ramey, S. (2014). Textbooks, assumptions, and us: Commentary on Jimmy Emanuelsson's "Islam and the sui-generis discourse: Representations of Islam in textbooks used in introductory courses of religious studies in Sweden." *Method and Theory in the Study of Religion, 26*(1), 108–110. https://doi.org/0.1163/15700682-12341285

Ramey, S. W. (2016). The critical embrace: Teaching the world religions paradigm as data. In C. R. Cotter & D. G. Robertson (Eds.), *After world religions: Reconstructing religious studies* (pp. 48–60). Routledge.

Roff, W. R. (1987). *Islam and the political economy of meaning: Comparative studies of Muslim discourse*. Croom Helm.

Shodhan, A. (1995). *Legal representations of Khojas and Pushtimarga Vaishnava polities as communities: The Aga Khan case and the Maharaj libel case in mid-nineteenth century Bombay* (Publication No. 9530799) [Doctoral dissertation, The University of Chicago]. ProQuest Dissertations Publishing.

Shryock, A. (2010). Introduction: Islam as an object of fear and affection. In A. Shryock (Ed.), *Islamophobia/Islamophilia: Beyond the politics of enemy and friend* (pp. 1–25). Indiana University Press.

Smith, W. C. (1991). *The meaning and end of religion*. Fortress Press.

Taira, T. (2016). Doing things with "religion": A discursive approach in rethinking the world religions paradigm. In C. R. Cotter & D. G. Robertson (Eds.), *After world religions: Reconstructing religious studies* (pp. 1–20). Routledge.

Tamdgidi, M. H. (2012). Beyond Islamophobia and Islamophilia as Western epistemic racisms: Revisiting Runnymede Trust's definition in a world-history context. *Islamophobia Studies Journal, 1*(1), 54–81. https://doi.org/10.13169/islastudj.1.1.0054

Tayob, A. (2018). Decolonizing the study of religions: Muslim intellectuals and the Enlightenment project of religious studies. *Journal for the Study of Religion, 31*(2), 7–35. https://doi.org/10.17159/2413-3027/2018/v31n2a1

SEVEN

# Queer Worlding as Historical Inquiry for Insurgent Freedom-Dreaming

*Tadashi Dozono*

> My family did not come all the way from Mexico in order for me to not be anything or to not make them proud. The thing that came out of my best friend's death was the fact that she told me that I can be anything I desire to be. So you know I'm tired of the stigma. I'm tired of being ashamed! I'm gonna run for prom queen. (Angel-Bello, 2019)

THIS IS HOW ELLA SANTOS, a Mexican American trans woman, explains to her new friends how she arrived in New York from San Antonio after her friend Ruby was murdered for being trans. She tells this to her friends on the Christopher Street pier, a historic site for New York's queer community haunted by decades of both community action and systemic violence. Ella is a fictional character in the short film *Ella for Prom Queen* (Angel-Bello, 2019) created by New York City teens through the after-school program of the Global Action Project (GAP). Ella's journey represents the queer world-making that students are doing in response to the worlds they inhabit and the histories they inherit, creating these works outside of school.

GAP is a New York City community-based organization with several after-school film-making programs for low-income new immigrant, trans, queer, and gender-nonconforming youth. GAP's Supafriends program specifically centers TLGBQ (transgender, lesbian, gay, bisexual, and queer[1]) youth, creating media about and of low-income POC (People of Color) TLGBQ communities. The students write and produce their own original films, not only rewriting narratives but also envisioning and generating new queer worlds. These narratives arise out of students agentively turning their readings of the world into new texts to be read by others.

I refer to this process as queer worlding, as the ways queer people (and queer POC in particular) create new worlds as an agentive response to the systemic violence and oppression of contemporary American society.

The term *queer* is an overarching term for TLGBQ peoples, but the term is also used as a verb, *to queer*. Queer embraces older connotations as strange and peculiar and references a broad critique of power, and the power of the category of "normal" to police that which lies outside that category. The students wrote and produced a film that moved beyond a narrative of revenge or retribution, embodying the complexities of both bullies and those who are bullied by them and reimagining these conflicts through reparation and reconciliation. In the end, Ella is chosen for prom queen, and Kayla, the straight cis bully, apologizes and tells Ella that she is beautiful inside and out. The students wrote a story that begins in the lived realities of violence against trans Women of Color in the United States but redresses that violence through agency, rewriting new narratives of reparation.

This sort of work would not be considered historical or historical thinking by many history education scholars. Some might say this topic should be in a volume about English language arts, not social studies. However, it is an important means for students from historically marginalized backgrounds and communities to confront and speak back to historical legacies. This chapter begins with an example of queer Youth of Color's generative capacity to make sense of their worlds to then consider how such inquiry links to world history. Rather than begin from world history and figure out how it might link to students who have been marginalized, this chapter flips the trajectory and driving force of inquiry to center the generative work that trans queer Youth of Color are doing and choosing to engage in outside of school. These students are synthesizing what they know of the world to be true, its systematic racism, exploitative capitalism, homophobia, transphobia, and cis-heteronormativity, against a world imagined otherwise, envisioning other worlds beyond their experiences of systemic violence.

I write this as a social studies teacher, deeply committed to the integrity of my discipline and a classroom environment of authentic disciplinary inquiry. I must admit though that some of my favorite moments were not in my content-area classes, but during meetings as the facilitator of my different schools' Gender and Sexuality Alliances (GSAs), Know Homo and Spectrum. Over 12 years in New York City's public schools, I taught in two small community-based Title I high schools with about 96% of the population being Black and Latino students. I became a social studies teacher not because I loved history but because my own experiences of racism and homophobia as a queer,

Japanese American, cis male resulted in my desire to speak back to history. Within these GSAs, the students and I created a world of our own amid the larger school community, emphasizing the safety to express and explore our true selves. And yet, that level of world-making did not occur in my social studies classrooms. This chapter is a challenge to my content-area self to question, What might happen when we bring queer worlding into social studies classrooms? What happens when we acknowledge queer worlding as an authentic assessment, as disciplined inquiry, as a real-world application?

When tasked with writing a chapter on queer world history for a book on insurgent social studies, I could not help but begin from the ways TLGBQ Youth of Color refuse the status quo order of things and reimagine the world. The films these Supafriends youth create are texts in conversation with other artworks from TLGBQ scholar/activist/artists globally who also create new queer worlds as responses to systemic state and societal violence. This chapter places their work in conversation with the theoretical frameworks and vocabulary of queer studies and cultural studies Scholars of Color. I turn to the works of Jose Muñoz, Saidiya Hartman, and Ronak Kapadia to frame queer worlding as an insurgent means to respond creatively to TLGBQ Youth of Color's experiences living in an oppressive world.

Queer worlding names this method of engaging the past, present, and future for many queer Youth of Color. GAP's queer Youth of Color embody this agentive act of taking control over one's relationality to the world and to the historical archive. It is a means of disassociating oneself from a world that negates them, a state that polices and vilifies them, to disrupt the permanence of contemporary overlapping systemic oppressions by engaging with historic legacies on one's own terms and reimagining potential futures.

The work these students already engage speaks to how Jose Muñoz (2009) framed queerness: "We have never been queer, yet queerness exists for us as an ideality that can be distilled from the past and used to imagine a future. The future is queerness's domain" (p. 1). I take Muñoz to imply that we have never been queer because we remain embedded in damaging systems of power and oppression. Queerness critiques those present power dynamics and serves as a future horizon of possibility, which we have yet to reach. Programs like Supafriends and the films these youth produce exemplify the intellectual and creative work TLGBQ Youth of Color already do, yet this work often remains outside of school. In this chapter, I link this creative work to academic and intellectual inquiries modeled by various queer and trans Scholars/Activists/Artists of Color.

This chapter asserts queer worlding as a mode of inquiry responsive to both the failure of world history and systemic marginalization and silencing of trans and queer Communities of Color. I first ground the notion of queer worlding in relation to world history. I then bring queer worlding in conversation with the theoretical frameworks of insurgent aesthetics, and freedom-dreaming. Third, I contextualize queer worlding within a broader community of artist/scholar/activists whose work speaks back to historical legacies of violence. Finally, I apply these conceptual frameworks to the work youth are already doing, and consider the implications for the social studies classroom.

## Beyond Queering World History to Queer Worlding as Historical Inquiry

I have written elsewhere about queering world history (Dozono, 2017), something that I value as an important endeavor. Yet, there is something deeply deflating about trying to do an inquiry into world history as a queer POC. Growing up as a queer, Japanese American, cis male, I sought to identify with others in the past, looking for the queer moments in world history. But one repeatedly confronts the limits of historical inquiry. The intersecting minoritizations of what it means to be queer and a POC today translate into overlapping erasures when it comes to historical inquiry. Gayatri Spivak's (1988) answer to the question, "Can the Subaltern Speak?" was a resounding no. The voices of the subaltern (the colonized, the underclasses, women, among a multitude of subaltern groups) cannot be recovered through history's intentionally exclusive archives. In David Halperin's (1993) work on the history of homosexuality, he posited that to write a history of homosexuality is anachronistic, applying our contemporary social constructs onto those in the past. We cannot redeem our present identities by seeking legitimate versions of ourselves in the past. One is left with the notion that one cannot fully construct a world history of homosexuality.

The framing of world history is already confined, determined through political interests of not only what places get included but who counts within those places as well. The non-Westernized regions of the world are already marginalized, let alone the subaltern within those non-white, non-Westernized spaces. To begin from world history and then queer it is to acknowledge the importance of the center, to begin from the foundation of a defined world history and then respond to it. Once we accept that the subaltern indeed cannot speak, where does inquiry lead for TLGBQ Students of Color? When the answer given is that you don't exist in the archives, and it's anachronistic to search in the past for your present identities, of what use is historical inquiry? Although there are wonderful scholarly works that engage world history through queerness, this chapter centers queerness's generative capacities as something not-yet-quite existing. For this volume on insurgent social studies, it seemed prescient to center those who conduct insurgent inquiries in the world and history.

Queer worlding is this generative capacity of queerness. When you don't fit into a world that doesn't seem to make sense of you anyhow, you create your own worlds. When you're not made sense of, there's a freedom to then make your own sense. Trans and queer POC generate new paths through the world. Queer Scholars and Artists of Color look to the past, not in order to re-create idealized utopias but as a means of breaking through the power of the status quo today.

TLGBQ peoples, racially and economically marginalized groups, have turned to the arts to imagine other possible futures and modes of existence. Many of these scholars mix historical inquiry with literary arts and other media including film, performance, visual arts, and music. Jose Muñoz's (2009) *Cruising Utopia* sparked further studies into queer world-making. Afrofuturism has grown from African American scholar/artists such as Sun Ra, Octavia Butler, and Samuel Delaney, whose work continues to resonate for various marginalized groups seeking to envision alternatives to the worlds we inhabit. This chapter invokes Richard Iton's (2008) *In Search of the Black Fantastic* in light of the ways my TLGBQ Students of Color are often already engaged in forms of the fantastic. The chapter title also invokes Robin Kelley's (2003) *Freedom Dreams: The Black Radical Imagination*, tracing the importance of imagination and freedom dreaming in the face of systemic oppression. Many of my queer Students of Color read fantasy literature, embracing anime worlds, cosplay, Sailor Moon, and vampire worlds, among many other realms of the fantastic.

As historical inquiry, queer worlding is a means for engaging with the archive, engaging the existing traces of evidence, but emphasizing, as Saidiya

Hartman (2008) framed it, "the subjunctive and conditional" modes (p. 11). Queer worlding as historical inquiry aligns more with a genealogical approach (Foucault, 1977), which attends to the dead-ends of history, emphasizing the unpredictable and unforeseen dynamism of historical contingency rather than the givenness of the past. A genealogical approach disrupts mainstream world history curricula that often reproduce a narrative of progress toward a (Hegelian) predetermined idealized endpoint (Dozono, 2020) only to reaffirm the inevitability of the status quo today. Through a subjunctive reimagining, queer worlding reinvigorates those historical dead ends. When the evidence trail has been "lost" or destroyed or not recorded in a form deemed legitimate, queer worlding takes up that trail, to move history into the subjunctive and conditional realm. Given the facts and evidence trails we do have, what else might have been? What stories might the lost and unaccounted evidence have told? To accept queer worlding as subjunctive is an acknowledgment that it is not fact in and of itself. Just as Muñoz framed queerness as not-yet-here, queer worlding as historical inquiry is a queerness of the not-yet-thence. Queer worlding as historical inquiry does not claim to reflect the past as it was; it does not claim to be fact. But in the face of systemic violence, it allows marginalized groups to dream a little. It is an act of refraction, not reflection. Queer worlding acts as a prism: the light shifts and refracts, revealing new wavelengths through which we might perceive our worlds and the past remembered.

In another Supafriends' (2012) film, *Past Forgotten, Future Unwritten*, the characters engage the past not so much as nostalgia but as a means to shatter the givenness of the present. The film plays off *A Christmas Carol*, wherein four TLGBQ Youth of Color find themselves in the same subway car. The conductor of the train is the ghost of the past and takes them through queer history in the city, starting with Harlem in 1927, to a Saturday night skiffle, or a rent party. The conductor explained, "This is how drag balls started. People were coming together to pay the rent so people had a space to make their art to speak their truth." One youth, Ebony, explained how she was kicked out of her friend's place where she's been sleeping. The past inspired Ebony to plan her own skiffle to raise money for rent. Next, the conductor takes them to 1995 to the Christopher Street Pier. The youth see the makeshift housing where trans and queer POC such as Sylvia Rivera lived. Sylvia Rivera was a trans Puerto Rican and Venezuelan activist who participated in the Stonewall riots and cofounded STAR (Street Transvestite Action

Revolutionaries). The film shows footage of Rivera, who tells how she stayed on the pier for as long as she could until she got thrown out in 1996. The second person, Steph, links it to their own experiences of getting evicted. This journey is not to equate the past with the present but to provide a provocation into the unwritten future. The youths arrive in the future to encounter the fourth queer youth, Katana, who is no longer homeless and seems happy. The film cuts just before Katana explains what changed to get to that future. The Supafriends youth use the visit to the past in order to disrupt the present condition, but they stop short of saying what the answers for the future are. Historical inquiry through queer worlding creates portals of possibility rather than reproducing a teleological narrative.

In schools, we talk about authentic assessments and real-world applications. Rather than focus on an exclusionary white majoritarian model of future capitalist production and job-market skills, I look to those TLGBQ Artists/Scholars/Activists of Color who professionally work through marginalization as a site of community intervention and care. The films these youth produce in an after-school program are in conversation with the "higher ordered thinking" of academia and the arts world.

## Queer Worlding as Insurgent Freedom-Dreaming

Queer worlding names that process of creating new unimagined and impossible worlds. When we do not feel that this world was made for us, then perhaps we are not of this world. Queer worlding allows that to be okay to not feel like queer individuals need to conform to the social order but can create their own relationalities to the world and create their own worlds. Queer worlding is an agentive thoughtful response to experiencing marginalization daily.

This section frames queer worlding as a method of insurgent freedom-dreaming. I turn to Ronak Kapadia's and Saidiya Hartman's works to frame insurgency as a means of making one's way through the world and through the archive. Queer worlding is a means of engaging historical legacies by inverting dominant narratives, embracing one's agency to speak against the forces of violence which police, monitor, and corral marginalized queer and trans Peoples of Color.

Kapadia built on Jose Muñoz's assertion of queerness as not-yet-here and how this notion enables a temporal calculus that utilizes "the past and the future as armaments to combat the devastating logic of the world of the here and now" (Muñoz, 2009, p. 12). For Kapadia (2019), "*Insurgent Aesthetics* is about the creativity and fugitive beauty that emanate from the shadows of terrible violence incited by forever war" and "freedom dreams flecked by inscriptions of wartime's death and dispossession" (p. 9). This statement applies similarly to the creative works of GAP's Supafriends program, of TLGBQ Students of Color speaking against the legacies of state violence incited against their communities.

Ronak Kapadia's (2019) *Insurgent Aesthetics* framed a larger movement of queer artists of the South Asian and Middle Eastern diasporas generating new queer worlds beyond their everyday experiences of intersecting oppressions. Kapadia (2019) explained that "the 'forever' in 'forever war' calls up a fantasy sense of temporal perpetuity in wartime's violence in the dystopian here and now that likewise mimics the uninterrupted and limitless spree of US global war-making across the long twentieth century" (p. 8). Although Kapadia applied the term "forever war" to the United States' destructive role on a global scale of international politics and imperialism, the notion of forever war applies as well to the marginalized lives of trans and queer Youth of Color who encounter state violence daily in the United States. The ubiquity of such forces instills this sense of givenness, inevitability, and inescapability from systemic oppression.

Kapadia's (2019) queer mode of inquiry involved assembling a new archive of diasporic works that speak against state and imperial power, which challenge "the explanatory power of dominant 'expert' knowledge about U.S. empire and its forever war" (p. 12). Artists from Iraq, Palestine, Afghanistan, and Pakistan speak back against drone warfare, redaction practices in military archives, military detention, confinement, and torture, among other terrorizing practices of the forever war. For example, Pakistani American Mahwish Chishty's artwork speaks back to drone warfare by creating paintings and sculptures of drones ornamented in the colorful style of Pakistani truck art (Kapadia, 2019, p. 4). Her work documents this interplay of warfare, folk art traditions, and interregional commercial shipping. As Kapadia (2019) explained,

> these insurgent aesthetics craft a queer calculus of US empire that makes intimate what is rendered distant, renders tactile what is made invisible, and unifies what

> is divided, thereby conjuring forms of embodied critique that can envision a collective world within and beyond the spaces of US empire's perverse logics of global carcerality, security, and war. (p. 10)

These works take official archives and technologies of war as their beginning point, creating conceptual and experimental art that speaks against and back to those archives.

Whenever I teach about the systemic suppression of voices and silencing through the archive, I simultaneously emphasize agentive responses to those silences. In the face of the forever war, Kapadia traces artistic creation as agentive acts against systemic and sustained violence. These become models of assessment, models of how others have assessed historic legacies and global phenomena, how others have made sense of their experiences through archival interrogations. As teachers, we can create opportunities for students to assess the current state of the forever war, and responses amidst their communities.

Moving from the global scale to the localized worlds of individual daily life, Saidiya Hartman offers a model of historical inquiry and living through insurgency. When the state works to dismantle one's being and way of life, Hartman turns to reconstructing the traces of those who have refused to abide by societal norms or for whom conforming was impossible. Saidiya Hartman's (2019) book *Wayward Lives, Beautiful Experiments: Intimate Histories of Riotous Black Girls, Troublesome Women, and Queer Radicals* aimed

> to recover the insurgent ground of these lives; to exhume open rebellion from the case file, to untether waywardness, refusal, mutual aid, and free love from their identification as deviance, criminality, and pathology; to affirm free motherhood (reproductive choice), intimacy outside the institution of marriage, and queer and outlaw passions; and to illuminate the radical imagination and everyday anarchy of ordinary colored girls, which has not only been overlooked, but is nearly unimaginable. (p. xiii)

Hartman retells these stories based on existing archival evidence, shifting the narrative from one told by police records and slum-gazers, to a narrative of human dignity and agency that speaks against dehumanization. Hartman uses those traces in the archives to recontextualize them into unimagined narratives. What results is a form of historical narrative in the subjunctive mode, taking archival dead-ends and allowing them to flourish.

For trans and queer Students of Color who are misread, mislabeled, and dismissed, Hartman offers a model of reinterpreting, renarrating, and repairing the trespasses of dominant society on those most marginalized. Students whose school files speak of truancy, bad grades, or chronic absence can take those archives of evidence and speak back against the school's narrative of who they are.

In *Ella for Prom Queen* (Angel-Bello, 2019), the conversation between Ella and her friends occurs on the Christopher Street pier on the Hudson River, a historic site of New York's TLGBQ community, a place that has shifted over decades, and has been gentrified. Ella's friend Kai sleeps on the pier, similar to how Sylvia Rivera called the pier home in the footage from Supafriends' earlier film. The film represents just one method through which New York City queer and trans Youth of Color speak against the violence to their communities and spaces. FIERCE (Fabulous Independent Educated Radicals for Community Engagement) was founded by primarily TLGBQ Youth of Color to speak collectively against plans to gentrify and rebuild the Christopher Street pier. FIERCE continues to fight against the policing of trans and queer Youth of Color along the pier and around the city. Supafriends' films not only rewrite the narrative of the high school experience for queer and trans Youth of Color but reclaim this historic space for the current and future generations of queer and trans Youth of Color in New York City. By telling her friends she will run for prom queen while sitting on the pier, Ella reinscribes that space from one of policing to one of queer-as-not-yet-here.

Queer worlding for insurgent freedom-dreaming can be applied as a pedagogic tool. Queer worlding can be understood pedagogically as a form of synthesizing and creating through critique, as a higher-ordered thinking task for assessment. It takes a great deal of comprehension, interpretation, analysis, and critique to get to the point of queer worlding. At the same time, for queer Students of Color who experience marginalization daily, that expertise might not stem from sitting in front of piles of primary sources, but from critical analysis on a daily level of systems that exclude and negate. Some of the most fantastic queer worlding I have witnessed in my students comes from those who tend to "fail" at traditional schooling. But what if schools served the needs of their most marginalized publics, and allowed fantastic queer worlding to flourish?

## Tourmaline's Queer Worlding and Freedom-Dreams

In this section, I apply queer worlding as insurgent freedom-dreaming to scholar/artist/activist Tourmaline's films which provide a model for what queer worlding can look like as a career and professional production. Tourmaline is an artist/activist/scholar who has created artworks and community spaces that honor the freedom dreams of trans and queer Black people. Her works engage the space between the trans and queer African diaspora and historical legacies and archives.

Tourmaline's films speak back to historical archives that have erased, villainized, and criminalized stories of trans and queer Black women. These films narrate the lives of "history's impossible women" (Tourmaline & Lax, 2020). Tourmaline drew on Hartman's method of "critical fabulation," which takes the basic elements of the story and rearranges them to disrupt the authorized account of an event. Hartman (2008) explained:

> The intent of this practice is not to give voice to the slave, but rather to imagine what cannot be verified, a realm of experience which is situated between two zones of death—social and corporeal death—and to reckon with the precarious lives which are visible only in the moment of their disappearance. It is an impossible writing which attempts to say that which resists being said (since dead girls are unable to speak). It is a history of an unrecoverable past; it is a narrative of what might have been or could have been; it is a history written with and against the archive. (p. 12)

A nod to Foucault's genealogical over historical methods, here historical inquiry occurs in the subjunctive and conditional, emphasizing the contingency, the dead-ends of history, breaking the narrow linear path of a teleological historical narrative.

Tourmaline's queer worlding through critical fabulation breaks the archive's hold over how we narrate those in the past, shattering the givenness of our current social order, and opening up the queer impossibilities of future freedom-dreams. Tourmaline's short films model this queer historical worlding as freedom dreaming. Two of her films in particular, *Salacia* (Tourmaline, 2019) and *Atlantic is a Sea of Bones* (Tourmaline, 2017), inquire into the historical archives and legacies of state violence.

The film *Salacia* (2019) tells the story of Mary Jones, a real-life Black trans sex worker and outlaw in New York City in the 1930s. The film is set in Seneca Village, a Black landowning community between 1825 and 1857 that was destroyed when the city used eminent domain to build what is now Central Park in Manhattan. C. Riley Snorton (2017) wrote about Mary Jones in his book *Black on Both Sides: A Racial History of Trans Identity*. Mary Jones was made infamous through a lithograph depicting her as "The Man-Monster" that was distributed across the city through print shops. Tourmaline takes aspects of the historical archive but also reimagines and recontextualizes those traces. By placing Mary Jones in Seneca Village,

> Tourmaline's re-placement is not only a feat of imagination—as Jones is not known to have found refuge in Seneca Village—but a political feat of class solidarity: Then, as now, women accused of thieving and making their money through sex were not always welcome by landowners, whatever their race. (Tourmaline & Lax, 2020, para. 2)

We also find solidarity through Kapadia's framing of the forever war. Although Mary Jones's life was vastly different from those of Black trans sex workers today, there is something of the forever war in how systemic racial, class, and gender oppression maintain continuous legacies into the present.

The film shifts to a dreamlike clip of Sylvia Rivera on the Christopher Street pier saying: "Every time you look at that damn river and meditate on the river you got to keep fighting, girly, 'cause it's not time for you to cross the River Jordan." Queer worlding becomes a portal across the forever war, wherein Tourmaline puts Sylvia Rivera, Mary Jones, and the viewer in the present in conversation across a vast expanse of systemic oppression and violence.

> As she analogizes the Hudson with the Old Testament's journey from slavery to freedom, as well as the New Testament site of Jesus's baptism, death, and resurrection, the video returns to Jones and those who remain warehoused with her, as if Rivera were speaking backwards in time, across the river to her foresister. (Tourmaline & Lax, 2020, para. 3)

Queer worlding as a method of inquiry into the past and the archive enables one to recontextualize archival traces, to disrupt the power of the forever war in our lives.

Tourmaline's (2017) film *Atlantic is a Sea of Bones* stars Egyptt LaBeija of the House of LaBeija and was a part of the *Alternative Endings, Radical Beginnings* series of events for 2017's Day With(out) Art created by the organization Visual AIDS. Tourmaline used the Hudson River as a nexus of history, as a node along the Atlantic slave trade, a home for New York's TLGBQ community, and a site of gentrification today. The film begins with Egyptt LaBeija peering from the Whitney Museum's windows overlooking the Christopher Street Pier, recounting when she was homeless and lived on the piers. Tavia Nyong'o (2018) explained how "*Atlantic is a Sea of Bones* thus posits history through the angular entanglements of transgender subjects who are caught up in non-linear temporalities and non-sovereign subjectivities. Stolen and disposable life finds new dispositions for itself and others" (para. 8). Through the rest of the short film, the two characters of Egyptt and Jamal move silently through dark interiors toward supporting each other's self actualization, punctuated with footage of Egyptt on stage.

Tracing the film's background becomes its own historical archive of Black women's artistry, activism, and epistemology. The film arose out of Tourmaline's collaboration with Egyptt through both the Sylvia Rivera Law Project and Audre Lorde Project's TransJustice program. Tourmaline (2018) explained how the idea came about through their conversations:

> We were also talking about loss . . . and how that can haunt a place. Loss has happened through gentrification and HIV criminalization and really intense "quality of life" policing on Christopher Street, in the Meatpacking District, in Chelsea, and in the West Village. (para. 2)

This conversation on loss coincided with Tourmaline listening to Alexis Pauline Gumbs's reading of Lucille Clifton's poem *Atlantic Is a Sea of Bones* as part of her "Lucille Clifton Rebirth Broadcast" Vimeo series. Gumbs explained her relation to the poem:

> violence, huge violence, systemic violence, genocidal violence remains present in the ocean, in the land. . . . And I'm interested this week in how we might think about the legacies that stay present in the landscape, in the structures that we live. What might that threat and that energy be offering in terms of a transformative imperative for how we shift in how we live today? (Gumbs, 2010, 02:22)

Tourmaline's film merged her background in community organizing with both Clifton's and Gumbs's calls to be transformed as we process those legacies of violence. She provokes us to shift how we live in the present, and our possible futures. Her queer worlding through historical inquiry is an agentive means to rearticulate how we relate to legacies of violence.

These films offer models of queer historical worlding, of how one engages with the past and the archive but on one's own terms. They model an agentive approach to one's relationality to state violence and historical erasure. After sharing her own insights about the poem, Gumbs (2010) provided a writing prompt to her audience: "write about some way that a legacy that urgently, poignantly, and tragically speaks to the necessary transformation of the place that you live. How is it palpable for you? How is it present for you? Where does a repressed history live in your life?" (03:42). Gumbs's videos and prompts could be adapted to social studies classrooms as well, as a form of assessment that allows students to inquire into the past through their particular present worlds.

## Queer Worlding as Reparative Inquiry Into the Past

Queer worlding is also a reparative practice linked to self-care. adrienne maree brown's various works are emblematic of this process, of both queer-worlding, and doing reparative self-care work for oneself and in community. brown's work speaks to the importance of science fiction for queer POC. adrienne maree brown and Walidah Imarisha's (2015) edited volume *Octavia's Brood: Science Fiction Stories from Social Justice Movements* called on activists/scholars embedded in various social justice movements to write stories inspired by Octavia Butler's speculative fiction, reimagining the world for the sake of new futures. Grounded in the daily work of activists embedded in systems of oppression, the activists then became authors daring to imagine the world otherwise, to imagine a world without police brutality, racial violence, prisons, and exploitative capitalism. In light of the toll from confronting systemic oppression daily, queer worlding is a part of a reparative process, to repair from that harm.

Why can't that sort of analysis, synthesis, and genesis that GAP youth do, why can't that occur within social studies classrooms? I do not mean that I believe that I or most other social studies teachers could do the work that

GAP has been doing. The people who have run GAP over the last two decades have been influential community members involved in many other artistic, scholarly, and activist spaces both locally and globally. But I do believe in funding the arts, valuing the work of artists, and employing artists as arts educators in schools. I believe in collaboration and solidarity work across movement spaces. As I write this, GAP is winding down its programming due to underfunding.

GAP has been able to support marginalized youth because it functions as an autonomous and safe space. I relate this to how, although many teachers are inspired by Paolo Freire's (1993) *Pedagogy of the Oppressed*, such a project is impossible under a compulsory education system that is simultaneously complicit in the prison system. Public schools ultimately serve the state, and a public school teacher cannot do the work of those in marginalized communities within their own safe and autonomous community spaces. But can we use schools as resources to support these programs, to work in collaboration with artists who help our students dare to imagine the world otherwise?

As social studies teachers, we can provide texts that model queer worlding for our students. To offer textual examples of speaking back to those silences. Insurgent social studies is not only teaching about the erasure of marginalized and subaltern peoples of the past but how marginalized peoples today move through a world that continuously and repeatedly erases them, mislabels them, and negates them. Some historians would argue that this is not "good" historical work, and I respond by arguing that this is important historical work. What good does it do for a student who lives marginalization daily, to be told that you cannot find resemblances of yourself in the past because you were not included in the archives? Why then, would marginalized students engage in history if it is not for them or of them? Queer worlding as historical inquiry is an engagement with the world that utilizes history to break the confines of the forever war in the present, for the sake of a queer future not yet realized.

## Note

1. This group purposefully places transgender peoples first, centering trans people rather than after sexual identities that have become more normalized in recent decades. I honor that work by following their lead.

## References


Angel-Bello, S. (Director). (2019). *Ella for Prom Queen* [Film]. Global Action Project. https://www.global-action.org/supafriends

brown, a. m., & Imarisha, W. (Eds.). (2015). *Octavia's brood: Science fiction stories from social justice movements*. AK Press.

Dozono, T. (2017). Teaching alternative and Indigenous gender systems in world history: A queer approach. *The History Teacher, 50*(3), 425–447. http://www.societyforhistoryeducation.org/pdfs/M17_Dozono.pdf

Dozono, T. (2020). The passive voice of white supremacy: Tracing epistemic and discursive violence in world history curriculum. *Review of Education, Pedagogy, and Cultural Studies, 42*(1), 1–26. https://doi.org/10.1080/10714413.2020.1721261

Foucault, M. (1977). Nietzsche, genealogy, history. In D. F. Bouchard (Ed.), *Language, counter-memory, practice: Selected essays and interviews* (pp. 139–164). Cornell University Press.

Freire, P. (1993). *Pedagogy of the oppressed* (M. Ramos, Trans.). Continuum.

Global Action Project. (2012). *Past forgotten, future unwritten* [Film]. Vimeo. https://vimeo.com/42407236

Gumbs, A. P. (2010, September 13). *Atlantic is a sea of bones: Lucille Clifton rebirth broadcast #12* [Video]. Vimeo. https://vimeo.com/14916291

Halperin, D. M. (1993). Is there a history of sexuality? In H. Abelove, M. A. Barale, & D. M. Halperin (Eds.), *The lesbian and gay studies reader* (pp. 416–431). Routledge.

Hartman, S. (2008). Venus in two acts. *Small Axe, 12*(2), 1–14. https://doi.org/10.1215/-12-2-1

Hartman, S. (2019). *Wayward lives, beautiful experiments: Intimate histories of riotous Black girls, troublesome women, and queer radicals*. W. W. Norton & Co.

Iton, R. (2008). *In search of the Black fantastic*. Oxford University Press.

Kapadia, R. (2019). *Insurgent aesthetics: Security and the queer life of the forever war*. Duke University Press.

Kelley, R. D. (2003). *Freedom dreams: The Black radical imagination*. Beacon Press.

Muñoz, J. E. (2009). *Cruising utopia: The then and there of queer futurity*. New York University Press.

Nyong'o, T. (2018, August 13). b.O.s. 6.2 / Atlantic is a sea of bones. *ASAP/J*. http://asapjournal.com/b-o-s-6-2-atlantic-is-a-sea-of-bones-tavia-nyongo/

Snorton, C. R. (2017). *Black on both sides: A racial history of trans identity*. University of Minnesota Press.

Spivak, G. (1988). Can the subaltern speak? In C. Nelson & L. Grossberg (Eds.), *Marxism and the interpretation of culture* (pp. 271–313). Macmillan Education.

Tourmaline. (2017). *Atlantic is a sea of bones* [Film]. Vimeo. https://vimeo.com/245608125

Tourmaline. (2018, January 29). *Alternative endings, radical beginnings: Video and artist statement: Tourmaline*. Visual AIDS. https://visualaids.org/blog/aerb-tourmaline-statement

Tourmaline. (2019) *Salacia*. Permanent Collection. Museum of Modern Art, New York, NY.

Tourmaline & Lax, T. J. (2020, June 25). Anything we want to be: Tourmaline's *Salacia*. *MoMA Magazine*. https://www.moma.org/magazine/articles/360

EIGHT

# Democracy Is Interdisciplinary: The Case for Radical Civic Innovation Across Content Areas

*Antero Garcia, Nicole Mirra, and Mark Gomez*

STUDENTS ARE VIVIDLY EXPERIENCING PROFOUND and seismic shifts in the world around them today. From a pandemic that fundamentally altered the lives of students and families in an inconceivable number of ways to radical domestic terror that attempts to dismantle the foundations of American democracy to the overdue necessity of addressing legacies of anti-Blackness coursing through the roots of U.S. democratic systems, students are routinely immersed in turmoil that requires civic imagination and action.

These heavy issues are not topics that are avoidable. They are not subjects that can be corralled solely in the texts and standards of a single discipline. And they are not issues that can wait for exploration in the later years of a student's K–12 schooling career. For every image of domestic terrorism, every message of misogynistic braggadocio shared by a political leader through social media, or every viral video of the murder of Black individuals in this country at the hands of the police, young people are learning profound lessons about the foundations of America, with or without the support and facilitation of schools. Frankly, these may not be the contexts that teachers are equipped or comfortable teaching within. They are, however, the lived experiences that face our students and schools today.

In light of these all-too-obvious facts, we write to urge for a cross-disciplinary focus on the sociopolitical needs of young people in *every* classroom and in *every* discipline. This call requires educators to embrace the discomfort that is otherwise elided in classrooms. Furthermore, we do not call for traditional forms of debate or argumentation that are often at the heart of how educators engage young people in "current events" in classrooms. The world is demanding new civic innovations that both preserve the central human tenets of democracy and rip apart the aspects of settler-colonial history that underscore the operations of an inherently inequitable government. This work has never been as important as it is in this moment when the current generation of young people weathers multiple catastrophes—the uncertain recovery from the pandemic, the confrontation of legacies of anti-Blackness in the United States, the ongoing devastation of the mounting climate crisis, and many others. And yet, despite these multiple, urgent demands for innovation, collaboration, and radical deviation from systemic responses that have only exacerbated these social, political, and environmental ills, schools have not risen to the present moment.

In the remainder of this chapter, we illustrate the kinds of speculative civic pedagogies that must function as the core for *every* subject area. In doing so, we do not turn our back on the allied efforts of justice-focused history educators. Offering an updated and actionable definition of *civics* to meet the historic inequities of the present moment, we briefly illustrate existing civic practices occurring in content areas such as English language arts, math, and science. Furthermore, we recognize that social studies still maintains a fundamental role in shaping youths' civic identities and we offer a nuanced reflection on ways history and social studies teachers must meet the same civic demands we explore in other subject areas. Ultimately, we contend that an intentional centering of civic education must be at the core of how classrooms shape the purposes of disciplinary education in all areas of young people's schooling and describe the specific needs in teacher education to respond to this pressing moment.

## New Civic Imaginations for Freedom

On January 6, 2021, hours after a violent mob of Donald Trump's supporters initiated an armed insurrection in the U.S. Capitol complex, *Education Week* published an article about the "dreaded, real-life lesson" facing educators the next morning. The lede of the article read, "As social studies teachers watched a violent, far-right mob breach the U.S. Capitol in an attempt to stop the formal certification of the election of President-elect Joe Biden, a daunting question loomed: How would they address this with their students tomorrow?" (Will & Sawchuk, 2021, para. 1).

Considering the ubiquitous rhetoric in school mission statements and policy discourse about the civic purpose of education writ large, this article led us to wonder: Why would a question about addressing a mortal threat to American democracy in the classroom be directed toward social studies teachers alone?

The answers to this question are complex; this situation speaks on a macro level to the general silo-ization of disciplinary learning within U.S. public schools and on a micro level to the specific designation of civic learning as the exclusive domain and responsibility of social studies teachers. State standards for civics are universally embedded within their discipline, they are tasked with teaching the stand-alone civics courses that students are often required to take to graduate, and curricula and other programs are overwhelmingly marketed toward them alone.

We suggest that the construction of civics as the sole responsibility of the social studies has two related effects. First, it defines *civics* as a discrete collection of knowledge and skills that can be neatly packaged into a school subject area, and second, it sends a message allowing other teachers to believe that the choices they are making in their classrooms are unrelated to visions of public life. Both of these effects are contrary to what research tells us about how young people come to understand their identities as civic actors and lead to models of teaching and learning that fail to meet their needs and desires for their futures in tumultuous and troubled times.

Most civic standards involve encyclopedic lists of facts and dates that seek to offer students the technical specifications of democratic governance in this country (think three branches of government, how a bill becomes a law, etc.). These are often not placed into any wider coherent narrative about the nature and purpose of democracy itself or its relationship to young people's daily lives (Torney-Purta & Vermeer, 2006). When a narrative is invoked, it is largely a simple one of heart-swelling patriotism and steady incremental liberal progress (National Assessment of Educational Progress Civics Framework, 2014). Situating this collection of facts within the discipline of social studies often leads to civic learning being measured as other forms of disciplinary learning are within neoliberal accountability structures—through indicators of knowledge recall on multiple-choice standardized exams (Shapiro & Brown, 2018; Youniss, 2011).

This approach runs counter to findings from the learning sciences, particularly in the area of sociopolitical learning, that young people develop civic identities by drawing on a wide range of sources across the interrelated ecologies of family, community, institutions, and broader historical and cultural forces (Nasir et al., 2020). These insights suggest that every subject area is and should be cultivated as a site for civic dreaming (Mirra et al., 2018). Narrowing this learning to the domain of social studies obscures opportunities for teachers in other subject areas to consider the messages about democracy that they are transmitting to students through the implicit and explicit choices they make in their classrooms regarding curriculum, instruction, and even classroom culture.

Narrow, procedural civics curricula also seek to downplay the lived experiences of young people—particularly those from minoritized communities—that demonstrate the contradictions and oppressive foundations of U.S. democracy (Banks, 2017). Without opportunities to critically analyze the gap between American rhetoric and reality, youth understandably may ask themselves why they should invest in mainstream civic structures at all (Watts & Flanagan, 2007). In response, more progressive and culturally responsive models have emerged; these include the lived civics approach, which seeks to ground civic learning in community life and foreground issues of power, inequity, and collective action (Cohen et al., 2018). Action civics programs also organize civic learning around inquiry projects that put knowledge to use in service of community uplift (Warren, 2019).

We argue that the next step needed in the reconstitution of civic learning is a shift in focus from incrementally reforming current democratic structures to imagining radically new social futures. Inspired by visionary artists and writers in the Afrofuturist tradition, we propose a paradigm of *speculative civic education* that centers student civic dreams, encourages expansive public storytelling, and rejects the constraints of the status quo (Garcia & Mirra, 2020; Mirra & Garcia, 2020). The work of speculative civics is already occurring as authors write of fantastic alternative worlds outside the realm of white supremacy and as community organizers engage in the "science fiction" of making those worlds our own (Imarisha & brown, 2015). The field of education now needs to transform by expanding what civic education can be and what it can look like across content areas.

### *Pedagogies of Speculative Civic Education*

In calling for a speculative approach to civic learning that builds expansively with young people, we recognize that the task at hand requires new kinds of pedagogical skills and supports that have, too often, been disregarded in teacher education and professional development programs. While we explore later in this chapter the possibilities for transforming the ways that teacher learning can responsibly accommodate the overdue needs of our young people's civic desires, we want to emphasize that the approach to engaging in this work builds on Au's (2021) articulation of a "pedagogy of insurgency" that names multidimensional aspects of sustaining speculative civic learning. Like Au's description, we see fundamental aspects of this work, including allyship and solidarity, intentionally elevate the task of collective civic learning in schools to an ongoing activity that is aligned with social movements and communities entrenched in work toward liberation. The contrasts between these urgent civic needs in classrooms and the traditional forms of civic instruction that students receive are stark.

As we continue to refer to the work in this chapter as civic instruction, we recognize that we have been getting more uncomfortable with the term *civics* in light of escalating threats to the lives and freedoms of historically marginalized communities in the United States.

As a label, the way that civics is bandied in schools today implies a passive integration of young people into the structures of democratic governance that persist today. The general expectations for civic learning in schools is a functional understanding of how a (broken) democracy is supposed to work historically. This is a dangerously low bar and the threshold for civics that ensure the safety of our polity and that can inspire young people are absolutely possible.

Civics is not just about transforming sociopolitical engagement at national and state levels. The vision we offer here centers individual and collective agency for influencing and changing one's place in society. For our students, this might be within their immediate family, the local community in which they reside, and even online communities dispersed across digital networks. All these are just as valid spaces that we must ensure young people are able to thrive and guide through civic thought, deliberation, and action. A civic education that is boiled down to calling a legislator or writing a letter to a local media source is the stripping of civic imagination from the expectations of youth capabilities.

Speculative civic instruction and learning offer the potential for abetting movements for freedom and abolition. Too, while such learning must intentionally be future-facing in terms of outcomes, this work is rooted in the present moment and the challenges we face through historical inequities; it is our murky and unjust past that drives us to imagine brighter futures. Simply stating one's commitment to justice-driven civic education is not enough in classrooms. We are under no illusions that, every day, well-intentioned teachers, administrators, and students may reify settler-colonialism anti-Blackness in classrooms, causing harm through efforts to move forward traditional civic lessons. As we describe in the remainder of this chapter, intentionally shaping a classroom experience for speculative civic dreaming and innovation is not only possible in every subject area but *always* necessary as well.

## Toward Speculative Civics in All Disciplines

As the discipline through which students interrogate history, encounter specific content knowledge about the functions of government, and that typically explores "current events," the burden of civic education has fallen entirely on the shoulders of history and social studies educators. This is unacceptable. As recent crises have revealed for some and reminded others of the important civic work that educators are uniquely situated to do, we hear the calls for a renewed emphasis on the long-standing civic mission of schools. However, contrary to the assumption that civics is the domain of history and social studies teachers (and is, indeed, still the title of some high school courses students may encounter), we recognize that every teacher is a civics teacher. Whether the lessons teachers choose to enact intentionally guide students toward exuding their agency in specific ways or not, students are learning lessons about how to persist in community with one another and about the power structures as funneled through the lens of disciplinary learning. In this way, a kind of civic education is already happening in every classroom, just not necessarily one that sparks hope, rebellion, direct action in the name of justice.

Through broad applications of rote, abstract knowledge and through hewing to standards to position students as docile and passive (e.g., Garcia & Mirra, 2019), students are recognizing disciplinary learning as divorced from meaningful aspects of their civic lives. This is a profound and lasting civic lesson that occurs daily. And while this unintended set of civic lessons does little to ignite passion, activism, and solidarity in students, it is also a malleable curriculum. Just as the Common Core Standards (National Governors Association Center for Best Practices, Council of Chief State School Officers,

2010) prescribed the role of literacy instruction as a base expectation in every discipline, we can ask no less of the expectations of civic learning across content areas.

As a bit of clarification, we are not calling for history and social studies teachers to abscond their responsibilities teaching toward transformative and speculative civics; in the following, we detail the ways this disciplinary space necessarily anchors aspects of civic learning alongside the work of other educators. Instead, we contend that it is the fundamental purpose of *every* teacher to engage in the task of sustaining powerful youth civic commitments to freedom. Additionally, these commitments spread across disciplinary axes that sharpen the spokes of democratic action.

We do not seek to offer definitive explanations of what constitutes "good" civic learning in each subject area. Instead, we offer a few examples of already-existing civic learning practices that are occurring in different subject areas. These reemphasize the point that civics learning is *already* transpiring across every subject area and act as encouragement for teachers to customize and shape their civic instruction—like all other content in their classrooms—around the knowledge of their students and local contexts.

### *English Language Arts*

The central commitments of English language arts (ELA) instruction are civic in nature. Communicating *for* particular purposes and *to* intended audiences is fundamentally about the incorporation of individuals into the actions and ideas of a broader polity. The ways we shape classroom dialogue, writing, and engagement with multimodal texts must reflect considerations of other people, social outcomes, and the power that our ideas and expressions have over others. This framing may deviate from a more prescribed understanding of disciplinary literacy, as reflected in broad standards and assessments, which focus on individual acquisition of textual mastery.

In work with high school teachers, extracurricular debate organizations, and informal communities, the tools of ELA classrooms can regularly engage in the transformative work of allowing young people's imaginations spark action and further justice movements and acts of solidarity (e.g., Garcia, 2017; Mirra & Debate Liberation League, 2020; Mirra & Garcia, 2020). Further, we believe that the unique emphasis on literature in ELA classrooms can also function as a powerful civic opportunity to confront the "windows, mirrors, and sliding glass doors" that allow young people to see themselves in the world around them (Sims Bishop, 1990). Centering stories and storytelling, ELA can center civic imagination as the foundation of what this subject focuses on. As a sister discipline with social studies as part of the humanities that students encounter in classrooms, it is unsurprising that the basic roots of ELA may coalesce smoothly with notions of civic dreaming. Likewise, long histories of the arts mediating, responding to, and instigating social change means that such classes must remain core courses offered in schools. However, such base assumptions about the role of *every* class as a site of civic learning extends to all subjects, as we note in our turn to examine the civic possibilities in math and science.

*Math*

We draw inspiration for the necessary ways that math functions as a site for justice and engagement from Robert Moses's work establishing the Algebra Project (Moses & Cobb, 2001). Focused on "establishing math literacy for freedom and citizenship" (Moses & Cobb, 2001, p. 13), the Algebra Project illustrates the ways that numeracy is tied to civic learning outcomes as well as to parallel movements ensuring that access to such powerful learning must be provided to all students, particularly Black youth in America. In our own enactment of the Algebra Project in community-based school design (Garcia et al., 2018), Moses's vision led to community asset mapping and measurement for students while simultaneously driving collaboration and solidarity with faculty across all disciplines. Importantly, this civics-driven approach to math reframes for many the purpose of math classrooms and the role of teachers as allies; this is one of the most profound contributions of the Algebra Project writ large: When educators see their discipline as a crucible through which to craft alloyed civic enthusiasm and action, engagement with the subject matter and academic outcomes can follow along naturally.

*Science*

Perhaps as representative of this natural outpouring of civic enthusiasm into disciplinary knowledge, recent explorations of the discourse and engagement around climate change in classrooms speak to how politicized yet urgent topics demand youth imagination. In one study, Zummo et al. (2020) focused on a set of youth writing advocating (from multiple ideological perspectives) for legislative action related to climate change. Tellingly, students appealing to the urgent need and building off popular viral images related to climate change like polar bears and the Great Barrier Reef demonstrated keen proficiency with the skills of scientific reasoning and content knowledge. Being able to communicate civic ideas empathetically and persuasively meant understanding and articulating complex disciplinary knowledge. As an additional point here, these communicative skills loop back to the possibilities for interdisciplinary and collaborative approaches *across* disciplines when developing civic action.

There are spillover effects from ensuring a dispersed and sustained focus on youth civic learning in every class. As the distribution of civic instruction falls equitably on the shoulders of all disciplines that students encounter, the role of social studies educators in young peoples' civic learning is pulled into sharper clarity. The grain of transformative civic learning can be more easily interpreted from the chaff of other kinds of disciplinary responsibilities in civics and so our return to social studies classrooms functions as a clarion call for what may not always be centered in teachers' curricular designs.

### *Reevaluating the Role and Responsibilities of Social Studies*

In the fields of history and social sciences, there is a logic that attempts to assign responsibility for civic instruction squarely within the realm of these disciplines. On the surface, this may seem to make sense. Where else do students get to spend an entire semester focusing their learning on everything there is to know about the complicated inner workings of government in all sectors of our lives? However, to many, the sarcastic nature in posing this question is not registered, because so many of us were only explicitly taught civics in this manner. There has been much written about the folly of thinking that relegates any real-time or strategic effort about effectively engaging students in what most people call "civic" learning to the domain of a government class in the final year of one's public education. But what about history and the social sciences affords the opportunity to expand our civic education infrastructure to center student agency through transformational learning in ways that other disciplines cannot? Where can history and social studies educators take the lead in reframing the discussion around powerful civic learning in all classrooms?

One might begin with an examination of what makes the history classroom different from the disciplines discussed earlier. While there is a recognition that historical literacy (the reading of the past and consequently the thinking about it) departs significantly from the kind of analytic reading taught in other disciplines (Wineburg, 2001), one of the main advantages history offers is the sheer volume of stories available in the historical record. Every day there are a plethora of new narratives generated by individuals engaged in the work of transforming and illuminating parts of the world through the multitude of activities that can be considered civics. This seemingly advantageous work becomes an Achilles' heel for many history teachers, however. The pressure to select which narratives to include soon becomes an overwhelming task, resulting in a return to the "tyranny of coverage" (Loewen, 2009), prompting many teachers to make the decision to default to the official, state-sanctioned and -published history of textbooks. The consequences of this have been explored thoroughly yet remain a real criticism of the teaching of history. There are opportunities for teachers to incorporate critical methodologies that help decenter the dominant narrative of whiteness within history classrooms. Ethnic Studies as a movement and a field has been a rich example of what can be done with students when a teacher explicitly decides to have them challenge the false notion of a singular official history that progresses slowly and in a linear fashion. Including more of everyone's stories is a transformative practice that history teachers can broadly embrace.

A stance for speculative civic learning can be built through examining the role that people play in social movements and how society and its institutions work in relation to individuals. We applaud how teachers pair a story of steady progress with narratives of people or groups that organized and fought for forward movement. The action of "civics" embedded in these movements is rarely explored in the manner in which other histories are learned about. More often than not, students learn about others' civic attributes and actions by reading the passages or chapters in the textbook and perhaps extending this distilled knowledge into a presentation or "project." Students are not usually afforded opportunities to engage with ephemera or archival sources (let alone the firsthand experiences of people who were there and are still alive to talk about it) that complicate the narratives, perspectives, and practices of civics. Furthermore, teaching about movements in certain ways risks sending our students the message that civics only happens in these watershed moments of historical significance, again restricting the aperture of our lens to include far less of what should be defined as civics. Rather than recycling these practices, we seek the casting forward of speculative possibilities that enrich history as a site of future dreaming informed by myriad histories and sources.

History may be unique in its potential to engage students with past movements for social justice and progress that offer blueprints for building students' civic schema. However, the interdisciplinary nature of the social sciences creates powerful opportunities for a special type of critical triangulation of the very fabric of our political, economic, social, and cultural structures. Exploring race, for instance, as W.E.B. Du Bois did through a sociological lens, students can not only learn from the questions and solutions that Du Bois and others in his time offered but also take this lens and begin to apply it to their lived experiences. Students, with the guidance and facilitation of teachers trained in this type of deep pedagogy, can utilize the frameworks and methodologies of sociology to better understand how race plays out in their schools and communities. They can more aptly identify the problems they have always seen through lived experience and better name them, utilizing disciplinary tools (interviews, surveys, etc.) to speak back to a reality that they wish to shape in a different way by speculating on solutions and unrealized designs fashioned more in the image of equality and justice. This is an imaginative activity that builds off understanding present conditions and the factors that brought them forth; from these origins, students can align themselves with activist movements and ongoing efforts of organizing for change in their own communities. In essence, these disciplinary tools are used not for the labeling of the present but as a means of assessing sites and possibilities for change in not-yet-imagined futures. Wondering, dreaming, and praxis-driven action must be layered atop these fundamental social studies activities.

Similarly, students can become critical geographers, utilizing cartographic practices to map out race, power, and inequity in the physical spaces they frequent. Juxtaposed with an exploration of the history of racial redlining in housing and lending policies, a much more nuanced and critical understanding of racial segregation and power is possible. Cultivating more critical geospatial awareness can lead to a more empowered and positive identification of self and community.

Likewise, using an economic lens to analyze not only past but present-day lending practices for communities of color can bring students back full circle to the histories and geographies of racially contested spaces in real time as students learn to name the push out practices of gentrification and newer iterations of red- or bluelining, referring to the effect climate change is having on flood zones. This could lead them back to a practice of speculation that puts them directly in the process of ideating and fighting for substantive policy changes that reinforces the most important civics lesson: that young people have agency. That much history has shown us time and time again.

What should a social studies teacher do when students pose questions about violence and extremism in our nation? This question requires social studies teachers to reevaluate where civic learning opportunities emerge within their current disciplinary focus. To explore the psychology of radicalization and sociological processes that unfold in a media landscape dominated by corporations motivated by profit might be just as prudent as comparing the events of 1812 to 2021. In helping students leverage more of the tools of history and the social sciences, teachers in these subject areas can help students better understand seemingly inconceivable events that they are living through now. Not only by venturing to the past to help connect and contextualize moments like the insurrection of our nation's capital on January 6, 2021, but by encouraging our students to expand their curiosity to incorporate a multitude of fields in helping them make sense of dissonance and discord.

As we have argued, civics is a speculative and interdisciplinary venture that, when done effectively, incorporates every discipline, whether from the humanities, social, physical, or mathematical sciences. All of these could and should be enlisted in the service of empowering youth to engage in spaces where they are welcomed and disrupt systems where they are not. Ultimately, however, it is not the inherent nature of these disciplines that offers the best case for civics, but the inherent curiosity of the human condition that is the best starting point for effective civic education. Classrooms and teachers that have a practice that not only invites but encourages the development of cross-disciplinary inquiry are the ones ripe for a more powerful civic engagement. Classrooms that continue to operate in an orientation of putting subject matter before what matters to students will further erode possibilities of educating an informed and engaged public, a truly perilous proposition in the light of this particular day.

## Speculative Civics as Professional Development

Looking across the different disciplinary approaches to civic instruction, it is clear that there are some (and sometimes abundant) examples of powerful learning happening for every age group and across every disciplinary area. However, in illustrating the needs for civic learning in this chapter, we have curated piecemeal examples to suggest pathways for instruction and rationales for engagement in this topic across students' K–12 schooling experiences. These are intentionally not definitive. We do not presume a minimum or specific set of limited civic instructions in classrooms but rather voice the need for fundamental practices of trust and mutuality for teachers and students to engage in local contexts of action and activism. In order to sustain a form of civic learning that undergirds each class students take requires a fundamental shift in how teachers are prepared and the kinds of professional development opportunities they are offered.

In discussing how Ethnic Studies has prepared and guided some social studies teachers earlier, it is clear that critical and liberatory civics instruction across subject areas requires reframing how disciplinary and pedagogical content knowledge are taught in every subject. If freedom is not the heart of why students are entering our classrooms, we are selling them a false promise on the possibilities of education in a time that needs direct action. As with other chapters in this volume, we recognize that such transformational approaches require clearly vocalized commitments to justice that mean refusing to consider our classrooms as neutral spaces with objective perspectives on the world and our human roles within it. Too much damage has been done, in every subject, through providing air to *both sides* of issues, false equivalencies that require students to diminish the humanity of themselves and others in order to preserve the civil over the civic. To shift beyond this is to ask teachers to love themselves and their students fully and to commit to that love *through* the subjects that we teach. Within teacher education, such work demands embedding civics as a core practice of what we prepare every teacher to engage in and sustain in classrooms.

Just as disciplinary literacy meant reading like the experts and professionals in a given field (Shanahan & Shanahan, 2008), doing civics through the lens of each class must be interrogated and can help invigorate the learning happening. Reframing what stories are told in each subject area and what tensions exist in these fields allows students to see themselves as part of thriving communities, some of which maintain roots in anti-Black and anti-Indigenous histories that must be interrogated and confronted. Ethnic Studies, as we noted earlier, is one disciplinary site that has sometimes taken up the kinds of critical questioning necessary for speculative progress. However, rather than rest on the laurels of building toward critical cognizance of the present, speculative civic learning—in ethnic studies and *all* content areas—must cast a gaze toward the uncertain and always lingering horizon of tomorrow. There is civic work, then, to be done *within* each discipline and *through* each discipline. Furthermore, the synergies that exist across each field make these different classes feel less like silos and more like affinity spaces that are all interlinked to different components of a wholly lived life committed to justice and freedom. If every class feels actionable, then school becomes invigorated around a collective civic purpose that builds on the passions of the students that we serve.

Admittedly, there are many teachers that may feel discomfort with the vision of civic education proposed here. This may not be what most teachers signed up for when they decided to become teachers; generations of passivity have rendered our schools as lacking in broad models of the kinds of civic change that we propose here and that are, frankly, overdue considering the fractured state of discourse and increasing forms of harm that are experienced today. We know that new possibilities spring eternal from the imaginations of young people; just because adults may not have myriad school-sanctioned examples of how to nurture these ideas yet does not mean that we can eschew this task. We must better integrate the hopeful with the practical in schools today. This is hard work and we return to the framing words of Robert Moses (2009) describing liberatory work like the Algebra Project. As he notes, invoking the title of this volume, "in this country, you have to earn your insurgency. You have to capture the imagination of the people in the federal government who actually want to close the gap between our espoused ideals and the practices that we tolerate" (Moses, 2009, p. 39). Further evoking this vision, we echo Moses's (2009) sentiments to those educators uncertain about the ways to tear up the docile civic lessons implicitly schooled into the lives of students: "Demanding educational rights requires courage in the face of terror" (p. 39).

## Freedom as the Core of Teacher Responsibilities

The foundations of every core subject area students encounter in their K–12 experience as well as the very structures of schools have been built from historically white perspectives and framed to instill docile passivity in the students that are schooled (e.g., Garcia & Mirra, 2019). Teachers, willingly or not, are complicit in the damage that schools sustain every day. And while harm is done in schools continually, teachers can begin to work toward repairing and healing the communities we serve and are a part of. This is a kind of civic action that we must bear as professionals in a field largely dictated by federal and statewide regulations. The subversive heart we beat within the settler-colonial machine of schooling pulses with life and possibility as we work toward freedom alongside the students in every classroom (e.g., la paperson, 2017).

The work of confronting U.S. legacies of anti-Blackness, of challenging the forms of racism and disinformation that have allowed the far right to flourish, of addressing climate crises, and of the myriad other urgent demands in classrooms must happen in each subject area students encounter, and it must happen persistently. The gravitational pull of schools back toward a normative center must be actively resisted—this is a center that has allowed domestic terrorism and insurrection to occur. A speculative civic approach to schooling requires a collaborative effort to imagine a new center of gravity that does not pull us toward legacies of harm. Rather, recognizing the constellations of freer possibilities that exist in the minds of students and teachers, we must re-center to whom and for what our civic efforts coalesce.

## References

Au, W. (2021). A pedagogy of insurgency: Teaching and organizing for radical racial justice in our schools. *Educational Studies, 57*(2), 1–15. https://doi.org/10.1080/00131946.2021.1878181

Banks, J. (2017). Failed citizenship and transformative civic education. *Educational Researcher, 46*(7), 366–377. https://doi.org/10.3102/0013189X17726741

Cohen, C., Kahne, J., & Marshall, J. (2018). *Let's go there: Race, ethnicity and a lived civics approach to civics education*. GenForward at the University of Chicago.

Garcia, A. (2017). *Good reception: Teens, teachers, and mobile media in a Los Angeles high school.* MIT Press.

Garcia, A., Gomez, M., & Briggs, K. R. (2018). Schools for community action: Public school design as a revolutionary act. In E. Mendoza, B. Kirshner, & K. D. Gutiérrez (Eds.), *Power, equity, and (re)design* (pp. 131–147). Information Age.

Garcia, A., & Mirra, N. (2019). "Signifying nothing": Identifying conceptions of youth civic identity in the English Language Arts Common Core State Standards and the National Assessment of Educational Progress' Reading framework. *Berkeley Review of Education, 8*(2), 195–223. https://doi.org/10.5070/B88235831

Garcia, A., & Mirra, N. (2020). Writing toward justice: Youth speculative civic literacies in online policy discourse. *Urban Education*. Advanced online publication. https://doi.org/10.1177/0042085920953881

Imarisha, W., & brown, a. (Eds.). (2015). *Octavia's brood: Science fiction stories from social justice movements*. AK Press.

la paperson. (2017). *A third university is possible*. University of Minnesota Press.

Loewen, J. W. (2009). *Teaching what really happened: How to avoid the tyranny of textbooks and get students excited about doing history*. Teachers College Press.

Mirra, N., Coffey, J., & Englander, A. (2018). Warrior scholars and bridge builders: Civic dreaming in ELA classes. *Journal of Literacy Research, 50*(4), 423–445. https://doi.org/10.1177/1086296X18784335

Mirra, N., & Garcia, A. (2020). I hesitate but I do have hope: Youth speculative civic literacies in troubled times. *Harvard Educational Review, 90*(2), 295–321. https://doi.org/10.17763/1943-5045-90.2.295

Mirra, N., & Debate Liberation League. (2020). Without borders: Youth debaters reimagining the nature and purpose of public dialogue. *English Teaching: Practice & Critique, 19*(3), 253–267. https://doi.org/10.1108/ETPC-07-2019-0102

Moses, R. (2009). An earned insurgency: Quality education as a constitutional right. *Harvard Educational Review, 79*(2), 370–381. https://doi.org/10.1763/haer.79.2.937m754251521231

Moses, R. P., & Cobb, C. E. (2002). *Radical equations: Civil rights from Mississippi to the Algebra Project*. Beacon Press.

Nasir, N., Lee, C., Pea, R., & McKinney de Royston, M. (Eds.). (2020). *Handbook of the cultural foundations of learning*. Routledge.

National Governors Association Center for Best Practices, Council of Chief State School Officers. (2010). *Common Core State Standards for English language arts and literacy in history/social studies, science, and technical subjects*. Washington, DC: National Governors Association Center for Best Practices, Council of Chief State School Officers.

Shanahan, T., & Shanahan, C. (2008). Teaching disciplinary literacy to adolescents: Rethinking content area literacy. *Harvard Education Review, 78*, 40–59. https://doi.org/10.17763/haer/78.1.v62444321p602101

Shapiro, S., & Brown, C. (2018). *The state of civics education*. Center for American Progress.

Sims Bishop, R. (1990). Mirrors, windows, and sliding glass doors. *Perspectives, 1*(3), ix–xi.

Torney-Purta, J., & Vermeer, S. (2006). *Developing citizenship competencies from kindergarten through Grade 12: A background paper for policymakers and educators*. Education Commission of the States.

Warren, S. (2019). *Generation citizen: The power of youth in our politics.* Counterpoint.

Watts, R., & Flanagan, C. (2007). Pushing the envelope on civic engagement: A developmental and liberation psychology perspective. *Journal of Community Psychology, 35*, 779–792. https://doi.org/10.1002/jcop.20178

Will, M., & Sawchuk, S. (2021, January 6). Insurgency at the U.S. Capitol: A dreaded, real-life lesson facing teachers. *Education Week.* https://www.edweek.org/teaching-learning/insurgency-at-the-u-s-capitol-a-dreaded-real-life-lesson-facing-teachers/2021/01

Wineburg, S. S. (2001). *Historical thinking and other unnatural acts: Charting the future of teaching the past.* Temple University Press.

Youniss, J. (2011). Civic education: What schools can do to encourage civic identity and action. *Applied Developmental Science, 15*(2), 98–103. https://doi.org/10.1080/10888691.2011.560814

Zummo, L., Gargroetzi, E. & Garcia, A. (2020). Youth voice on climate change: Using factor analysis to understand the intersection of science, politics, and emotion. *Environmental Education Research, 26*(8), 1207–1226. https://doi.org/10.1080/13504622.2020.1771288

NINE

# Cultural Bombs and Dangerous Classes: Social Studies Education as State Apparatus in the War on Terror

*Jennice McCafferty-Wright*

CLASS AND CAPITALISM POSITION EVERY social studies teacher, student, and scholar within structures of power that are global. As critical scholars of social studies education have challenged the systems and policies that produce exploitation in our communities, our broader field has been nearsighted with its critical gaze. We cannot ignore the ways that we are materially connected to global communities of struggle. As we resist oppressive domestic policies through our research, our discipline must also expand our approach to account for global systems of power and exploitation and the state-sponsored foreign policies that support them. In this critical foreign policy analysis, I examine annual reports to Congress from the U.S. Bureau of Counterterrorism and Countering Violent Extremism (CT-CVE). I consider class and capitalism in the ways social studies education is leveraged, even weaponized, in foreign policy and the scope and ends to which social studies education operates as an apparatus of state in post-9/11 counterterrorism initiatives for youths outside of the United States. I argue that since 9/11, classrooms, curricula, and instruction for non-elite children and youths have been designated as theaters of war and that the United States tactically uses social studies education as cultural bombs against non-elite and Muslim youths within the War on Terror. Finally, I call on education scholars to take up "the weapon of theory" so that we can dismantle the cultural bombs used against non-elite youths around the world who are engaged in a broader global class struggle.

## Education as an Apparatus of the State and Theater of War

Louis Althusser (1970/2006) wrote of education being one of the most influential ideological state apparatuses. According to Althusser, ideological state apparatuses are social institutions such as schools, churches, and families. Unlike repressive state apparatuses, ideological state apparatuses such as schools fall within civil society but support the state's power through social control rather than coercion. However, in the context of programs implemented by a state with military occupation, colonization, or other hegemonic behavior, it might also be argued that features of the educational programs found in U.S. counterterrorism reports fall as much within Althusser's repressive state apparatuses as they do ideological state apparatuses. Coercion and repression through education can be found throughout colonial and imperial projects. For example, the history of North America's colonization bears witness to the use of education as a hegemonic and exploitative weapon against Indigenous cultures and toward the interests of the state (Miller, 1996; Razack, 2015; Reyhner & Eder, 2015; Schissel & Wotherspoon, 2003). Supporting the notion that education operates as an apparatus of state (ideological or repressive), this critical policy analysis demonstrates that the Bureau of CT-CVE uses U.S.-centric social studies education as a tactical strategy in its military theaters and among populations considered to pose a threat to U.S. interests.

When approaching education within federal counterterrorism policies and programs, I began to think of classrooms as a *theater of war*—not just a war of ideas but, in many cases, physically within places facing armed conflict or where the United States has military interests in the War on Terror. A *theater of war* is an "area that is or may become involved directly in war operations" (Merriam-Webster, 2017). Just as the Pacific Theater of World War II engaged naval aircraft and marine infantry units, the classroom theater of the War on Terror engages curricula and educators through public diplomacy programs. Unlike traditional diplomacy, which advances national interests through relationships between heads of state and their officials, the United States and other countries use *public* diplomacy to pursue national interests by influencing and shaping public opinion and behavior in foreign nations. Public diplomacy programs are developed in a variety of ways to respond to specific foreign policy interests and have been initiated by legislative bodies, federal agencies, and consulates. It is important to note that not all public diplomacy programs weaponize education. Some, such as the Fulbright Teachers for Global Classrooms program, the Stevens Initiative, and the British Council's Connecting Classrooms program, are designed to grow cultural literacies, disrupt dangerous narratives about "the other," and teach for intercultural cooperation and global understanding through meaningful projects. As an educator, I have personally benefited from some of these programs, and I have recommended them to others. This analysis focuses on the most problematic, widespread, and hegemonic education initiatives and narratives described in counterterrorism reports.

## Dangerous Classes

The post-9/11 *Country Reports on Terrorism* situate aggrieved youths, especially non-elite Muslim youths as a threat, both to the present and the future. This depiction of youths calls to mind historic examples of similarly situated *dangerous classes*. The concept of "the dangerous classes" was used heavily in 19th-century literature and social theory as poverty concentrated in industrial centers. The dangerous classes or *lumpenproletariat*, as used by Marx and Engels, were often characterized by poverty, crime, immigration, and immorality (Bussard, 2012; Morris, 1994; Standing, 2011/2016; Wacquant, 1996). This common theme of the dangerous classes reverberates throughout the post-9/11 *Country Reports on Terrorism* so that, like the street youths of Charles Dickens and Victor Hugo, the dangerous classes of underprivileged Muslim youths become potential victims to the "conveyor belt" of terrorism and threats to the state. Examples from struggles against imperialism and colonialism in Africa shed light on how social class operates in resisting economic and cultural domination from foreign state actors. Amilcar Cabral (1973/1994), having experienced Guinea-Bissau's war for national liberation against the Portuguese, writes that he encouraged resistance leaders' immersion into the non-elite classes of their culture to strengthen their resistance. For Cabral (1973/1994), in addition to armed resistance, the anti-colonial struggle is also a battle with and for one's culture for "to take up arms to dominate a people is, above all, to take up arms to destroy, or at least to neutralize, to paralyze, its cultural life" (p. 53). Cabral saw that acquiring cultural attributes of the colonizer confers social privileges on the assimilated and that the assimilated become the *petite bourgeoisie*. Cabral describes this as happening with Indigenous elites, leaving non-elite Indigenous peoples less affected. He also observed that the greater the cultural differences between the oppressed and the oppressor, the greater the possibility of successful resistance because it is easier to bring assimilated peoples into a system of domination and control. Essentially, Indigenous culture helps people resist foreign domination, and domination can only be sustained by repressing Indigenous culture.

Franz Fanon also accounts for social class and resistance to foreign powers. In *The Wretched of the Earth* (1963/2004), he discusses national consciousness and national culture, paying special attention to how they intersect with social class in Algeria's War of National Liberation. For example, he reworks Marx's term *lumpenproletariat* to include not just the criminal class (as described by Marx) but also the peasantry who "solemnly sets about cleansing and purifying the local face of the nation" from imperial cultural corruption (Fanon, 1963/2004, p. 83). For Fanon, because the peasantry falls so far outside of the ruling class's ideological power, they are more likely to launch a successful insurgency. Cabral's and Fanon's observations help us connect historic mechanisms of imperialism and colonization to contemporary U.S. education as an apparatus of state. They help us consider the ways exploitation reverberates from colonization to present times and how culture operates as resistance.

## Cultural Bombs

Framing education as a weapon is hardly a new phenomenon (Loewen, 2009; von Feigenblatt et al., 2010). Regarding post-apartheid futures, Nelson Mandela (2003) stated that "education is the most powerful weapon which you can use to change the world" (para. 24). However, I amended Mandela's words with "for better or worse" because education has indeed been used to change the world with its capacity to systematically create and sustain the compliance and exploitation of large populations of people within the historical contexts of imperialism, colonialism, and industrialization, as well as the contemporary contexts of late capitalism (Chibber, 2013) and the growing global precariat (Standing, 2011/2016). When considering the War on Terror, education should still be regarded as the most powerful weapon which can be used to change the world.

Supporting Fanon's (1963/2004) and Cabral's (1973/1994) observations, Kenyan author Ngũgĩ wa Thiong'o (1986/2003) reiterates this point, writing that "economic and political control can never be complete or effective without mental control. To control a people's culture is to control their tools of self-definition in relationship to others" (p. 16). Wa Thiong'o (1986/2003) writes that controlling relationships to foreign powers is accomplished daily in classrooms by deploying education as a "cultural bomb" (p. 3). Through programs described in annual reports from the CT-CVE, education operates as a *cultural bomb* by shifting how non-elite youths define themselves in relation to the United States. The cultural bomb as wa Thiong'o describes it *works* when students outside of the United States, whose interests might even be counter to U.S. interests, begin to identify with it.

## Annual Reports From the CT-CVE

The U.S. Bureau of CT-CVE works under a broad mission which includes developing and implementing "counterterrorism strategies, policies, and operations" and overseeing "programs to counter violent extremism, strengthen homeland security, and build the capacity of partner nations to deal effectively with terrorism" (CT-CVE, 2017). I examined all of the bureau's annual reports that have occurred since the launch of the U.S. War on Terror. They were produced by leadership from the Bush, Obama, and Trump administrations. While education can be found throughout the reports, the chapters on Terrorist Safe Havens include the most, with subsections such as "Struggle of Ideas in the Islamic World," "Outreach through Foreign Broadcast Media," and "Basic Education in Muslim Countries." The content of the reports, although used to support the direction of U.S. foreign policy in the years after declaring the War on Terror, contain descriptions of market-based reforms, educational initiatives such as *Sesame Street*, and descriptions of bombings and grisly beheadings. This reminds us that the topic of this chapter falls within especially sinister territory for education research—that classrooms, curricula, and instruction have been designated as theaters of war within the War on Terror.

## Entering the Theater of the Classroom

Focusing on the strategic use of education within the War on Terror and the power differentials between the government of the United States of America and the children of other nations situates my work within the intellectual landscape of critical policy analysis identified by Diem et al. (2014). It interrogates the symbolism and rhetoric surrounding education policy (Edelman,

1971; Fischer, 2003; Moses & Gair, 2004; Winton, 2013), how these programs evolve to support the dominant culture (Brewer, 2014; Gale, 2001; Scheurich, 1994), and how policies work toward the internalization of dominant cultures (Anderson, 1989; Bourdieu, 1991; Gillborn, 2005; McLaren & Giarelli, 1995).

I approach these reports through critical hermeneutic interpretation and analysis. This encompasses a broad range of interpretive processes "to understand the historical and social ways that power operates to shape meaning and its lived consequences" (Kincheloe, 2004, p. 11). Furthermore, critical hermeneutics designates "an understanding of how power inscribes the word and the world" (Kincheloe, 2004, p. 82). Thus, I seek to draw connections between my data, the cultures that produced it, and the breathing human beings connected to it. Additionally, the ethnographic research I conducted while reading many of the counterterrorism reports profoundly enhanced my analysis of them. I lived in Morocco for a year while working with teachers and youths who participated in the English Access Microscholarship Program, one of the most celebrated education programs found in the reports, and I continue to return for other projects. Essentially, I examined my own country's foreign policy documents in the company of people deeply impacted by them. Negotiating this dynamic requires acknowledging that I, as a white U.S. citizen, have benefited from U.S.-centric education in public diplomacy and my fields' decades-long disregard for social studies in foreign policy initiatives. My research now requires a sustained commitment to relationships in which I continue to learn with and from communities of educators and students brought into public diplomacy programs, and I remain engaged with several agencies and organizations implementing them.

I approached the reports using concepts such as education as an apparatus of state and theater of war, the dangerous classes as a threat to dominant states, and weaponizing education via cultural bombs. While reading, I also considered history, culture, and capital with the assumption that these reports are both products and producers of power.

## Cultural Bombs for Dangerous Classes

Data from the *Patterns of Global Terrorism* and *Country Reports on Terrorism* annual reports demonstrate that the phenomenon of education within the War on Terror has grown by leaps and bounds over the past two decades. I focus on two broad themes that illustrate the direction, scope, and intent of this growth: (1) the War on Terror weaponizes social studies education to shift students' cultural values and affinity toward the United States, and (2) the War on Terror situates youths, especially Muslim youths from non-elite backgrounds, as a dangerous class of people, a threat to future U.S. interests, and thus a target within a war of ideas.

### *Weaponizing Social Studies Education to Shift Cultural Values*

Within the *Country Reports on Terrorism*, classrooms, curricula, and instruction are all subject to *weaponizing*. The earliest reports to appear after 9/11 refer to education primarily as a threat, especially within foreign, religious schools. For example, the first post-9/11 report notes Pakistan's policy to crack down severely on madrassas—"In December President Pervez Musharraf announced to the Government a proposal to bring Pakistan's madrassas (religious schools)—some of which have served as breeding grounds for extremists—into the mainstream educational system" (Office of the Coordinator for Counterterrorism [S/CT], 2002, p. 12). Attention to the domestic education policies of countries in the Middle East, North Africa, and beyond spread in subsequent years. Following a similar pattern, the Yemeni government "integrated formerly autonomous private religious schools—many of which were propagating extremism—into the national educational system and tightened requirements for visiting foreign students" (S/CT, 2003, p. 63). However, within three years after 9/11, reports began to include education, especially U.S.-centric social studies education, as public diplomacy in counterterrorism strategy.

Reports written after 2004 indicate significant efforts by government programs to influence public behavior through education initiatives. For example, in East Africa, "to counter extremist influence and diminish the conditions terrorists seek to exploit for safe haven and recruitment," a program operates to provide "teacher education in disadvantaged Muslim communities" (S/CT, 2005, p. 29). This early example points to concerns that will later appear throughout education programs—disadvantaged or non-elite populations and Muslim communities.

By 2004, there are indications that the success of an English-language program that began in Casablanca in 2003 (the English Access Microscholarship

Program) has strongly influenced the direction of public diplomacy strategies for youths—"Media and information outreach and English language teaching are expanding, both to put forward a more accurate picture of the United States and its values, and to serve as a counterweight to Islamist-controlled media outlets" (S/CT, 2005, p. 29). In 2008, as the program expands beyond Morocco and into other Muslim-majority countries, the *Country Reports on Terrorism* describes the United States' "increased focus on education in predominantly Muslim countries and those with significant Muslim populations" (S/CT, 2009, p. 264). The dual appearance of both concerns for the impact of domestic education in contributing to violent extremism and the concerted effort to expand education programs through public diplomacy demonstrates that the United States, in agreement with Mandela, reaffirms education as a "powerful weapon which you can use to change the world" *for better or worse.*

**Social studies education.** Education in public diplomacy can feature a variety of subjects such as science, technology, and the performing arts. One popular program in North Africa even sends kids to space camp. However, one subject in particular, social studies, is tactically used as a cultural bomb. According to the National Council for the Social Studies (NCSS), "social studies is the integrated study of the social sciences and humanities to promote civic competence" (NCSS, 2017, "What Is Social Studies?"). This can include subjects such as history, civic education, and geography. Programs that fall within the NCSS's definition are especially well suited to shifting students' relationship to the United States and are thus deployable as cultural bombs.

Social studies education is a natural fit for the goals of public diplomacy (such as intercultural understanding and cooperation) for these goals are grounded in civic values and cultural narratives communicated through multicultural social studies education. It is no surprise, then, that the importance of education programs with social studies components grows as the War on Terror incorporates a parallel "war of ideas" along with its military tactics.

Although, initially, education only appears in the context of schools being "breeding grounds for extremists" (S/CT, 2002, p. 12), being of poor quality, or being tactical targets in military operations, social studies education as public diplomacy appears rather abruptly and substantially in 2004. Surrounded by accounts and images of graphic violence such as beheadings, bombings, and executions in Jeddah, Karbala, and Beersheba, a new

"Public Diplomacy" section presented the case for developing "support for and understanding of the United States" because it goes "hand-in-hand with strengthening moderate voices as an antidote to extremism" (S/CT, 2005, p. 58). In subsequent reports, the Bureau of Counterterrorism continues to highlight the importance of social studies education in its *Country Reports on Terrorism* when describing how "the U.S. government approach stressed mobilizing public and private resources as partners to improve the access, quality, and relevance of education, with a specific emphasis on youth and on developing civic-mindedness in young people" (S/CT, 2009, p. 264).

The reach of education programs featured in the bureau's reports has continued to grow. Examples of ongoing programs with social studies themes include broadcasts and shows such as *Voice of America* and *Sesame Street*, as well as academic centers and classroom instruction such as American Corners and the English Access Microscholarship Program. Broadcasted programs certainly merit discussion. However, due to size limitations and the ways this analysis connects with my ethnographic research with students and teachers, I will focus on the latter two programs which occur in the physical spaces of formal education.

**American Corners.** The 2004 *Country Reports on Terrorism* features "American Corners," a program the U.S. Department of State writes originated "just past the millennium" (American Spaces, n.d.). The remarkable growth of American Corners and the narratives delivered through them make this program a strong example for illustrating the significance of traditional, U.S.-centric social studies content in post-9/11 foreign policy. The depiction of American Corners in the 2004 *Country Reports on Terrorism*, the online catalog that provides its design elements and learning materials, and personal experiences shed light on the growth and mission of the program.

Highlighting its importance in the War on Terror, the 2004 report asserts that "one of the most effective public diplomacy tools is American Corners. Often housed in educational institutions, American Corners in 201 cities in 89 countries serve as platforms for public outreach, especially to young people" (S/CT, 2005, p. 58). At this time, American Spaces, the coordinator for American Corners and similar programs, does not list the number currently operating, however, the U.S. Embassy in Ethiopia, a country with four American Corners, writes on its webpage that

> Currently, there are 413 American Corners: 164 in Europe and Eurasia, 59 in East Asia, 75 in Africa, 43 in South and Central Asia, 50 in the Middle East, and 22 in Latin America. Enthusiasm for American Corners continues to grow as more visitors are exposed to their benefits. (U.S. Embassy in Ethiopia, n.d.)

The inclusion of American Corners' growth in *Country Reports on Terrorism* incorporates social studies education into counterterrorism discourse. The sheer number of American Corners suggests that the U.S. Department of State sees a tactical value in using social studies education to promote positive narratives about the United States—narratives capable of endearing youths to it. They have the capacity to rapidly expand such programs, are committed to this strategy, and have promoted its growth for more than a decade.

The messages delivered through such programming demonstrates the promotion of traditional social studies narratives as a cultural bomb in the War on Terror. It grounds these narratives in "knowledge about life in the United States, American government, and American culture through computers, books, magazines, and information" (S/CT, 2005). Not unlike social studies classrooms in the United States, American Corners are filled with U.S.-themed decorations and murals. These murals can be ordered through an online store set up by American Spaces. Design options for outfitting an American Corner include wall-sized murals of Mount Rushmore, the Capitol building, George Washington, Thomas Jefferson, Steve Jobs, Martin Luther Kings, Jr., flags, maps, and more—all in dominant color themes of red, white, and blue. American Corners are also stocked with books and media that can be ordered through American Spaces. These include titles for children and adults in English, French, and Spanish on subjects ranging from Columbus Day to entrepreneurship.

**The English Access Microscholarship Program.** Access's origin makes it significant to the recent history of education in counterterrorism policy. In 2003, 15 non-elite male youths took their own lives and the lives of others by bombing international sites throughout Casablanca. Twelve of the youths and 33 civilians died in the blasts. More than 100 Moroccans were injured ("Moroccans March Against Terror," 2003). The U.S. Department of State responded by launching what would become the English Access Microscholarship Program with 17 non-elite male youths from the same neighborhood as those who carried out the attacks (U.S. Department of State, 2014).

In its second year, the United States brought girls into Access, implemented it in other cities throughout Morocco, and expanded the program to 12 other countries in the Middle East and North Africa, incorporating more than 1,500 youths. The 2005 *Country Reports on Terrorism* noted that "because of the program's initial success, the program size is being increased to reach a total of 13,000 people, with an added focus on civic responsibility" (S/CT, 2006, p. 28). A year later, the 2006 report announced that "during FY-2006, U.S. embassies selected schools in 45 countries" to enroll students in the program (S/CT, 2007, p. 216), and the 2007 reports specified that this is a program for non-elite students from "countries with significant Muslim populations" (S/CT, 2008, p. 248). The *Country Reports on Terrorism* indicate that like American Corners, Access expanded rapidly. Within its first 10 years, the Access program grew to operate in more than 85 countries and included more than 100,000 students (Bureau of Educational and Cultural Affairs, 2014).

Today, the program continues to provide English language instruction for non-elite youths in a "civic education context" (S/CT, 2008, p. 284). This is reflected in Access's official mission statement: "The mission of the Access Program is to provide a foundation of English language skills to bright, 13- to 20-year-old students from economically disadvantaged sectors, and to help participants gain an appreciation for U.S. culture and democratic values through cultural enhancement activities" (English Access Microscholarship Program-Headquarters, n.d.; U.S. Embassy in Morocco, 2010). Rather specific concerns and strategies in the War on Terror are packed into the components of the Access program's mission statement. These components include *non-elite youths, U.S. culture, democratic values,* and *cultural enhancement*.

The development and expansion of Access demonstrate the United States' intentionality and commitment in combating violent extremism through education. It also reiterates the United States' attention to non-elite youths and focus on Muslim youths in the post-9/11 era. In addition to shifting students' relationships to the United States, programs such as American Corners and the English Access Microscholarship program essentialize U.S. culture. Essentializing any culture, including "U.S. culture," results in obscuring diversity in the United States (Gorski, 2016; Ladson-Billings, 2006; St. Denis, 2009). Furthermore, privileging a monolithic appreciation of "culture" has been used in multiple fields to decenter or hide from issues of justice and inequity faced by peoples of the cultures studied (Beach et al., 2005; González, 2005; Gorski, 2009, 2016; Kamoea, 2003, Kumagai & Lypson, 2009; St. Denis 2009). For non-elite youths in the global South, hiding inequities and exploitation behind this thin veneer of "culture" obscures economic injustices.

The growth of the American Corners and Access programs demonstrates a clear trajectory and commitment to using social studies education in foreign policy. The rest of this analysis more closely examines the *target* of social studies education as a cultural bomb in the War on Terror.

*Disarming the Dangerous Classes*

Throughout counterterrorism reports, non-elite youths in the Muslim world represent an especially dangerous class of people, and policies designed to mitigate the threat through education reflect concerns about social class and class struggle. For example, non-elite youths become the focus of specific programs, such as the English Access Microscholarship Program, from the start. According to the reports, this is because aggrieved Muslim youths are prone to weaponization by a "conveyor belt [of radicalization which transforms youths] by stages, to increasingly radicalized and extremist viewpoints, turning them into sympathizers, supporters, and ultimately, in some cases, members of terrorist networks" (S/CT, 2007, p. 11). Subsequent reports not only identify Muslim youths as a dangerous class of people, but also indicate that *future* Muslim youths will also be dangerous and part of "the threat environment of the future" because of "demographic and technological trends in countries where terrorism is already endemic" (S/CT, 2010, p. 12). Of special concern, "the youth population throughout South Asia and the Middle East is rapidly expanding" and "Europe may continue to be a fertile recruitment ground for extremists if sizable numbers of recent immigrants and, in particular, second- and third-generation Muslims continue to experience integration problems" (S/CT, 2010, p. 12). The demographic problem of current and future Muslim youths poses enough of a threat to "underscore the need to look beyond the immediate—and genuinely pressing—challenges of tactical counterterrorism toward the longer term [*sic*] developments shaping the threat environment of the future" (S/CT, 2010, p. 12).

Including social studies instruction in annual counterterrorism reports to Congress signals its significance to policymakers' thinking about the roles social studies education can play in mitigating what it deems to be a threat—current and future aggrieved non-elite Muslim youths. Without addressing their grievances, the S/CT identifies solutions for disarming the dangerous classes by indicating that cultural bombs such as "the application of media and academic resources are key components of our response to the threat" (S/CT, 2007, p. 11). The U.S. approach to the dangerous classes also includes (in language that evokes the paternalism of the 19th-century bourgeoisie) helping "wean at-risk populations away from subversive manipulation" (S/CT, 2007, p. 13). Furthermore, social studies education is used as a corrective, an additive, or "cultural enhancement" to use the Access program's mission statement, suggesting a cultural deficit makes non-elite Muslim youths dangerous.

In my previous study on the implementation of Access (McCafferty-Wright, 2020), I describe examples of educative psychic violence, a process also described by Leonardo and Porter (2010) and King and Woodson (2017). Troubling examples of educative psychic violence in Access include

> students tearing down their own dignity and worth of who they were prior to participating in the program, paired with rebuilding their dignity and worth through their participation. . . . This process brings students into a position of defining themselves in relationship to a more powerful and/or exploitative apparatus, in this case a foreign nation state, so that they may identify with it. In a much more literal sense of *tearing down*, some content is connected to countries that have been physically damaged by U.S. bombings and/or through economic exploitation in global market systems. (McCafferty-Wright, 2020, p. 74)

Some examples of students shifting how they identify with the United States include students celebrating the Fourth of July/U.S. Independence in a country where children were being bombed in a unilateral, U.S drone war, students posing with the U.S. Seal in a country suffering from the generational effects of exposure to Agent Orange dropped by the United States, and Indigenous children in Southeast Asia celebrating Columbus Day.

I have seen similar patterns of creating distance between students and their cultures through my experiences in American Corners. Once, I arrived at a university in North Africa as Marxist students were gathering on campus with drums and chants for a demonstration against certain campus policies.

Upon entering the suite housing the American Corner, I faced a colorful, wall-sized map of the United States and about 30 university students. The wall behind the stage where I stood for my talk displayed a mural of Steve Jobs. There, in a place deeply and continuously shaped by colonization and imperialism and in front of students whose diverse ethnicities—including Arab, Amazigh, and Hassani—are part of colonial and imperial struggles for power and existence, this mural of Steve Jobs, a wealthy white man from the global North, encouraged us all to "GO **INVENT TOMORROW** INSTEAD OF WORRYING ABOUT WHAT HAPPENED **YESTERDAY** [caps and emboldened as displayed]." For an hour, I stood in front of that quote facilitating a discussion about diversity in the United States, what happened "yesterday," and why we should care about it. Meanwhile, the students outside concluded their demonstration, a demonstration hopefully guided by an understanding of what happened "yesterday" *as well as* a concern for "inventing tomorrow."

By specifically focusing on *non-elite* youths, U.S.-centric social studies education for the dangerous classes supports antiterrorism goals by undermining cultural resistance and therefore rendering disaffected youths less dangerous to U.S. interests. Cabral (1973/1994) and Fanon (1963/2004) both noted that those most isolated from the culture of the colonizers played a critical role in generating and sustaining resistance to colonization. While Cabral and Fanon wrote prior to education through U.S. public diplomacy programs in the War on Terror, today, U.S.-centric social studies education operates around the world, *specifically targeting non-elite students*, thus undermining sources of cultural resistance, and rendering "the threat environment of the future" or, rather, Muslim youths engaged in the global class struggle, compliant.

As a result, civic education for democratic values, or in the case of one policy recommendation, "market-based democracy" (S/CT, 2007, p. 224), brings non-elite youths into the specter of democratic processes without the structure or even the promise of a democratic system that will work for them. Indeed, it is possible that enfranchising non-elite youths into the specter of market-based democratic processes can remove them from more immediate, organic, and effective methods of resistance (such as social movement citizenship), rendering organic, non-elite leaders less likely to emerge and dangerous classes of aggrieved non-elite youths easier to control.

## Taking Up the Weapon of Theory

Education bears a history as a hegemonic and exploitative apparatus of state, from who has access to different kinds of education, to its content and the coercion imposed on students to acquire it. Ngũgĩ wa Thiong'o (1986/2003) describes "the cultural bomb" of education as a weapon deployed daily in colonized children's lives (p. 3). This is because education played a key role in many colonial tasks, from manufacturing consent among the colonizers to "getting the 'natives' to love them" (Sartre, 1961/2004) or at the very least, keeping them compliant. As we see in the counterterrorism reports, policymakers still consider education to have the power to manufacture compliance by shifting cultural identities, values, and students' relationships to state actors.

From pushing educational reform in foreign countries to providing education intended to counter unfavorable narratives about the United States, the CT-CVE's reports illustrate the role that public diplomacy plays in shaping intended futures through the education of non-elite students. While the use of social studies education as a state apparatus in the War on Terror may only be a decade and a half old, elements of its goals and ends reverberate from the past. The cultural battles that fuel the War on Terror bear powerful resemblances to historic examples of imperialism and its resistance.

Joseph Masco (2014) writes that "counterterror constitutes itself today as endless, boundless, and defensive—a necessary means of protecting American interests in a world of emergent and violent dangers" (p. 1). As U.S. foreign policy demonstrates, the *boundlessness* of counterterrorism incorporates classrooms and curriculum. Additionally, Masco (2014) describes a security state apparatus that "no longer recognizes national boundaries or citizenship as the defining coordinates of its governance" (p. 1). In the context of the theater of classroom in the War on Terror, the coordinates of the security state's attention have fallen on non-elite children and youths in more than 85 countries from American Corners and the English Access Microscholarship Program alone. As of the date of this writing, these two programs are still in operation. Time will tell whether they will grow, shrink, or be cut altogether. However, the significance given to education programs in the CT-CVE's reports suggests that they or similar programs will remain integral to U.S. foreign policy.

Although the phenomenon has been largely ignored by education scholars for more than a decade, U.S.-centric social studies education has become an essential part of the never-ending War on Terror. As counterterrorism programs work to bring marginalized youths of other countries into the democratic franchise and endear them toward pro-U.S. narratives, I wonder which "democratic values" these youths might find appealing. When they enter the specter of "market-based democracy," will it undermine popular power? Privilege corporate and state power? Or accomplish other goals?

Although social studies scholars have missed the initial growth of U.S.-centric social studies education in counterterrorism policy, we are uniquely positioned to understand, critique, and shape its future outcomes. Scholars of critical pedagogy can engage with the makers and shapers of policies that bring education into public diplomacy initiatives, name systems of oppression and exploitation, call out deficit orientations to students and their cultures, and push for culturally sustaining education. Critical policy analysis, by showing how programs benefit the dominant culture (Brewer, 2014; Diem et al., 2014; Gale, 2001; Scheurich, 1994) and work toward the internalization of the dominant culture (Anderson, 1989; Bourdieu, 1991; Gillborn, 2005; McLaren & Giarelli, 1995) can help us better resist the use of social studies education in the War on Terror and the ends to which education is used as a cultural bomb.

Revisiting and reconsidering critical theories and concepts born in response to historic uses of cultural hegemony, imperialism, and class struggle helps us understand the ways in which social studies education can be wielded as an apparatus of state in foreign affairs. Finally, we must remember that the commitment to weaponizing education in the War on Terror demonstrates a reaction to the potential power of education to be wielded *by* communities *resisting* hegemonic cultures and systems. In this way, education and critical theory can help dismantle hegemonic systems. As Amilcar Cabral articulated in his 1966 speech, *The Weapon of Theory*, "every practice produces a theory" and "nobody has yet made a successful revolution without a revolutionary theory" (para. 8). Every insurgency needs its weapons. As we find our field broadly wielded against non-elite youths resisting exploitative global power structures, we must take up the weapon of theory, consider reverberations from the past, and dismantle cultural bombs for dangerous classes.

## References

Althusser, L. (2006). Ideology and ideological state apparatuses (notes towards an investigation). In A. Sharma & A. Gupta (Eds.), *The anthropology of the state: A reader* (pp. 86–111). Blackwell Publishing. (Original work published in 1970)

American Spaces. (n.d.). *American Spaces history.* https://americanspaces.state.gov/home/about/american-spaces-history/

Anderson, G. L. (1989). Critical ethnography in education: Origins, current status, and new directions. *Review of Educational Research, 59*, 249–270. https://doi.org/10.3102/00346543059003249

Beach, M. C., Price, E. G., & Gary, T. L. (2005). Cultural competence: A systematic review of health care provider educational interventions. *Medical Care, 43*(4), 356–373. https://doi.org/10.1097/01.mlr.0000156861.58905.96

Bourdieu, P. (1991). *Language and symbolic power.* Harvard University Press.

Brewer, C. A. (2014). Historicizing in critical policy analysis: The production of cultural histories and microhistories. *International Journal of Qualitative Studies in Education, 27*(3), 273–288. https://doi.org/10.1080/09518398.2012.759297

Bureau of Counterterrorism and Countering Violent Extremism. (2017). *Who we are.* https://www.state.gov/j/ct/about/index.htm

Bureau of Educational and Cultural Affairs. (2014). *Celebrating 10 years: The English Access Microscholarship Program.* Bureau of Educational and Cultural Affairs. http://eca.state.gov/files/bureau/Access/index.html

Bussard, R. L. (2012) The "dangerous class" of Marx and Engels: The rise of the idea of the *Lumpenproletariat. History of European Ideas, 8*(6), 675–692. https://doi.org/10.1016/0191-6599(87)90164-1

Cabral, A. (1966, January). *The weapon of theory* [Address]. The First Tricontinental Conference of the Peoples of Asia, Africa and Latin America, Havana, Cuba. https://www.marxists.org/subject/africa/cabral/1966/weapon-theory.htm

Cabral, A. (1994). National liberation and culture. In P. Williams & L. Chrisman (Eds.), *Colonial discourse and post-colonial theory* (pp. 53–65). Columbia University Press. (Original work published in 1973)

Chibber, V. (2013). *Postcolonial theory and the specter of capital.* Verso.

Diem, S., Young, M. D., Welton, A. D., Mansfield, K. C., & Lee, P. L. (2014). The intellectual landscape of critical policy analysis. *International Journal of Qualitative Studies in Education, 27*(9), 1068–1090. https://doi.org/10.1080/09518398.2014.916007

Edelman, M. (1971). *Politics as symbolic action: Mass arousal and quiescence.* Markham.

English Access Microscholarship Program-Headquarters. (n.d.). *About.* https://www.facebook.com/AccessProgramHQ/info?tab=page_info

Fanon, F. (2004). *The wretched of the Earth* (R. Philcox, Trans.). Grove Press. (Original work published in 1963)

Fischer, F. (2003). *Reframing public policy: Discursive politics and deliberative practice.* Oxford University Press.

Gale, T. (2001). Critical policy sociology: Historiography, archaeology and genealogy as methods of policy analysis. *Journal of Education Policy, 16*(5), 379–393. https://doi.org/10.1080/02680930110071002

Gillborn, D. (2005). Education policy as an act of white supremacy: Whiteness, critical race theory and education reform. *Journal of Education Policy, 20*(4), 485–505. https://doi.org/10.1080/02680930500132346

González, N. (2005). Beyond culture: The hybridity of funds of knowledge. In N. González, L. C. Moll, & C. Amonti (Eds.), *Funds of knowledge: Theorising practices in households, communities, and classrooms* (pp. 26–37). Routledge.

Gorski, P. C. (2009). Good intentions are not enough: A de-colonizing intercultural education. *Intercultural Education, 19*(6), 515–526. https://doi.org/10.1080/14675980802568319

Gorski, P. C. (2016). Rethinking the role of "culture" in educational equity: From cultural competence to equity literacy. *Multicultural Perspectives, 18*(4), 221–226. https://doi.org/10.1080/15210960.2016.1228344

Kaomea, J. (2003). Reading erasures and make the familiar strange: Defamiliarizing methods for research in formerly colonized and historically oppressed communities. *Educational Researcher, 32*(2), 14–25. https://doi.org/10.3102/0013189X032002014

Kumagai, A. K., & Lypson, M. L. (2009). Beyond cultural competence: Critical consciousness, social justice, and multicultural education. *Academic Medicine, 84*(6), 782–787. https://doi.org/10.1097/ACM.0b013e3181a42398

Kincheloe, J. L., & Berry, K. S. (2004). *Rigor and complexity in educational research: Conceptualizing the bricolage.* Open University Press.

King, L. J., & Woodson, A. N. (2017). Baskets of cotton and birthday cakes: Teaching slavery in social studies classrooms. *Social Studies Education Review, 6*(1), 1–18.

Ladson-Billings, G. (2006). It's not the culture of poverty, it's the poverty of culture: The problem with teacher education. *Anthropology & Education Quarterly, 37*(2), 104–109. https://doi.org/10.1525/aeq.2006.37.2.104

Leonardo, Z., & Porter, R. K. (2010). Pedagogy of fear: Toward a Fanonian theory of "safety" in race dialogue. *Race Ethnicity and Education, 13*(2), 139–157. https://doi.org/10.1080/13613324.2010.482898

Loewen, J. W. (2009). *Teaching what really happened: How to avoid the tyranny of textbooks and get students excited about doing history.* Teachers College Press.

Masco, J. (2014). *The theater of operation: National security affect from the cold war to the War on Terror.* Duke University Press.

Mandela, N. (2003, July). *Lighting your way to a better future* [Speech transcript]. http://db.nelsonmandela.org/speeches/pub_view.asp?pg=item&ItemID=NMS909

McCafferty-Wright, J. (2020). "It changes me from nothing to something": Educative psychic violence in a public diplomacy program for nonelite youths. *Journal of International Social Studies, 10*(3), 66–85. https://iajiss.org/index.php/iajiss/article/view/493/407

McLaren, P., & Giarelli, J. M. (1995). Introduction: Critical theory and educational research. In P. McLaren & J. M. Giarelli (Eds.), *Critical theory and educational research* (pp. 1–22). SUNY Press.

Miller, J. R. (1996). *Shingwauk's vision: A history of Native residential schools*. University of Toronto Press.

Morris, L. (1994). *Dangerous classes: The underclass and social citizenship*. Routledge.

Moroccans march against terror. (2003, May 25). BBC News. http://news.bbc.co.uk/2/hi/africa/2936918.stm

Moses, M. S., & Gair, M. (2004). Toward a critical deliberative strategy for addressing ideology in educational policy processes. *Educational Studies, 36*(3), 217–244. https://doi.org/10.1207/s15326993es3603_3

National Council for the Social Studies. (2017). *National Council for the Social Studies: About*. https://www.socialstudies.org/about

Office of the Coordinator for Counterterrorism. (2002). *Patterns of global terrorism 2001*. https://www.state.gov/j/ct/rls/crt/2001/

Office of the Coordinator for Counterterrorism. (2003). *Patterns of global terrorism 2002*. https://www.state.gov/j/ct/rls/crt/2002/

Office of the Coordinator for Counterterrorism. (2005). *Country reports on terrorism 2004*. https://www.state.gov/j/ct/rls/crt/2004/

Office of the Coordinator for Counterterrorism. (2006). *Country reports on terrorism 2005*. https://www.state.gov/j/ct/rls/crt/2005/

Office of the Coordinator for Counterterrorism. (2007). *Country reports on terrorism 2006*. https://www.state.gov/j/ct/rls/crt/2006/

Office of the Coordinator for Counterterrorism. (2008). *Country reports on terrorism 2007*. https://www.state.gov/j/ct/rls/crt/2007/index.htm

Office of the Coordinator for Counterterrorism. (2009). *Country reports on terrorism 2008*. https://www.state.gov/j/ct/rls/crt/2008/index.htm

Office of the Coordinator for Counterterrorism. (2010). *Country reports on terrorism 2009*. https://www.state.gov/j/ct/rls/crt/2009/index.htm

Razack, S. (2015). *Dying from improvement: Inquests and inquiries into Indigenous deaths in custody*. University of Toronto Press.

Reyhner, J., & Eder, J. (2015). *American Indian education: A history*. University of Oklahoma Press.

Sartre, J. (2004). Preface. In F. Fanon, *The wretched of the Earth* (pp. xliii–lxii). Grove Press. (Original work published in 1961)

Scheurich, J. J. (1994). Policy archaeology: A new policy studies methodology. *Journal of Education Policy, 9*(4), 297–316. https://doi.org/10.1080/0268093940090402

Schissel, B., & Wotherspoon, T. (2003). *The legacy of school for Aboriginal people: Education, oppression, and emancipation*. Oxford University Press.

Standing, G. (2016). *The precariat: The new dangerous class*. Bloomsbury Academic. (Original work published in 2011)

St. Denis, V. (2009). Rethinking cultural theory in Aboriginal education. In C. Levine-Rasky (Ed.), *Canadian perspectives on the sociology of education* (pp. 163–182). Oxford University Press.

Theater of War. (n.d.). In *Merriam-Webster*. Retrieved December 15, 2021, from https://www.merriamwebster.com/

U.S. Department of State. (2014). *U.S. Department of State English Access Microscholarship Program in Morocco*. http://photos.state.gov/libraries/morocco/ 19452/pdfs/AccessMorocco.pdf

U.S. Embassy in Ethiopia. (n.d.). *American Corners*. https://et.usembassy.gov/education-culture/american-corners/

U.S. Embassy in Morocco. (2010). *Access Microscholarship Program in Morocco*. http://morocco.USembassy.gov/root/pdfs/access-in-morocco-info-sheet.pdf

von Feigenblatt, O. F., Suttichujit, V., Shuib, M. S., Keling, M. F., & Ajis, M. N. (2010). Weapons of mass assimilation: A critical analysis of the use of education in Thailand. *Journal of Asia Pacific Studies, 1*(2), 292–311. https://www.japss.org/journal-asia-pacific-studies

Wacquant, L. (1996). The rise of advanced marginality: Notes on its nature and implications. *Acta Sociologica, 39*(2), 121–139. https://doi.org/10.1177/000169939603900201

wa Thiong'o, N. (2003). *Decolonizing the mind: The politics of language in African literature*. Heinemann. (Original work published in 1986)

Winton, S. (2013). Rhetorical analysis in critical policy research. *International Journal of Qualitative Studies in Education, 26*(2), 158–177. https://doi.org/10.1080/09518398.2012.666288

TEN

# Whiteness and White Responsibility in Social Studies

*Andrea M. Hawkman*

When first invited to contribute a chapter about whiteness within the realm of insurgency, I (a) was not sure if there should be a chapter focused on whiteness within this volume about insurgency and, if there was, (b) questioned whether I, a queer white woman, should be writing it. Is the whole point of this book to disrupt the ways that whiteness and white supremacy dominate social studies curriculum and pedagogy? Not to mention the fact that white women and white queer people have not taken appropriate responsibility for their role in perpetuating white supremacy in society. I mean, really, why is this chapter in this book? Simply put, insurgency is needed because of whiteness. A volume about insurgency without a chapter directly addressing why insurgency is necessitated would be incomplete. I open with these thoughts not as a slight to the editors of this volume. The collection of chapters in the text offer powerful examples of what insurgency can look like and the impact it can have on social studies teaching and learning. Rather, I seek to begin with recognition of the damage inflicted in the name of whiteness and white supremacy in social studies.

## *Note to Readers*

Before moving forward, I must acknowledge that this chapter will have two audiences: Black, Indigenous, and People of Color (BIPOC)–identified/ing readers and white-identified/ing readers. Although people of all racial identities need to account for the ways that whiteness shapes their experiences, they come to this work from their own positions and interlocking identities. To BIPOC-identified/ing readers, what follows may be a recounting of things you already know or have experienced as individuals involved in social studies education. This chapter is not meant as a culminating essay about your experiences with whiteness and white supremacy in social studies. Nor do I wish to speak "on behalf" of you. Those are not efforts for which I should be a part. However, reading this chapter may shine light on ways that you unknowingly aid in promoting whiteness in social studies teaching or research.

To white-identified/ing readers, if you have selected to read a book about insurgency, and a chapter about whiteness, you are in some way interested in disrupting white supremacy in social studies. You may already be engaged in that work, or you may be at the beginning of your journey to take responsibility for your connection to whiteness. This chapter is intended to name the ways that whiteness exists and persists within the field and to call readers to account for their investments in whiteness, whether they be conscious or unconscious. Therefore, reading this chapter will likely evoke varied responses, emotions, and reflections. But let me be clear, this is not a chapter that ascribes "good white person's medals" or allyship merit badges (Hayes & Juárez, 2009). After reading this chapter, you will not be an antiracist social studies educator. But hopefully, you will dig in and further commit to wrestling with your relationship to/with whiteness and take responsibility for its presence in the field of social studies education.

## What is Whiteness?

Whiteness is more than skin color. It is a system used to obfuscate the humanity of people deemed not to be white. Whiteness is largely understood as an identity construct and power structure that is dehumanizing, ever-shifting, hierarchical, and hegemonic (Bonilla-Silva, 2010; Leonardo, 2009; Roediger, 1991). Operationally, whiteness functions in at least three ways. First, whiteness thrives through the adoption of a color-evasive ideology. Annamma et al. (2017) suggest that viewing the world through whiteness is situated on the conscious attempt to avoid acknowledging the presence of race/ism. Unlike previous framings that have identified this ideology as "colorblindness," color-evasiveness centralizes the intentional act of avoidance within this ideological position. It is not that race/ism is not seen, it is that people, institutions, and policies are choosing not to reckon with it. Referring to this refusal as "colorblind" also improperly associates visual impairment with the more insidious act of deliberately choosing not to recognize or engage with racism (Annamma et al., 2017). Choosing to not talk about race/ism has nothing to do with (dis)ability—it has to do with protecting the comforts of whiteness. White people, in fact, spend a great deal of time talking about race, although often through coded or veiled language that allows them to express white racial/ist opinions without feeling uncomfortable (Leonardo & Zembylas, 2013).

Second, sociologist Charles Mills (2007) suggests whiteness is rooted in an epistemology of ignorance. The common understanding of ignorance, for example, a lack of knowledge or awareness, does not adequately capture how whiteness shapes epistemological awareness. According to Mills (2007), whiteness requires that we recalibrate our understanding of ignorance:

> *Ignorance is usually thought of as the passive obverse to knowledge,*
>
> *the darkness retreating before the spread of Enlightenment.*
>
> *But . . .*
>
> *Imagine an ignorance that resists.*
>
> *Imagine an ignorance that fights back.*
>
> *Imagine an ignorance militant, aggressive, not to be intimidated, an ignorance that is active, dynamic, that refuses to go quietly—not at all confined to the illiterate and uneducated but propagated at the highest levels of the land, indeed presenting itself unblushingly as* knowledge. (p. 13)

White ignorance, unlike its more general iteration, is an active epistemological position used to perpetuate white norms, ways of knowing, and privileges. Through this epistemological frame, whiteness minimizes the violence and pain caused by racism and allows white people the privilege of selectively engaging with race/ism as they find it most palatable (Mills, 2007). In this way, white ignorance aggressively asserts the historical reality that "Whiteness is originally coextensive with full humanity, so that the nonwhite Other is grasped through a historic array of concepts whose common denominator is their subjects' location on a lower ontological and moral rung" (Mills, 2007, p. 26).

Third, due to the widespread embodiment of white ignorance, white ways of knowing, or white common sense have been widely adopted, expected, and enshrined. Leonardo (2009) suggests the construct of white common sense is a hegemonic understanding of white notions of truth, knowledge, and power. While white common sense may appear to be "just how it is" for white people, these norms are rooted in anti-Black racism and seek to minimize information, experiences, or knowledge that disrupts white ignorance or challenges color-evasiveness. Therefore, the ontological frame of white common sense builds on white ignorance and is implemented in ways that universalize the white experience, making it difficult to refute, despite its inherent shortcomings (Leonardo, 2009). Moreover, as white common sense fills the ether—from popular discourse to legislative policy to curriculum and pedagogy—white people, then, are positioned as knowledgeable about race. In this way, white understandings of race/ism are utilized to determine the rules of engagement around racialized issues.

Fourth, despite claims that whiteness is superior, whiteness is, in actuality, quite insecure (Packnett Cunningham, 2021). Whiteness is constantly shifting, reassigning itself to new groups of people, asserting itself in varied ways and places (Roediger, 1991). In order to further enshrine white supremacy, whiteness protects the racialized feelings of white people (Leonardo & Zembylas, 2013). In this sense, white people are invested in whiteness retaining its privileges and power (Lipsitz, 1995). These investments have persisted since before the creation of the United States, as Lipsitz (1995) noted:

> From the start, European settlers in North America established structures encouraging possessive investment in whiteness. The colonial and early-national legal systems authorized attacks on Native Americans and encouraged the appropriation of their lands. They legitimated racialized chattel slavery, restricted naturalized citizenship to "white" immigrants, and provided pretexts for exploiting labor, seizing property, and denying the franchise to Asian Americans, Mexican Americans, Native Americans, and African Americans. (p. 371)

Investments in whiteness have continued into the contemporary era, albeit, as racism has evolved, so too has the nature of these efforts. Many of the social, political, and economic initiatives of the 20th and 21st centuries have operated in service of maintaining the influence of whiteness in society (e.g., the Social Security Act's exclusion of farm and domestic workers from coverage; the Federal Housing Administration's involvement in real estate redlining; urban renewal efforts that promote gentrification and place environmental burdens on communities of color; Leonardo, 2009; Lipsitz, 1995).

In order to maintain this possessive investment in whiteness, it often operates in correlation or collaboration with other forms of oppressive systems, such as sexism, ableism, patriarchy, xenophobia, and heteronormativity.

Mayorga et al. (2020) suggest white supremacy can be understood as a hydra, the multiheaded creature from Greek mythology, nearly impossible to defeat because removing one head causes the growth of two more in its place. Therefore, whiteness and white supremacy are difficult to disrupt because of this multifaceted attack.

## Whiteness in Social Studies

The functions of whiteness also operate within social studies curriculum and pedagogy. As Mills (2007) suggested when arguing for an articulation of white ignorance, the "mapping" of whiteness in social studies is necessary to articulate a new path forward that exists outside of the limits of whiteness (p. 16). And yet, discussing whiteness in a way that does not centralize it, rely on it, or uplift it can be a difficult ropewalk (Leonardo, 2009). Social studies must be willing to articulate the ways that whiteness exists and persists before insurgent efforts can be effective in transforming the field (Hawkman & Shear, 2020). The critique that traditional social studies narratives have centralized whiteness is not new. Scholars have long critiqued the white ways that social studies functions (e.g., Ladson-Billings, 2003; Pang et al., 1998). In fact, the chapters in this volume offer suggestions for how to engage in this disruptive teaching.

That said, in order to take account for the ways that whiteness persists in social studies, we must articulate its presence, decenter its position, and replace it with racially literate representations. In doing so, we must acknowledge that two social studies exist: one dominated by white knowledge, white histories, white expectations, and pedagogies that protect whiteness and a second social studies grounded in racial realism that builds racial literacy, and centralizes concern and care for BIPOC students' stories, histories, and emotions. These two forms of social studies have always existed. At times, they operated in distinct segregated schools or communities due to de jure segregation policy (Hudson & Holmes, 1994). As de facto segregation and gentrification supplemented legal forms, these two social studies persisted, albeit perhaps in new locations. In other circumstances, the two social studies exist within the same hallway at the same school. The former refers to the social studies that has been situated as "traditional," "mainstream," or, as is the case recently, "under attack" from the critical race theory boogeyman in state legislatures across the United States. Chandler and Branscombe (2015) referred to the former as white Social Studies, henceforth WSS. The latter—a racially literate social studies—has been utilized in not only classrooms but also community centers, Freedom Schools, homeschooling, and education co-ops established by BIPOC communities uninterested in the social studies offerings provided by their public school (King & Simmons, 2018; Ray, 2015). Both have always existed; however, their utilization has varied over time.

### *White Social Studies*

According to Chandler and Branscombe (2015), WSS has less to do with any particular curricular resource or pedagogical approach that a teacher utilizes, and rather refers to the "(1) approved, sanctioned messages and the silences on *how and why* certain *raced* episodes in [history] occurred; and (2) the power of 'mainstream academic knowledge' (Merryfield, 2011, p. 72) and its ability to mask racial knowledge" (p. 65, emphasis in original). In this way, WSS refers to the ways that whiteness is operationalized within social studies classrooms. For example, WSS utilizes white common sense to reify white understandings of the past and reify the racist status quo. This approach to social studies is rooted in nationalistic assumptions about the founding of the United States and seeks to discredit any attempt to challenge this limited and inaccurate view of the past (e.g., 1619 Project).

WSS often focuses on conservative or libertarian understandings of civics and history, although it positions these ideologies as a neutral universal foundation to "good" social studies teaching. Moreover, beyond teaching U.S. history, WSS centralizes concern for white U.S.-ians, their perspectives, and their individualism within all courses that fall under the umbrella of social studies (i.e., geography, world history, sociology, economics, psychology). Within a WSS-driven course, whiteness is both perpetually present and never formally acknowledged. In short, the purpose of WSS is to transmit race-evasive understandings of the past, present, and future (Chandler & Branscome, 2015). As a result, WSS has been one of the largest purveyors of white ideology within the history of schooling (Chandler & Branscombe, 2015; King & Chandler, 2016; King & Woodson, 2017).

Rather than utilizing the breadth of social studies courses available to students to advance racial literacy, teachers engaged in WSS perpetrate harm to students and educators, specifically educative-psychic violence.

Educative-psychic violence refers to the negative impact that can accompany racially unjust teaching about race/ism and whiteness (King & Woodson, 2017; Leonardo & Porter, 2010). King and Woodson (2017) suggest that within social studies, racialized educative-psychic violence occurs in five ways:

1. Standardizing and centralizing white European cultures within social studies curriculum, pedagogy, and assessment;
2. Including people of color exclusively in oppressed or subordinate positions;
3. Universalizing the experiences, behaviors, and actions of all people of color;
4. Providing simplistic or superficial accounts of people of color that relegates them to heroification of the race and within certain fixed historical time periods; and
5. Disassociating racialized violence from white actors, white policies, or white decision-making.

Through the promulgation and enshrinement of WSS, whiteness uplifts the contributions, histories, and perspectives of white people while simultaneously minimizing their racialized responsibilities and diminishing their efforts to promote white supremacy. Concurrently, through educative-psychic violence, WSS marginalizes the humanity of people, communities, and issues that are not white. The centering and reliance on WSS allow racial illiteracies to flourish, causing generations of white students to engage with mis/disinformation, walking away from school uninterested in social studies fields of study and underprepared for reckoning with the racism in their lives. In this way, teaching through WSS harms BIPOC students and fails to prepare white students for developing antiracist racial literacy, therefore perpetuating white supremacy from generation to generation.

*Resisting White Social Studies*

As noted, there has always been resistance to WSS, particularly within communities of color—those who have been most harmed by the relentless application of this form of social studies. Using creativity and flexibility while recognizing the racist utilization of WSS in many public social studies classrooms, BIPOC communities, families, and organizations have created social studies spaces rooted in racial realism and literacy. Whether at a community center or around the kitchen table, people of color have always found ways to situate learning as resistance, and even as survivance (Patel, 2016).

Scholarship addressing the pernicious presence of racism in social studies has laid a strong foundation from which critical treatments of whiteness have been established. Edited collections from Ladson-Billings (2003), Woyshner and Bohan (2012), Chandler (2015), Chandler and Hawley (2017), alongside a full-length manuscript from Epstein (2009), have all created space for scholars and teachers to engage deeply with the racial realities of social studies history, teaching, pedagogy, curriculum, learning, and policy. Articles and chapters from several scholars of color have also insisted that racial literacy be centralized in social studies teaching (King, 2016), called for attention to nuanced ways that racism impacts various racialized communities (e.g., Sohyun An's use of AsianCRT to explore experiences of Asian Americans in social studies, or Christopher Busey's scholarship exploring race/ism in Afro-Latin@representations), or insisted that Black feminist thought be centralized in theoretical and pedagogical considerations within the field (Vickery, 2019).

Across social studies scholarship, researchers have also sought to take up the work of acknowledging, decentering, and dismantling whiteness in social studies. Broadly, scholars have addressed the ways that whiteness shapes pedagogy (Chandler & Branscombe, 2015; Crowley & Smith, 2015; Hawkman, 2019; Smith & Crowley, 2015), self-reflection (Hawkman, 2018), and student engagement with racialized topics (Buchanan, 2015; Crowley, 2016, 2019; Hawkman, 2020; Martell, 2016). Furthermore, in a book I recently edited with Sarah Shear, *Marking the "Invisible": Articulating Whiteness in Social Studies Education* (2020), more than two dozen scholars account for the way that whiteness infiltrates social studies teaching, pedagogy, curriculum, policy, and spaces across the K–20 landscape. Across the volume, authors reflected on their own relationships to/with whiteness while presenting examples of what interrogating whiteness can look like. Engaging varied theoretical frames, methodologies, and contexts, each of these studies have sought to shine light on the presence, influence, and problems relating to whiteness in social studies.

But, as Ladson-Billings (2003) acknowledged, despite relative depth regarding racialized research, the field largely continues to situate race/ism and whiteness scholarship as external to what counts as *essential* social studies research:

"The social studies can serve as a curricular home for unlearning the racism that has confounded us as a nation. Yet, we still find teachers continuing to tell us lies" (p. 8). The other chapters in this book, albeit not all directly focused on whiteness, offer ways forward that stop telling lies and abandon WSS through centralizing BIPOC, queer, and non-U.S.-ian voices and perspectives. In order for insurgency to take hold of the field, it must be as wide-reaching, persistent, and aggressive as white supremacy continues to be.

## Presumed Allies/Embodied Enemies

Hopefully, so far, I have demonstrated why acknowledging whiteness is important in order to engage in insurgency against it. Before I conclude, however, I do want to return to the personal thoughts I shared regarding being asked to write this chapter about whiteness. I want to reiterate that whiteness and white people are not synonymous. But, as the group that benefits from whiteness and its supremacy, white people are responsible for the ways that whiteness is crafted, protected, weaponized, and utilized. Therefore, it makes sense to briefly address the ways that white people, particularly white women and white queer people, situate themselves in relation to whiteness.

From a distance, some may conclude that white women and queer people should see solidarity with people of color who are the targets of racism and racialized oppression. After all, gender and sexuality are identities that traverse racial categorization. Yet, historians have long documented the pernicious relationship white women have maintained with whiteness and white supremacy. As you read this chapter, women of color and queer people of color are facing intersectional forms of oppression not experienced by white women or white queer people. In fact, a major tactic of white supremacy is to create fissures where opportunity for solidarity exists. From brutality on the plantation (Jones-Rogers, 2019) to anti-Black suffragettes (Giddings, 2008) to perpetuating white violence during the mid-20th-century civil rights movement (Little, 2013) or white women supporting 21st-century white nationalist paramilitary organizations (Darby, 2020), overwhelmingly, white women have chosen their racial privilege when provided the opportunity to stand in solidarity with women of color. Look no further than voting turnout in the 2016 presidential elections to see that white women cling to their whiteness (Jaffe, 2018).

I remember the performative shock of "progressive" white women who could not believe so many of their friends and neighbors voted for the man who became the 45th president. A close family member confessed to me in 2017 that she had regretfully voted for him. I surmised that her vote was due to internalized sexism she projected toward Hillary Clinton. The 2016 Republican candidate consistently used sexist, racist, xenophobic, and ableist dog whistles to whip up support among the white electorate. My family member was willing to disregard all that racist nonsense to cling to the protection she amassed when whiteness and sexism intertwined. At the same time, "progressives" were surprised by the consistency with which Black women turned out to vote for the Democratic candidate. Black women were performatively thanked and celebrated for their efforts to save U.S. democracy (Scott, 2017). Because of whiteness and white supremacy, the political engagement of Black women was positioned as a surprise, when in reality statistics demonstrated that Black women vote for Democrats more consistently than any other demographic group. At the same time, white women clutched their pearls and cried out in surprise that other white women voted for a racist, sexist, white man, when all historical data indicated that this would most likely happen (Jackson, 2020).

Similarly, queer people are also the target of the white supremacist hydra, insofar that anti-queerness ultimately supports white heteronormativity. Queer people of color have long been leaders in intersectional movements for racial justice, recognizing that the liberation of queer people is connected to the liberation of people of color (Arriola, 1995). At the same time, white queer people have asserted and enshrined a white queer universalism, or white homonormativity (Duggan, 2002; Ward, 2008). This means white queer people too often assume that their way of knowing, living, and thinking is universally embodied by all queer people, regardless of other identities. This single-axis understanding of oppression is inaccurate and ultimately serves whiteness (Crenshaw, 1991). As a result, white queerness has long been used to police and silence the experiences of queer people of color, particularly as they seek to articulate a queer critique of whiteness and white supremacy. Here, I share a personal anecdote to demonstrate how whiteness functions in queer spaces:

> On June 13, 2016, my wife, our 4-month-old daughter, and I attended a local memorial to honor the victims of the tragic act of domestic terror at the Pulse

> Night Club in Orlando, Florida. The previous day, nearly 49 queer folks and their allies, most of whom were Latinx, were murdered. Our hearts were broken, not only for the horrific loss that had occurred but also because, like many other queer-identified folks, *Pulse* was synonymous with the LGBTQ-welcoming havens of our past.
>
> Upon arrival to the memorial, we were surprised to see a crowd of nearly 500 people, considering the event was planned hastily and in a midwestern college town during summer break. By this point, it was widely known that the attack at Pulse occurred on Latinx night, meaning the victims of the violence were Latinx and queer. Reflecting this reality, many of the speakers at the memorial were also Latinx, and the theme of the speeches and performances focused heavily on the intersections of sexuality and race.
>
> Midway through the 60-minute memorial, a middle-aged white man sitting in the audience angrily yelled at the top of his lungs, "WHY ARE YOU MAKING THIS ABOUT RACE? WE ARE ALL GAY HERE. THIS WAS ABOUT BEING GAY!" The speakers milling around the podium, most of whom were college-aged Latinx queer people, quickly took control of the discourse by reminding the audience of the racialized identities of the Pulse victims and asked the man to leave if he was uncomfortable recognizing this reality. The white man, and the group he was with, huffed away from the event and the speakers continued with the program. My wife and I were a bit in shock at the way that even in moments of deep tragedy brought on by horrific racialized queer violence, this group of white queer people were unwilling to decenter their whiteness from the conversation.

This is how whiteness functions in society. It sucks all the air out of the room. It has to be the center of attention, the lens through which all justice and injustice are determined. Just because someone shares an identity with a group that is oppressed or is in some way marginalized by white supremacist systems, they are not inherently positioned or knowledgeable regarding how to disrupt that which oppresses them. However, they are positioned in a way to stand in solidarity with others, if they are willing to divest from whiteness.

## Conclusion

Let me be clear: The world is in its current state, one driven by a white supremacist hydra set on protecting whiteness, because of white people. Leonardo

(2009) quipped that "it is not just that people *think* they are white, but that they *act* on it" (p. 62, emphasis in original). In calling out white people, white women, and white queer people specifically, I fully acknowledge that I am not off the hook. I have not earned, nor do I seek, a "good white person's medal," allowing me to claim to be a white person that "gets it" (Hayes & Juarez, 2009). I am implicating myself in this because resisting whiteness must be intentional, wide-ranging, and never-ending work. I view my efforts in researching and teaching about whiteness as a responsibility associated with the privileges I am afforded based on my racial identity. That said, I often wonder if I am doing enough. The very fact that I have the ability to ask this of myself is indicative that an on/off switch exists for white people. Because of the way that whiteness functions, white people can choose when, where, and how they wish to acknowledge and engage with race. As the group that benefits from whiteness and its supremacy, white people are responsible for the ways that whiteness functions and is operationalized within social studies classrooms. With this in mind, social studies cannot be facilitated through whiteness. Social studies researchers, teachers, students, and policymakers must be able and willing to take responsibility for whiteness's role in the field.

Taking responsibility means more than admitting that white privilege exists, engaging in a privilege walk with students, or joining a book club. Responsibility necessitates long-term commitment to destroy the white supremacist hydra through insurgency. Broadly, an insurgent approach to whiteness should include (1) naming the ways that whiteness has functioned and continues to function in social studies; (2) replacing whiteness with an ideology rooted in an intersectional understanding of justice, with experiences, histories, perspectives, theories, and emotions of people of color and queer people of color; and (3) creating space for a social studies future that centralizes the experiences, histories, perspectives, theories, and emotions most marginalized by whiteness.

Building from the six commitments offered by Shear and Hawkman (2020), I offer several action items to be adopted in pursuit of insurgency against white supremacy:

- Situate scholarship within and beyond the field of social studies. As social studies scholars and teachers, there is a great deal we can learn from other fields (e.g., Black Feminist Thought, Sociology, Queer Studies) and vice versa. Racialized scholarship and curricula are stronger when they are informed by multiple disciplines, perspectives, and approaches.

- Engage deeply with theory(ies) and method(ologies). It is essential to honor the theoretical and methodological contributions that come before us. For example, Critical Race Theory is a foundational theory to critical scholarship examining race in education. That said, it is not the only theory that can be used to account for race/ism in social studies. Nor is it always appropriate to utilize, based on circumstances, participants, or communities. Reading deeply and widely can push the field to more adequately respond to whiteness in our midst.
- Involve K–12 teachers in work to dismantle white supremacy in social studies. Dismantling whiteness cannot be left to academic productions designed to generate tenure dossiers. This work must involve practicing teachers and community members committed to shared goals. This can include the clinical placements of our teacher education students and can continue with developing partners in local schools to initiate racially just social studies pedagogies.
- Participate in perpetual critical self-reflection. The ideology of whiteness is persistent and shifty. Racialized self-reflection is key for taking personal and institutional responsibility as whiteness is reformulated and reasserted over time.
- Interrogate our teacher education courses and syllabi. "Race week" on a methods syllabus is not enough to prepare preservice teachers to dismantle whiteness in their future classrooms. Whiteness and white supremacy should be accounted for from the first draft of the syllabus through the final course session.
- Advocate for organizational and institutional change. Asserting influence within professional organizations can lead toward systemic change. As social studies educators, we must determine our personal spheres of influence and push forward through insurgent means to advance antiracism.
- Learn from those already blazing a path of insurgency. Efforts to disrupt white supremacy already exist. White responsibility requires that existing approaches to challenging white supremacy, particularly those

initiated within BIPOC communities or spaces, should be acknowledged, centralized, and built on. Racially just schools do not squash the efforts that already exist within communities or around kitchen tables.

It is important to remember that insurgency is not an end goal but rather an ongoing commitment to pursuing justice.

*Note to Readers*

As you engage with the other chapters in this book, hold these commitments in your mind. Reflect on how whiteness has shaped your understanding of the issues put forth by the authors. I urge you to see that which may have been invisible to you before—the active machinations of whiteness within social studies teaching, learning, and research.

## References

Annamma, S. A., Jackson, D. D., & Morrison, D. (2017). Conceptualizing color-evasiveness: Using dis/ability critical race theory to expand a color-blind racial ideology in education and society. *Race Ethnicity and Education, 20*(2), 147–162. https://doi.org/10.1080/13613324.2016.1248837

Arriola, E. R. (1995). Faeries, marimachas, queens, and lezzies: The construction of homosexuality before the 1969 Stonewall riots. *Columbia Journal of Gender and Law, 5*(1), 33–77.

Bonilla-Silva, E. (2010). *Racism without racists: Color-blind racism and racial inequality in contemporary America (3rd ed.).* Rowman & Littlefield.

Buchanan, L. B. (2015). "We make it controversial": Elementary preservice teachers' beliefs about race. *Teacher Education Quarterly, 42*, 3–26.

Chandler, P. T. (Ed.). (2015). *Doing race in social studies: Critical perspectives*. Information Age.

Chandler, P. T., & Branscombe, A. (2015). White social studies: Protecting the white racial code. In P. T. Chandler (Ed.), *Doing race in social studies: Critical perspectives* (pp. 61–87). Information Age.

Chandler, P. T., & Hawley, T. S. (Eds.). (2017). *Race lessons: Using inquiry to teach about race in social studies*. Information Age.

Crenshaw, K. (1991). Mapping the margins: Intersectionality, identity, politics, and violence against women of color. *Stanford Law Review, 43*(6), 1241–1299. https://doi.org/10.2307/1229039

Crowley, R. M. (2016). Transgressive and negotiated white racial knowledge. *International Journal of Qualitative Studies in Education, 29*(8), 1016–1029. https://doi.org/10.1080/09518398.2016.1174901

Crowley, R. M., & Smith, W. (2015). Whiteness and social studies teacher education: Tensions in the pedagogical task. *Teaching Education, 26*, 160–178. https://doi.org/10.1080/10476210.2014.996739

Darby, S. (2020). *Sisters in hate: American women on the front lines of white nationalism*. Little, Brown.

Duggan, L. (2002). The new homonormativity: The sexual politics of neoliberalism. In R. Castronovo, D. D. Nelson, D. E. Pease, J. Dayan, & R. R. Flores (Eds.), *Materializing democracy* (pp. 175–194). Duke University Press.

Epstein, T. (2009). *Interpreting national history: Race, identity, and pedagogy in classrooms and communities*. Routledge.

Giddings, P. J. (2008). *Ida: A sword among lions*. HarperCollins.

Hawkman, A. M. (2018). Exposing whiteness in the elementary social studies methods classroom: In pursuit of developing antiracist teacher education candidates. In S. B. Shear, C. M. Tschida, E. Bellows, L. B. Buchanan, & E. E. Saylor (Eds.), *(Re)Imagining elementary social studies: A controversial issues reader* (pp. 49–71). Information Age.

Hawkman, A. M. (2019). "Let's try and grapple all of this": A snapshot of racial identity development and racial pedagogical decision making in an elective social studies course. *The Journal of Social Studies Research, 43*(3), 215–228. https://doi.org/10.1016/j.jssr.2018.02.005

Hawkman, A. M. (2020). Swimming in and through whiteness: Antiracism in social studies teacher education. *Theory & Research in Social Education, 48*(3), 403–430. https://doi.org/10.1080/00933104.2020.724578

Hawkman, A. M., & Shear, S. B. (2020). Taking responsibility, doing the work. In A. M. Hawkman & S. B. Shear (Eds.), *Marking the "invisible": Articulating whiteness in social studies education* (pp. xxv–xxxvi). Information Age.

Hayes, C., & Juarez, B. G. (2009). You showed your whiteness: You don't get a "good" white people's medal. *International Journal of Qualitative Studies in Education, 22*(6), 729–744. https://doi.org/10.1080/09518390903333921

Hudson, M. J., & Holmes, B. J. (1994). Missing teachers, impaired communities: The unanticipated consequences of *Brown v. Board of Education* on the African American teaching force at the precollegiate level. *Journal of Negro Education, 63*(3), 388–393. https://doi.org/10.2307/2967189

Jackson, J. M. (2020, November 14). Yes, 55 percent of white women voted for Trump. No, I'm not surprised. *Truthout*. https://truthout.org/articles/yes-55-percent-of-white-women-voted-for-trump-no-im-not-surprised/

Jaffe, S. (2018). Why did a majority of white women vote for Trump? *New Labor Forum, 27*(1), 18–26. https://doi.org/10.1177/1095796017744550

Jones-Rogers, S. E. (2019). *They were her property: White women as slave owners in the American south*. Yale University Press.

King, L. J. (2016). Teaching Black history as a racial literacy project. *Race Ethnicity and Education, 19*(6), 1303–1318. https://doi.org/10.1080/13613324.2016.1150822

King, L. J., & Simmons, C. (2018). Narratives of Black history in textbooks: Canada and the United States. In S. A. Metzger & L. M. Harris (Eds.), *The Wiley international handbook of history teaching and learning* (pp. 93–116). Wiley.

King, L. J., & Woodson, A. N. (2017). Baskets of cotton and birthday cakes: Teaching slavery in social studies classrooms. *Social Studies Education Review, 6*(1), 1–18.

Ladson-Billings, G. (2003). (Ed.). *Critical race theory perspectives on social studies: The profession, policies, and curriculum*. Information Age.

Leonardo, Z. (2009). *Race, whiteness, and education*. Routledge.

Leonardo, Z., & Porter, R. K. (2010). Pedagogy of fear: Toward a Fanonian theory of "safety" in race dialogue. *Race Ethnicity and Education, 13*(2), 139–157. https://doi.org/10.1080/13613324.2010.482898

Leonardo, Z., & Zembylas, M. (2013). Whiteness as technology of affect: Implications for educational praxis. *Equity & Excellence in Education, 46*(1), 150–165. https://doi.org/10.1080/10665684.2013.750539

Lipsitz, G. (1995). The possessive investment in whiteness: Racialized social democracy and the "white" problem in American studies. *American Quarterly, 47*(3), 369–387. https://doi.org/10.2307/2713291

Little, K. K. (2013). *You must be from the North: Southern white women in the Memphis civil rights movement*. University Press of Mississippi.

Martell, C. C. (2016). Divergent views of race: Examining whiteness in the U.S. history classroom. *Social Studies Research and Practice, 11*(1), 93–111.

Mayorga, E., Aggarwal, U., & Picower, B. (2020). Introduction to the second edition. In E. Mayorga, U. Aggarwal, & B. Picower (Eds.), *What's race got to do with it: How current school reform policy maintains racial and economic inequality* (2nd ed., pp. 1–12). Peter Lang.

Mills, C. W. (2007). White ignorance. In S. Sullivan & N. Tuana (Eds.), *Race and epistemologies of ignorance* (pp. 13–38). SUNY Press.

Packnett Cunningham, B. [@MsPackyetti]. (2021, March 26). *White supremacy is deeply insecure. That's why it resorts to violence and constant revision to maintain itself* [Tweet]. Twitter. https://twitter.com/MsPackyetti/status/1375497074104533001?s=20

Pang, V. O., Rivera, J. J., & Gillette, M. (1998). Can CUFA be a leader in the national debate on racism? *Theory & Research in Social Education, 26*(3), 430–436. https://doi.org/10.1080/00933104.1998.10505858

Patel, L. (2016). Pedagogies of resistance and survivance: Learning as marronage. *Equity & Excellence in Education, 49*(4), 397–401. https://doi.org/10.1080/10665684.2016.1227585

Ray, B. D. (2015). African American homeschool parents' motivation for homeschooling and Black children's academic achievement. *Journal of Choice, 9*(1), 71–96. https://doi.org/10.1080/15582159.2015.998966

Roediger, D. (1991). *The wages of whiteness: Race and the making of the American working class*. Verso.

Scott, E. (2017, November 9). The Democratic Party owes Black female voters a big "thank you." *Washington Post*. https://www.washingtonpost.com/news/the-fix/wp/2017/11/09/the-democratic-party-owes-black-women-voters-a-big-thank-you/

Shear, S. B., & Hawkman, A. M. (2020). Committing forward: In lieu of an epilogue. In A. M. Hawkman & S. B. Shear (Eds.), *Marking the "invisible": Articulating whiteness in social studies education* (pp. 735–738). Information Age.

Smith, W. L., & Crowley, R. M. (2015). Pushback and possibility: Using a threshold concept of race in social studies teacher education. *Journal of Social Studies Research, 39*, 17–28. https://doi.org/10.1016/j.jssr.2014.05.004

Vickery, A. E. (2019). "Still I Rise": A Black feminist teacher's journey to (re)member in the teaching of national history. *Race Ethnicity and Education, 24*(4), 485–502. https://doi.org/10.1080/13613324.2019.1579183

Ward, J. (2008). White normativity: The cultural dimensions of whiteness in a racially diverse LGBT organization. *Sociological Perspectives, 51*(3), 563–586. https://doi.org/10.1525/sop.2008.51.3.563

Woyshner, C., & Bohan, C. H. (Eds.). (2012). *Histories of social studies and race: 1865–2000*. Palgrave Macmillan.

AFTERWORD

# Insurgent Social Studies and Dangerous Citizenship

*E. Wayne Ross*

PAUL STREET RECENTLY REFLECTED ON the boundaries of permissible reflection regarding political discourse in the media, while also referencing a core argument made by Hermann and Chomsky (1988) about the media's role in the manufacturing of consent:

> One of the doctrinal principles behind U.S. corporate-imperial news coverage and commentary and mainstream U.S. politics is that the United States is a fundamentally benevolent force for good facing difficulties created by evil others and challenging situations not of Washington's own making. Debate is permissible on immediate strategy and tactics but is not allowed on these core American Exceptionalist positions. (Street, 2021, para. 1)

For example, while there is contestation in the media over how to respond to the waves of migrants seeking entry into the United States along the southern border, there is "little if any serious mainstream discussion of and critique of the long and many-sided role the U.S. capitalist imperialism has played in imposing abject misery on millions of people across Central America and Mexico" (Street, 2021, para. 2).

Social studies curricula and teaching have long been subject to strict boundaries of what is permissible to discuss as well as dominated by hegemonic social, political, cultural, and economic perspectives that focus on the enculturation of students into the status quo. There have always been a few cracks where the light gets through from progressive or radical curriculum programs such as the New Social Studies (Stern, 2009), disability studies (Erevelles, 2010), and critical multiculturalism (Busey & Dowie-Chin, 2021), awareness of and broader acceptance of diversity regarding sexuality and gender orientation and LGBTQ+ human rights (Schmidt, 2010), Indigenous peoples and worldviews (Four Arrows, 2014), and, more rarely, attempts to teach social studies from anarchist or Marxist perspectives (DeLeon, 2010; Queen, 2014). But for the most part, politically progressive and radical social studies has always been domesticated or neutered by schools and the boundaries of permissible reflection carefully delineated by official curricula, bureaucratic accountability systems, and hegemonic beliefs about schools as a tool of capitalism and the ruling class and culture.

The initial challenge for anyone interested in the creation of schools that serve the public interest (e.g., promoting racial and economic justice) is to negate the prevailing image of a successful school and what has come to constitute good learning and teaching in the neoliberal era. Schools are continually threatened because they are autocratic, and they are autocratic because they are threatened—from within by students and critical parents and from without by various and disparate social, political, and economic interests. These conditions divide teachers from students and the community and shape teachers' attitudes, beliefs, and action. Teachers, then, are crucial to any effort to improve, reform, or revolutionize curricula, instruction, or schools. The transformation of schools must begin with the teachers, and no program that does not include the personal/collective rehabilitation of teachers can ever overcome the passive resistance of the old order.

Schools are sites of an unresolved ambiguity, the source of domination and alienation and—at least potentially—emancipation. Are public schools the source of hidden riches and starting points for the transformation of society or are they impoverished zones to which the construction of real education can only be opposed? My own response to this question is ambiguous; the optimist in me agrees with Gibson (2016) that "schools are the centripetal organizing point of de-industrialized North American life, and much of life elsewhere" (para. 7). On the other hand, schools are, as Illich (1970/1972) put it, "the advertising agency which makes you believe that you need the society as it is (p. 113).

Insurgent pedagogy is a way of understanding and responding to the unresolved ambiguities that define the landscape of schools and social studies education, encouraging a revolt against the constituted authority of traditional social studies and the terrors of white supremacist violence, xenophobia, homophobia, homelessness, and assaults on workers, migrants, and the environment (Au, 2021). Armed with ideas and willing to adopt subversive tactics, social studies insurgents embrace the contradictions of school while working in collaboration with colleagues and school communities for social, racial, and economic justice.

Following on from Au's (2021) conceptualization of insurgent pedagogies, this book is a manifesto for insurgent social studies education that is both powerful and groundbreaking in its conceptualization and articulation of social justice teaching and learning. Insurgent teaching is built on a critical analysis of power and learning about social and educational injustices. It recognizes and embodies the idea that teaching for social justice is intrinsically linked to working for change through active organizing, protest, and demonstrations, actions that are both political and pedagogical. Activism, particularly on the part of students, has long played an important role in political, social, and educational environments, and insurgent pedagogy is by definition a pedagogy that transcends the boundaries of the classroom.

Learning is a product of human experiences, and curiosity is the trigger of the kind of learning that is long lasting and meaningful. Social movements—like the movement for social and educational justice at the heart of insurgent pedagogy—are spaces where interaction among learning experiences, social engagements, and political practices are united. Student movements, as a form of collective action, also constitute a similar educational space that combines elements and potentialities for learning, creation, and curiosity. Students' (and teachers') repertoires of contention and direct action involve both pedagogy and politics because they encompass direct action that confronts authority and received knowledge, but these movements also include working within a community and critically reflecting and creatively producing knowledge in ways that merge theory and practice. Social action allows students to interact—teaching and learning from each other as part of an exercise of political and educational engagement. These experiences of resistance and collectivity can transform schools into spaces that potentially transcend its role as an advertising agency for the status quo (Delgado & Ross, 2016).

The repertoires of contention and direct action that emerge from insurgent teaching and learning contribute to the development of citizens who are dangerous to the status quo. The pedagogical power of dangerous citizenship resides in its capacity to encourage students and others

> to challenge the implications of their own education or work, to envision an education that is free and democratic to the core, and to interrogate and uncover their own well-intentioned complicity in the conditions within which various cultural texts and practices appear, especially to the extent that oppressive

conditions create oppressive cultural practices, and vice versa. (Ross & Vinson, 2013, p. 15)

Insurgent pedagogies create the conditions for the development of dangerous citizens—people who individually and collectively take actions that transcend activities of traditional/spectatorial democratic citizenship and adopt a praxis-inspired mindset of opposition and resistance. The practice of dangerous citizenship is dangerous to existing hierarchical power structures and the oppressive and socially unjust status quo. Being an insurrectionist is itself a dangerous practice, which requires bravery and acceptance of risk. This, in turn, highlights the importance of working in solidarity with allies and accomplices and the importance of conceptualizing pedagogy not as an activity of a single person but rather collectively creating the conditions that lead to critical awareness, political engagement, and intentional actions to create a more just world.

## References

Au, W. (2021). A pedagogy of insurgency: Teaching and organizing for radical racial justice in our schools. *Educational Studies*. Advanced online publication. https://doi.org/10.1080/00131946.2021.1878181

Busey, C. L., & Dowie-Chin, T. (2021). The making of global Black anti-citizen/citizenship: Situating BlackCrit in global citizenship research and theory. *Theory & Research in Social Education, 49*(2), 153–175. https://doi.org/10.1080/00933104.2020.1869632

DeLeon, A. (2010). Anarchism, sabotage and the spirit of revolt: Injecting the social studies with anarchist potentialities. In A. P. DeLeon & E. W. Ross (Eds.), *Critical theories, radical pedagogies, and social education* (pp. 1–12). Brill.

Delgado, S., & Ross, E. W. (2016). Students in revolt: The pedagogical potential of student collective action in the age of the corporate university. *Knowledge Cultures, 4*(6), 141–158. https://www.addletonacademicpublishers.com/997-knowledge-cultures/volume-4-6-2016/2980-students-in-revolt-the-pedagogical-potential-of-student-collective-action-in-the-age-of-the-corporate-university

Erevelles, N. (2010). Embattled pedagogies: Deconstructing terror from a transnational feminist disability studies perspective. In A. P. DeLeon & E. W. Ross (Eds.), *Critical theories, radical pedagogies, and social education* (pp. 13–24). Brill.

Four Arrows. (2014). Social studies, praxis, and the public good. In E. W. Ross (Ed.), *The social studies curriculum: Purposes, problems, and possibilities* (4th ed., pp. 161–180). State University of New York Press.

Gibson, R. (2016, August 16). *Why have school? Blood and money versus reason.* CounterPunch. https://www.counterpunch.org/2016/08/16/why-have-school-blood-and-money-versus-reason/

Hermann, E. M., & Chomksy, N. (1988). *Manufacturing consent: The political economy of the mass media.* Pantheon.

Illich, I. (1972). *Deschooling society.* Harrow Books. (Original work published 1970)

Queen, G. (2014). Class struggle in the classroom. In E. W. Ross (Ed.), *The social studies curriculum: Purposes, problems and possibilities* (4th ed., pp. 313–334). State University of New York Press.

Ross, E. W., & Vinson, K. D. (2013). Resisting neoliberal education reform: Insurrectionist pedagogies and the pursuit of dangerous citizenship. *Works & Days, 20*(1–2), 27–58. https://ojs.library.ubc.ca/index.php/clogic/article/view/190890

Schmidt, S. J. (2010). Queering social studies: The role of social studies in normalizing citizens and sexuality in the common good. *Theory & Research in Social Education, 38*(3), 314–335. https://doi.org/10.1080/00933104.2010.10473429

Stern, B. S. (2009). *The new social studies: People, projects, perspectives.* Information Age.

Street, P. (2021, August 17). *The United States, Afghanistan, and the doctrinal boundaries of permissible reflection.* CounterPunch. https://www.counterpunch.org/2021/08/17/the-united-states-afghanistan-and-the-doctrinal-boundaries-of-permissible-reflection/

# About the Authors

**Wayne Au** is a professor in the University of Washington Bothell School of Educational Studies. He is a longtime editor for the social justice teaching magazine, *Rethinking Schools*, and his work focuses on both academic and public scholarship about high-stakes testing, charter schools, teaching for social justice, and antiracist education. Recently, Dr. Au has been working in the Seattle area to support Black Lives Matter and Ethnic studies in Seattle Schools and surrounding districts. His recent books include *Unequal By Design* (2nd ed., Routledge, 2022), *Rethinking Ethnic Studies* (coedited with Tolteka Cuahatin, Miguel Zavala, & Christine Sleeter, Rethinking Schools, 2019), *Teaching for Black Lives* (coedited with Dyan Watson & Jesse Hagopian, Rethinking Schools, 2018), and *A Marxist Education* (Haymarket, 2018).

**Tadashi Dozono** is an assistant professor of history/social science education at California State University Channel Islands. Through cultural studies, ethnic studies, queer theory, and critical theory, Tadashi, in his research, emphasizes accountability toward the experiences of marginalized students by examining the production of knowledge in social studies classrooms. His work centers the theorizing that Black, Indigenous, People of Color, and LGBTQ students engage daily as a result of their marginalization. His work draws on his experiences as a queer, Japanese American, cis male, his family's internment during World War II, and more than 12 years of teaching in New York City public schools. He received his Ph.D. in social and cultural studies from the University of California Berkeley's Graduate School of Education, where his dissertation focused on "troublemaker" students of color in world history classrooms. Tadashi applied his dissertation findings by returning to teach in Brooklyn, New York, at a small public school focused on restorative justice. His research has been published in journals such as *Critical Studies in Education, Race Ethnicity and Education, Educational Theory, The Social Studies*, and *The History Teacher*.

**Antero Garcia** is an associate professor in the Graduate School of Education at Stanford University. Antero received his Ph.D. in the Urban Schooling division of the Graduate School of Education and Information Studies at the University of California, Los Angeles. His work explores how technology and gaming shape learning, literacy practices, and civic identities. His recent books include *Everyday Advocacy: Teachers Who Change the Literacy Narrative* (Norton, 2020), *Annotation* (MIT Press, 2021), and *Compose Our World: Project-Based Learning in Secondary English Language Arts* (Teachers College Press, 2021).

**Mark Gomez** is a history/social science curriculum specialist in Salinas, California. Mark has taught both middle/high school history classrooms for the last 18 years. He has also taught within teacher education programs at the University of California, Los Angeles; Antioch University; California State, Dominguez Hills; and California State, Monterey Bay. He is a founding design team member of Augustus Hawkins High School in South Central Los Angeles. His curricular and instructional expertise include action civics, effective integration of technology, critical media and literacy studies, restorative justice, ethnic studies, and community-driven school design.

**Natasha Hakimali Merchant** is an assistant professor of social studies and multicultural education at the University of Washington–Bothell, where she teaches courses exploring critical diversity studies and educational equity. Natasha's research interests focus on how othered bodies are taught about in social studies curricula. Her most recent work explores the practice of justice-oriented social studies teachers as they plan, teach, and reflect on lessons about Islam and Muslims.

**Andrea M. Hawkman, Ph.D.** (she/her), is an associate professor of social studies education, department of language, literacy, and sociocultural education at Rowan University. Her research explores the influence of race/ism and whiteness on social studies teaching, learning, and policy. She enjoys spending time with her family, traveling, sports, and pretending to be a gardener.

**Esther June Kim** is an assistant professor in the School of Education at William & Mary. Her teaching and research focus is on social studies education and Asian American representation in curricula, as well as how ideologies, race, and religion shape student enactment of citizenship.

**La Familia Aponte-Safe Tirado Díaz Beltrán Ender Busey Christ** is the chosen name for a scholarly collective shining a light on critical Latinx scholarship in social studies. This collective includes the following individuals: Gerardo J. Aponte-Safe (University of Wisconsin–La Crosse), Jesús Tirado (Auburn University), Ana C. Díaz Beltrán (University of Texas Rio Grande Valley), Tommy Ender (Rhode Island College), Christopher L. Busey (University of Florida), and Rebecca C. Christ (Florida International University). With all contributing equally to the scholarship, we see our thoughts and writing as inseparable from each other and would like to be insurgent against the idea of "authorship order."

**Jennice McCafferty-Wright** is an assistant professor in the College of Education at Missouri State University where she researches and teaches for critical civic engagement and global understanding. Her commitments include learning from and with teachers working in public diplomacy initiatives, education associations, and nongovernmental organizations. Her current projects include developing a virtual exchange for future teachers in Missouri and Morocco, research on the development of youth civic voice, and learning to play the spoons.

**Nicole Mirra** is an assistant professor of urban teacher education in the Graduate School of Education at Rutgers, the State University of New Jersey. She previously taught high school English Language Arts in Brooklyn, New York, and Los Angeles, California. Her research explores the intersections of critical literacy and civic engagement with youth and teachers across classroom, community, and digital learning environments. She is the author of *Educating for Empathy: Literacy Learning and Civic Engagement* (Teachers College Press, 2018) and a co-author (with Antero Garcia and Ernest Morrell) of *Doing Youth Participatory Action Research: Transforming Inquiry with Researchers, Educators, and Students* (Routledge, 2015).

**Tiffany Mitchell Patterson, Ph.D.,** is a manager of social studies at District of Columbia Public Schools (DCPS). Prior to joining the DCPS social studies team, she was an assistant professor of secondary social studies at West Virginia University. She has 10 years of experience teaching middle school social studies in the D.C. area and earned her doctorate in multilingual/

multicultural education and education policy from George Mason University. Advocacy, activism, intersectionality, and antiracist/anti-oppressive education lie at the core of her research, teacher practice, and community work. Education is her revolution.

**Noreen Naseem Rodríguez** is an assistant professor of Teacher Learning, Research, and Practice in the School of Education and affiliate faculty in the Department of Ethnic Studies at the University of Colorado Boulder. Her research interests include the culturally sustaining pedagogies of Asian American and Latinx teachers and the teaching of so-called difficult histories to young learners through children's literature. She has authored multiple peer-reviewed articles and is the coauthor of *Social Studies for a Better World: An Anti-Oppressive Approach for Elementary Educators* (2021) with Katy Swalwell.

**E. Wayne Ross** is a professor in the Department of Curriculum and Pedagogy at the University of British Columbia in Vancouver, Canada. His books include *Rethinking Social Studies: Critical Pedagogy in Pursuit of Dangerous Citizenship* (2017); *The Social Studies Curriculum: Purposes, Problems and Possibilities* (5th ed., 2022); and, with Stebastián Plá, *The New Social Studies Research in Latin America: Critical Perspectives from the Global South* (2022).

**Hanadi Shatara** (she/her/هي) is an assistant professor at the University of Wisconsin–La Crosse. She received her doctorate in social studies education at Teachers College, Columbia University. Her research focuses on critical global education, teacher education, teacher positionalities, and the representations of Southwest Asia and North Africa in education. Dr. Shatara was a middle school social studies teacher for 7 years in Philadelphia public schools and a National Board Certified teacher.

**Sarah B. Shear** is an associate professor of social studies and multicultural education at the University of Washington–Bothell. She earned her doctorate in learning, teaching, and curriculum from the University of Missouri in 2014, with concentrations in social studies education and Indigenous studies. Dr. Shear examines K–12 social studies curricula within Indigenous contexts, as well as race/ism and settler colonialism in K–12 social studies teacher education, popular media, and qualitative methodologies. As a member of the

Turtle Island Social Studies Collective, Dr. Shear is committed to collective action to combat oppression in education and academia. She and colleagues are published in *Theory and Research in Social Education*; *Journal of Social Studies Research*; *Knowledge Cultures*, *Social Studies and the Young Learner*; and *Qualitative Inquiry*. In addition, Dr. Shear coedited *(Re)Imagining Elementary Social Studies: A Controversial Issues Reader* (2018) and *Marking the Invisible: Articulating Whiteness in Social Studies Education* (2020). Dr. Shear and colleagues have presented their collaborative work at the College and University Faculty Assembly of the National Council for the Social Studies, the American Educational Research Association, the International Congress of Qualitative Inquiry, the National Association for Multicultural Education, and the Native American and Indigenous Studies Association. These efforts have also been featured by the Zinn Project, Teaching Tolerance, the *Huffington Post*, and several other media outlets. In addition, Dr. Shear has been a featured speaker at the Smithsonian's National Museum of the American Indian in Washington, D.C.

**The Turtle Island Social Studies Collective** (TISSC) is a collective of Indigenous studies scholars committed to countering colonialism and amplifying the work of Indigenous scholarship within social studies education. Our collective approach is inspired by the Combahee River Collective and Quechua scholar Sandy Grande's call to "commit to collectivity." As a collective that includes Anishinaabeg scholars, scholars from other Native nations, and non-Native allies, we use the term *Turtle Island* to draw attention to the importance of ongoing relationships between Indigenous peoples and lands and to the importance of land in Indigenous theories and practices of decolonization. The members of TISSC are Dr. Meredith McCoy (Turtle Mountain Band of Chippewa descent), Lakota Pochedley (Citizen Band Potawatomi), Dr. Leilani Sabzalian (Alutiiq), and Dr. Sarah B. Shear.

# Index